The Heirloomist

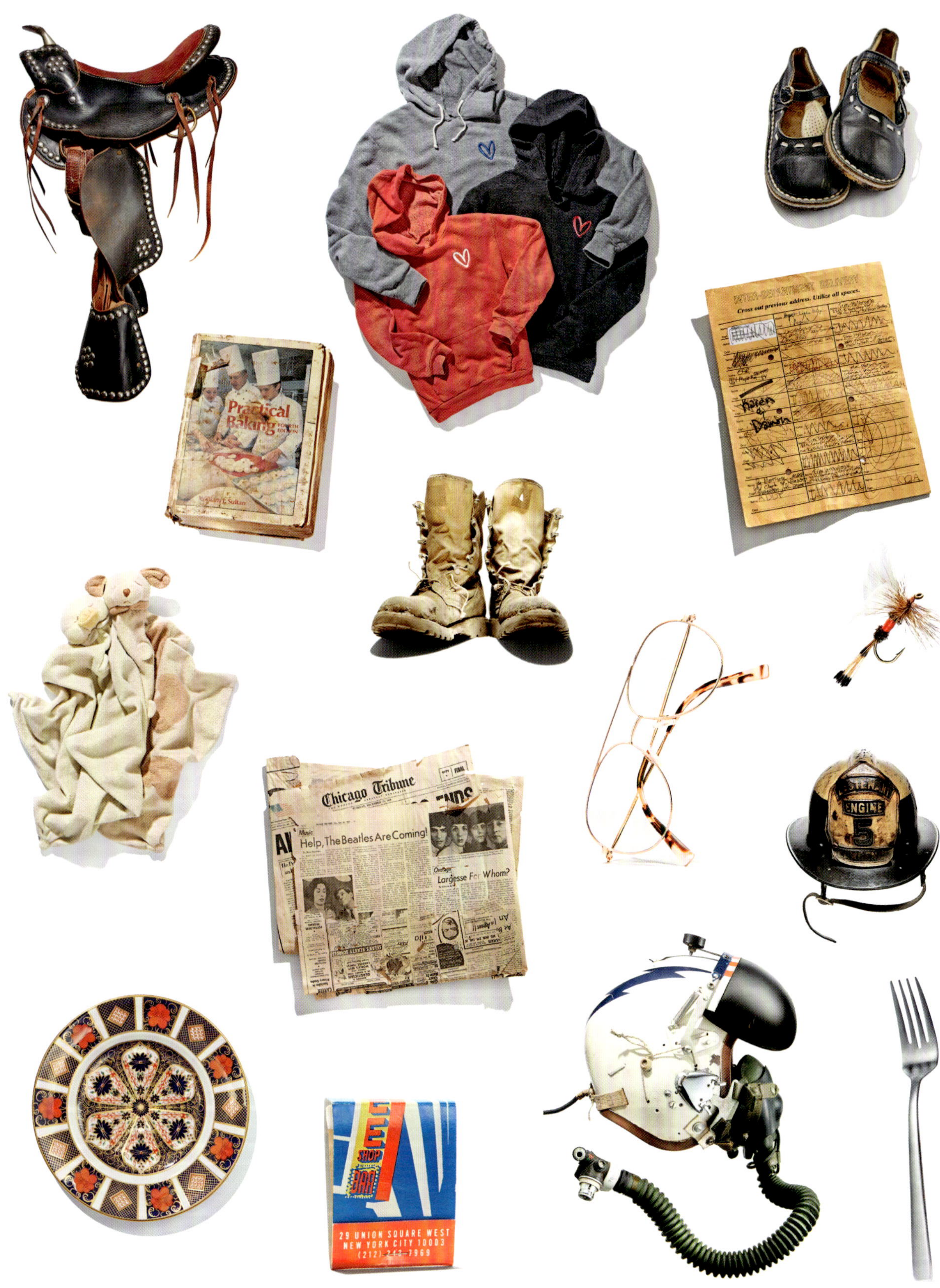
Practical Baking
INTER-DEPARTMENT DELIVERY
Cross out previous address. Utilize all spaces.
Chicago Tribune
Help, The Beatles Are Coming!
Largesse For Whom?
ENGINE
5
29 UNION SQUARE WEST
NEW YORK CITY 10003

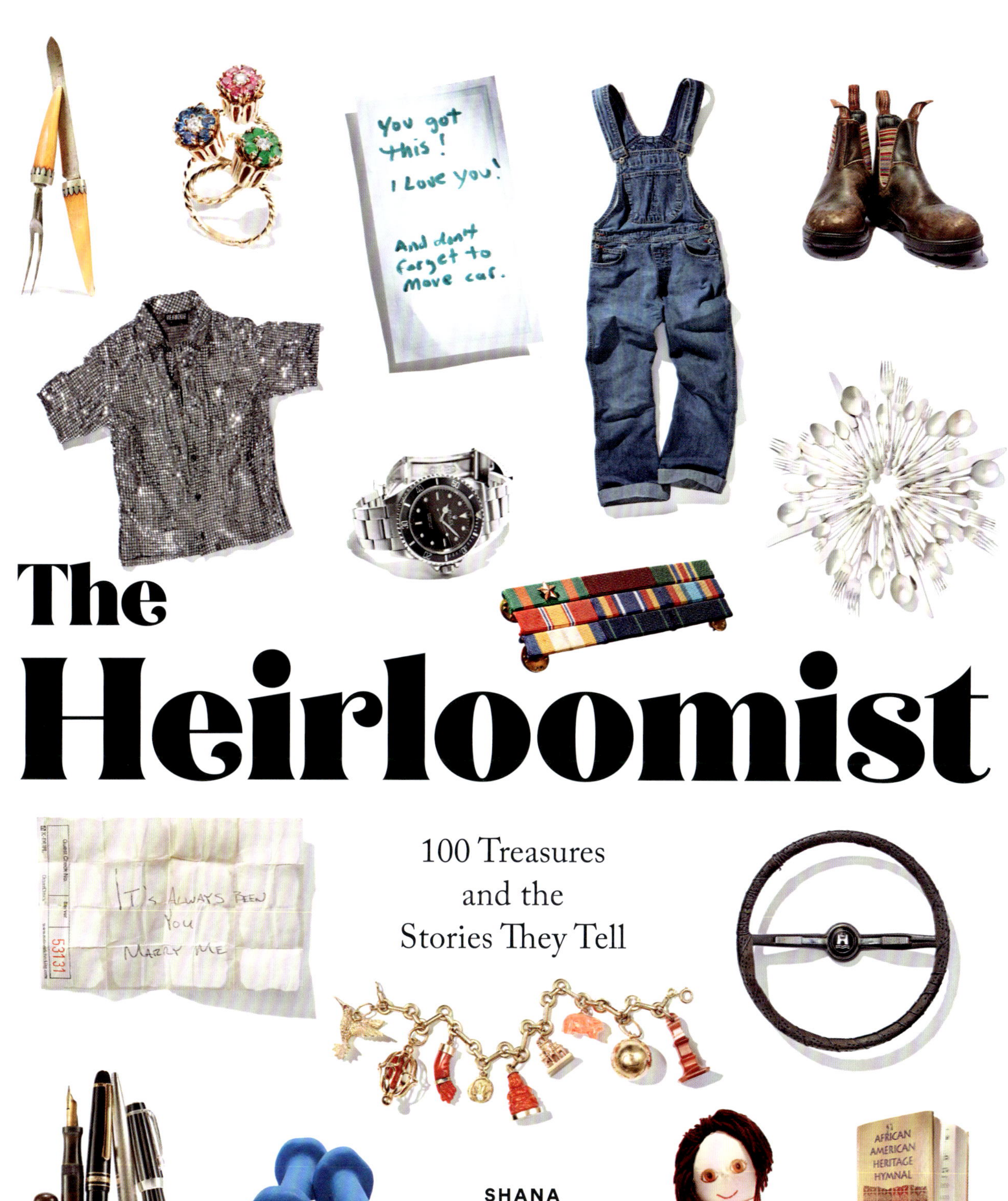

The Heirloomist

100 Treasures and the Stories They Tell

SHANA NOVAK

CHRONICLE BOOKS
SAN FRANCISCO

Library of Congress Cataloging-in-Publication Data available.

ISBN 978-1-7972-2440-4

Manufactured in China.

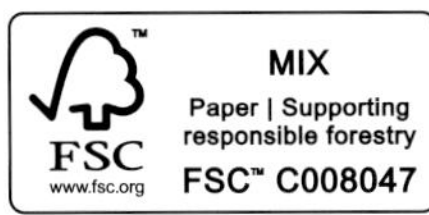

Design by Vanessa Dina.
Typesetting by Frank Brayton.

10 9 8 7 6 5 4 3 2 1

Chronicle books and gifts are available at special quantity discounts to corporations, professional associations, literacy programs, and other organizations. For details and discount information, please contact our premiums department at corporatesales@chroniclebooks.com or at 1-800-759-0190.

Chronicle Books LLC
680 Second Street
San Francisco, California 94107
www.chroniclebooks.com

For my grandmother Phyllis, the keeper of the past.

For Juniper, the keeper of what comes next.

And for Den, the one who keeps this train on the tracks.

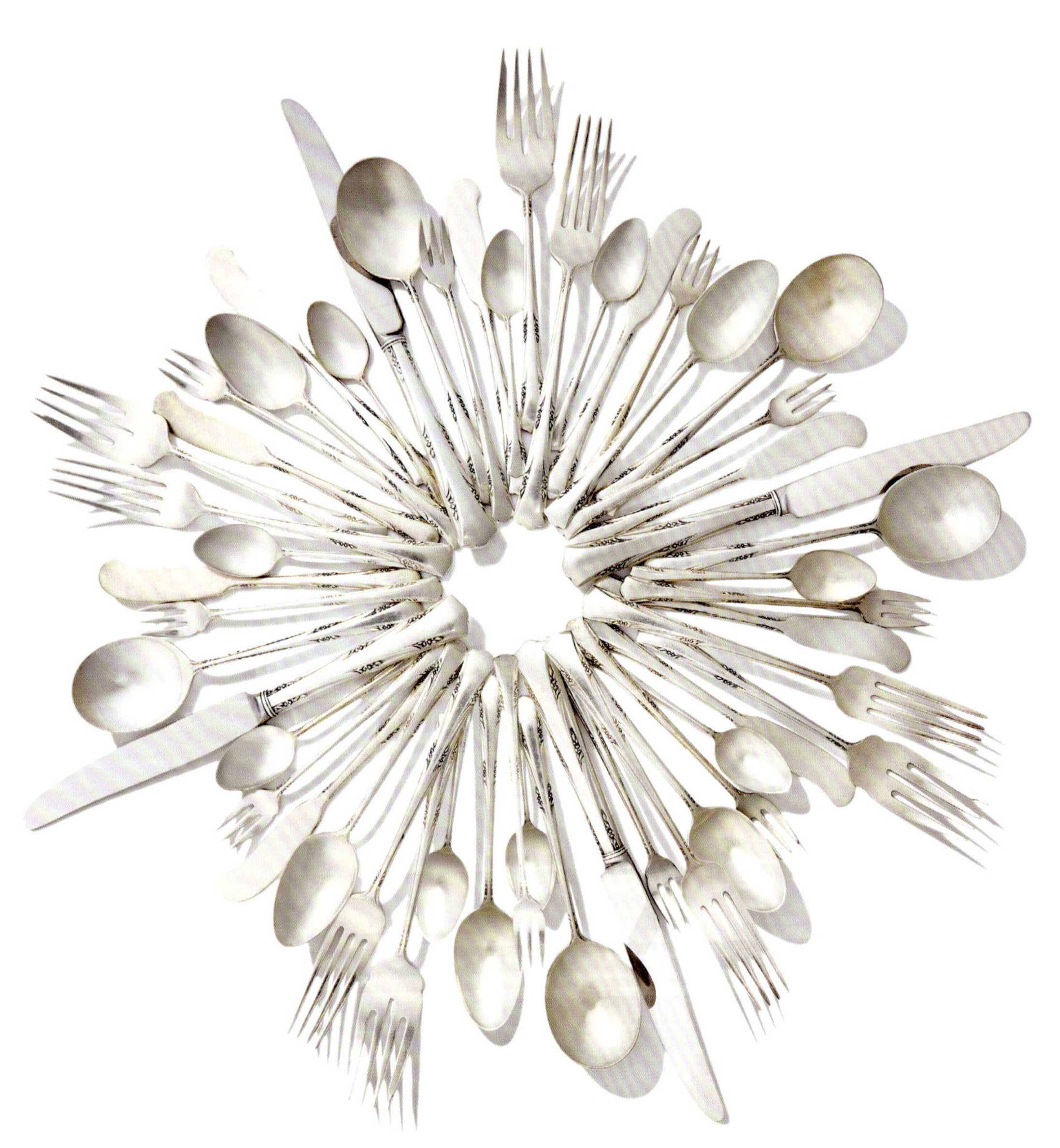

From Phyllis Neuswanger, my grandmother, I inherited a set of Lenox china, a crate of crystal stemware, and twelve sterling silver table settings. I was also the lucky recipient of my grandfather Gene's gold tooth fillings and the metal plate a surgeon put in my grandmother's leg when she was run over by a golf cart in Palm Springs sometime in the late 1980s.

The definition of heirloom, in my family, is clearly open to interpretation.

These silver table settings were the very first heirlooms my grandmother passed down to me. She told fabulously detailed stories about many of our family's heirlooms, but for the silver, she could recall dinner parties where it was used, right down to where guests were seated and what was served.

In an act of wild disregard for their perceived preciousness, I too started using the silverware—every day. To this day, I stir my coffee with her spoons. I slurp take-out noodles off the forks. And sometimes I even have a cheeseburger and French fries off a china plate. It feels delightfully decadent, which she was, and makes me feel connected to her every single time. (Use the heirlooms!)

Living with these heirlooms, knowing their special story, and enjoying them in my own way, was exactly why she left them to me. She wanted me to have a greater sense of myself, beyond my skin and bones. Heirlooms can be a great vehicle for that.

Being entrusted with her belongings came with a sense of reverence, and the desire to carry on their history felt like a deep responsibility. As my grandmother grew older, she began to feel her mortality, so I did the only thing I knew how to do—I started photographing her things. She would not live forever, but her stories could. A seed for my future as the Heirloomist was planted.

When she died, I couldn't look at an heirloom for a year. But in time, the universe brought everything back into focus. I needed to pick my camera up again and get back to my calling. In my heart, I knew she would insist. "Shake it off, dear," I could hear her say. "We have pictures to take."

I had experience working in the commercial photography industry at the time and had learned so much about the business from amazing creative professionals all around me, but the early *Heirloomist* website was rudimentary and self-made,

Shake it off, dear. . . . We have pictures to take.

—Phyllis Neuswanger

populated with photographs of stuff I convinced friends to send in. Photographing other people's treasures brought me a lot of joy. One of my first commissions was from a college friend who asked me to photograph a pair of jeans for her husband's fortieth birthday—he was wearing them when a campfire exploded right in front of him. The jeans saved him from being terribly burned. The make of the jeans, ironically, was "Lucky Brand," giving a wink to an otherwise seriously existential image. That tiny Heirloomist seed had sprouted.

The jeans reaffirmed what my grandmother had instilled—an heirloom can be anything, as long as it tells your story. And *everyone* has stories that deserve to be acknowledged. So, in my grandmother's honor, and in my family's spirit of free will and entrepreneurship, I formally founded a little business and called it The Heirloomist. Its goal was simple—to celebrate our stuff and the stories it tells.

Through word of mouth, and the joy of social media, the idea behind The Heirloomist began to resonate with a lot of people quickly. Before I knew it, it had become something bigger than me. (This still humbles me.)

Since 2015, I have photographed over 1,500 heirlooms. I got to be on TV, see my work in a museum, have a monthly column in a magazine, and write this book. But I still often feel like a kid who just misses her grandma, armed only with a camera and a desire to hold on. That's what keeps me searching for the magic; there is joy in all the heartbreaking, formative, and inspiring things that happen to us on this spinning rock we call home. I intend to share as much of it as I can.

In this book, I'm telling the stories of 100 treasures. Some are traditional heirlooms; others will totally surprise you. Some treasures are expensive; many have no monetary value. But all are priceless, precisely because their stories will play your heartstrings like a symphony. And that's the point—there is no one way to define "heirloom." You get to do it.

Putting these stories out into the universe is the most outrageous honor I could have ever dreamed up. I hope they make you smile. They'll probably make you cry. But mostly, I hope you close this book and feel a little joy knowing that we are all here together—to celebrate, to honor, and to be a part of each other's stories.

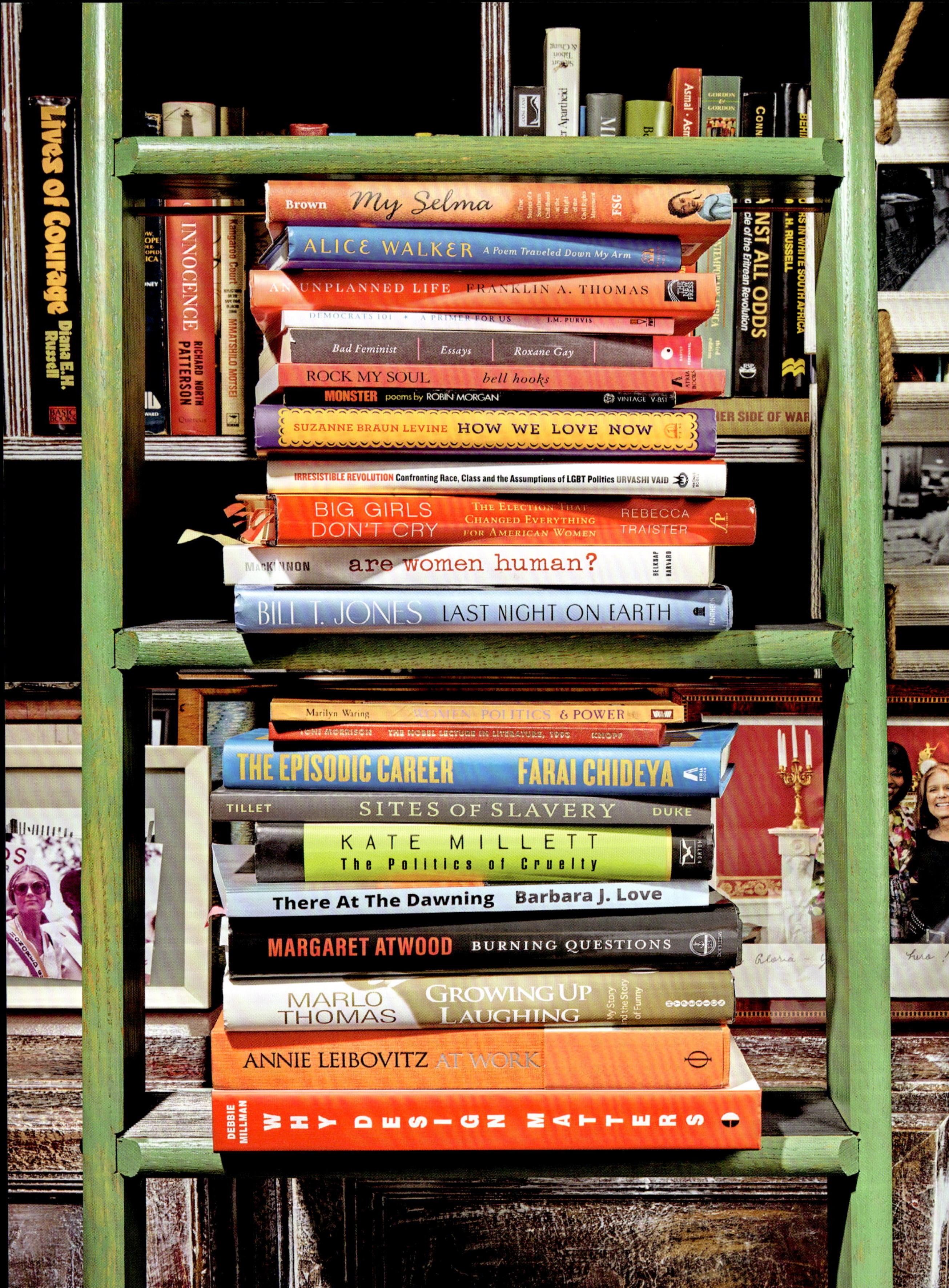

Lives of Courage Diana E.H. Russell
INNOCENCE RICHARD NORTH PATTERSON
Brown My Selma FSG
ALICE WALKER A Poem Traveled Down My Arm
AN UNPLANNED LIFE FRANKLIN A. THOMAS
DEMOCRATS 101 • A PRIMER FOR US I.M. PURVIS
Bad Feminist Essays Roxane Gay
ROCK MY SOUL bell hooks
MONSTER poems by ROBIN MORGAN VINTAGE
SUZANNE BRAUN LEVINE HOW WE LOVE NOW
IRRESISTIBLE REVOLUTION Confronting Race, Class and the Assumptions of LGBT Politics URVASHI VAID
BIG GIRLS DON'T CRY The Election That Changed Everything for American Women REBECCA TRAISTER
MACKINNON are women human?
BILL T. JONES LAST NIGHT ON EARTH
Marilyn Waring WOMEN, POLITICS & POWER
TONI MORRISON THE NOBEL LECTURE IN LITERATURE, 1993 KNOPF
THE EPISODIC CAREER FARAI CHIDEYA
TILLET SITES OF SLAVERY DUKE
KATE MILLETT The Politics of Cruelty NORTON
There At The Dawning Barbara J. Love
MARGARET ATWOOD BURNING QUESTIONS
MARLO THOMAS GROWING UP LAUGHING My Story and the Story of Funny
ANNIE LEIBOVITZ AT WORK
DEBBIE MILLMAN WHY DESIGN MATTERS

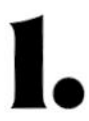

Gloria Steinem | NEW YORK, NEW YORK

"Books were my first everything—my first teachers, my first friends," says Gloria Steinem. She spent a lot of her childhood absorbing as much literature as she could. She also spent much of her childhood absorbing the reality that her mother, despite being an accomplished journalist, suffered from not being able to progress in a profession she very much enjoyed. At the time, a woman's path was limited by societal constructs.

Gloria's awareness of those constructs perhaps sparked the activist and advocate we all know today. She suspects that choosing a writing career was her way of living the career her mother never realized.

When Gloria bought her current home in New York City, she recalls being particularly charmed by one of the building's details—the high ceilings. It wasn't just for looks. "I thought, oh great, there will finally be room for all of my books."

She would spend the next several decades effecting change and inspiring progress from those book-lined walls. As her contributions grew, her book collection grew as well.

Pictured is her treasured library ladder, portions of the extensive bookshelf, and titles by some of her dearest friends. The books and ladder symbolize community and, especially, the richness that comes with diversity.

"I've grown up to have wonderful friends who write wonderful books, and it's a great point of pride to see them line the walls of my home," Gloria adds.

When she thinks of her book collection, it brings to mind the film based on *Fahrenheit 451*, the dystopian novel about censorship and book burning.

"When I look at my books, I think about the Truffaut film, *Fahrenheit 451*—about an authoritarian society that had outlawed books. As a counter or a rebellion to that, every person in that society memorized one entire book," Gloria says. "I loved that idea—having a whole book inside you. The last scene is of all of these people, walking in a circle, reciting the book that they had learned by heart. To keep the book alive."

"It's clear as ever how desperately we need books; we need other voices, other whole perspectives," Gloria says. "We're communal animals, and we learn more from difference than we do from sameness."

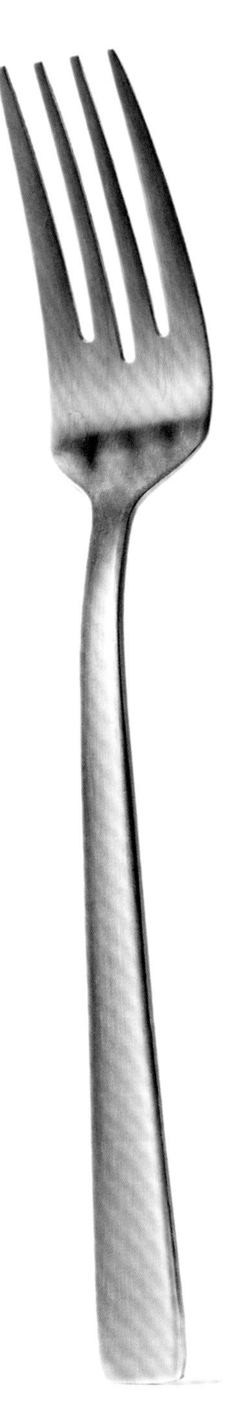

2. Nora McInerny | PHOENIX, ARIZONA

Nora McInerny was at work one day when the guy she had a huge crush on showed up at her office. He was holding coffee and a slice of cake, and they were both for her. It was the most thoughtful thing a man had ever done for her.

"No fork?" was her response. But the snark landed humorously. Nora and Aaron had their first official date a week later. He brought her another gift that night—a fork.

"It wasn't a nice fork," Nora jokes. "It was the kind that bends under the slightest amount of pressure." But Aaron's dating game held up.

"We had the kind of first date where you talk about how many kids you want to have. He wanted two, I wanted four, we did a handshake deal at three," she jokes. "I knew I'd get him to change his mind eventually."

"Ours was the kind of annoying love story people tell you about—the kind where 'it was just so easy,' and I'm sorry to be that annoying person, but it's true," Nora says.

They were soon engaged. It happened at the hospital . . . on the night Aaron was diagnosed with brain cancer.

After Aaron's diagnosis, the universe pitched a few more curveballs to the couple. They had a son during his treatment, then a miscarriage, and Nora's father passed away.

Aaron died in 2014.

These events made Nora a unique voice on the subject of grief and loss. She has published five books and is host of the podcast *Terrible, Thanks for Asking*. On the podcast and in her books, Nora's message veers from the societal construct that, after trauma, you're supposed to work your way back to being OK again. She's more focused on allowing the not-OK-ness to be OK on her website.

Nora remarried and is busy these days raising the kids and traveling for book tours and speaking engagements. The first-date fork sits quietly tucked away in Nora's jewelry box, but its meaning has never diminished.

"It's garbage to anyone else but me," she says with her trademark raw honesty. "But things don't have to be valuable to be valuable to you."

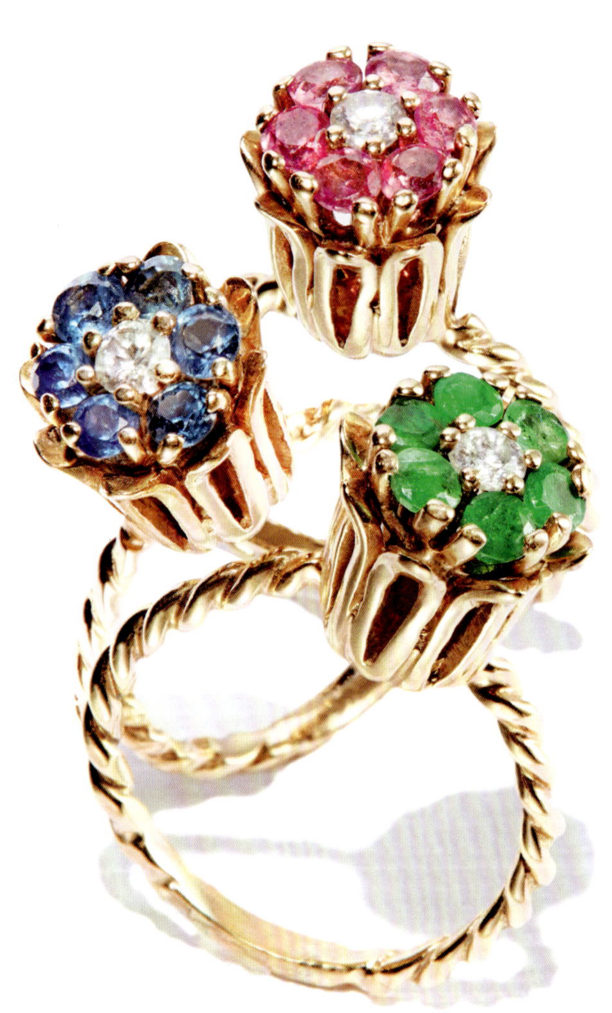

Some of Dana Gordon's most cherished memories of her grandmother are of the times she was allowed to try on her glamorous jewelry, often during their frequent lunch dates at the Cheesecake Factory.

"I was *always* drawn to her jewelry," Dana says of her grandmother, whom she lovingly refers to as Nana. "She was so stylish. And she had stories for all her jewels."

Dana always found herself especially entranced by Nana's grouping of tulip rings. Worn together, the three flower designs, each anchored by a diamond in its center, nested in one another.

When Dana was older, her grandmother developed Alzheimer's disease. Although the disease took a lot of her grandmother's mind, Dana notes that Nana always kept up her impeccably stylish appearance.

"She was still just as glamorous as she always was, and always dressed to the nines, but she was nothing like herself," Dana remembers. Nana began to hide things, the tulip rings included.

"I never saw the rings again," Dana says.

Years later, Dana met and fell in love with Jonathan Gordon, a handsome guy from the state next door, Indiana, whom she would eventually marry. On the night their families gathered to honor their engagement, Dana's connection to her grandmother came roaring back to life—and in high fashion.

Renee Gordon, Dana's future mother-in-law, walked into the room wearing three flower-shaped rings, nested in one another, anchored by diamonds in the middle. They were the very tulip rings Dana so vividly remembers Nana wearing.

"I screamed," Dana jokes. "I screamed for my mother to come and see."

The moms figured out that Nana had shopped at the same Chicago jewelry store, Shapiro Jewelers, around the same time as Jonathan's mother. They may have even worked with the same friend who was a sales associate at the store at the time.

"It felt like my grandma was there with me, and it was just incredible," Dana says.

On their wedding day, Jonathan's mother gave Dana a gift: the rings. And even though these days Dana Gordon is an accomplished jewelry designer in her own right, the tulip rings still hold a place as the most important pieces in her collection.

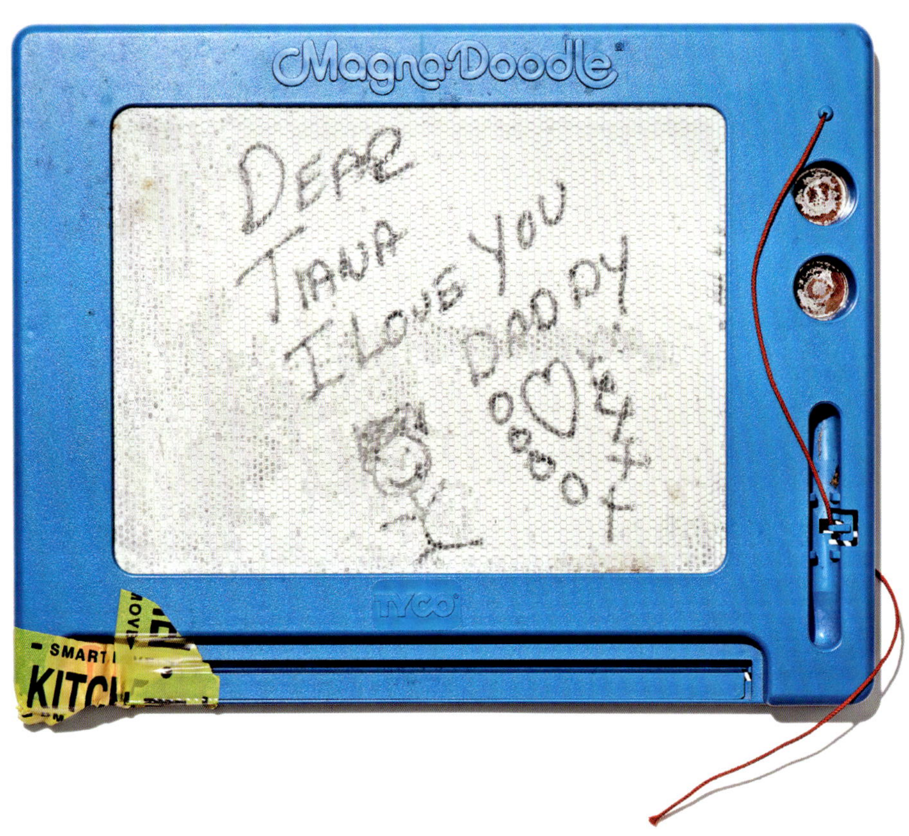
Magna Doodle
DEAR
TIANA
I LOVE YOU
DADDY
TYCO

Tiana Santore freely admits she was a daddy's girl—one who constantly tested her father and pushed his buttons because she always trusted him to love her back.

Her father, John Santore, was a New York City firefighter with Engine 24 Ladder 5 Battalion 2, Greenwich Village. Despite his fireman's schedule, he was always present for Tiana when she was a kid. John was running late for work on the morning of September 11, 2001, because he was helping her cover her new schoolbooks with contact paper.

Before rushing off, he popped his head into the bathroom where Tiana was getting ready for school and demanded a kiss good-bye.

"See you later," he said. John and his company were called to the World Trade Center that morning and did not return to their firehouse. Tiana was the last person in her family to see her father alive. She was thirteen.

Two days after the terrorist attacks, still hoping John would be found alive, Tiana, her mother, and her aunt (John's sister) went to John's firehouse. It was there that his firehouse brothers shared the news. John's remains had been found. And in a horrible way, Tiana remembers, they were actually the lucky ones. So many others would never get that closure.

Tiana remembers being asked that day if she and her family wanted to go up to John's locker to get his things.

As they were led to the firehouse's locker room, Tiana recalls, "I don't know why, but I looked at my dad's locker . . . and I just wanted it. It didn't make sense to me as a thirteen-year-old, but I wanted the whole locker. I didn't want anyone else to ever use it."

John's brothers obliged. Days after he was buried, they delivered his entire locker to the family's Staten Island home. For reasons so personal and deeply emotional, the locker still sits, untouched, with John's belongings in the same exact place he left them in 2001.

You would think that locker would now be considered a most treasured heirloom, and it is. But a few years later, Tiana happened across something else that was, in many ways, a more tangible memory of her father.

In 2005, while helping her mom pack up the family's home to prepare for a remodel, Tiana found an old wooden chest in the basement full of her childhood toys. At the bottom, sitting untouched for years, was a Magna Doodle—a toy tablet that could be drawn on using a magnetized stylus.

There, on the Magna Doodle's screen, was an old note from her dad: *Dear Tiana, I love you. —Daddy.* "It was frozen in time," Tiana says.

"Ever since that morning when my dad was late for work," Tiana says, "when he said, 'see you later,' that little clip has always stayed in my memory. This was a message for me. I was like 'Alright, Dad. I got it. I know you love me. I love you too.'"

John Santore is remembered by his daughter for many things—his love of Diet Coke and fanny packs, his always giving nature, and being a man of his word. "See you later," he said. And he meant it.

Alright, Dad. I got it. I know you love me. I love you too.

—Tiana Santore

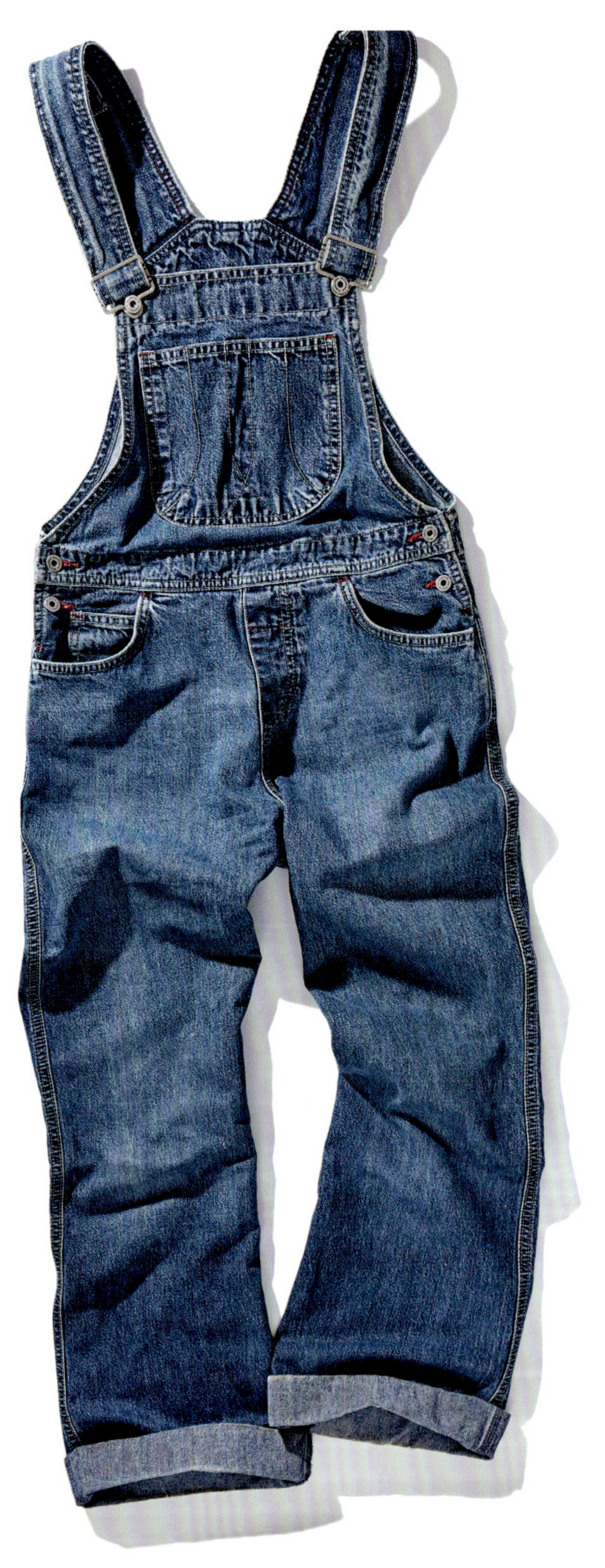

The five boroughs of New York City wake up to Jamie Stelter, co-anchor of Spectrum News *NY1 Mornings on 1,* every morning. But one fall evening, thirteen years ago at a concert in Central Park, she was just a kid on a date, rocking what would one day become some very special overalls.

When they first began dating, Jamie and her now husband, Brian, a Harvard fellow, author, and former CNN anchor, were also high-level professionals at the art of the good, old-fashioned phone call—talking endless dreams and life plans in the evenings after work. In September of 2011, the night before they were to attend a Ray LaMontagne concert, Jamie confided a secret wish to Brian on one of their marathon calls: She dreamed of living on a farm one day.

"I told him I'd trade my TV clothes for overalls," she says. "For open air. Animals. A slower life." Brian seemed all in on the farm dream. But just to make sure, Jamie wore overalls to the concert. "To give him a glimpse of the real, future Jamie," she jokes.

That night, on a blanket in the park in her overalls, as Ray LaMontagne played his sets, the real event was happening in Jamie's heart.

"Something came over me. That night, everything changed. I decided I wanted to marry him," she says. (Next, she did what any girl in love is inclined to do—she didn't tell Brian she wanted to marry him, but she told all her best girlfriends in the morning.)

By 2014, the Stelters had married. It wasn't exactly a picnic in the park from there. The couple struggled through several miscarriages and fertility treatments even as their careers grew and became more demanding. But their plans for each other never once changed.

"The thing you need to understand about Brian is that he is all in on me. Anything I want to do—anything I dream of," Jamie says.

They now have two kids (their oldest child's middle name is Ray, in honor of that fateful night under the stars), and in 2020, they made good on the plans they made that night on the phone—they bought a farm.

Jamie still puts on her TV clothes each day, but the overalls are the star of her closet.

"It all started with those overalls. The overalls that showed him the real me," Jamie says.

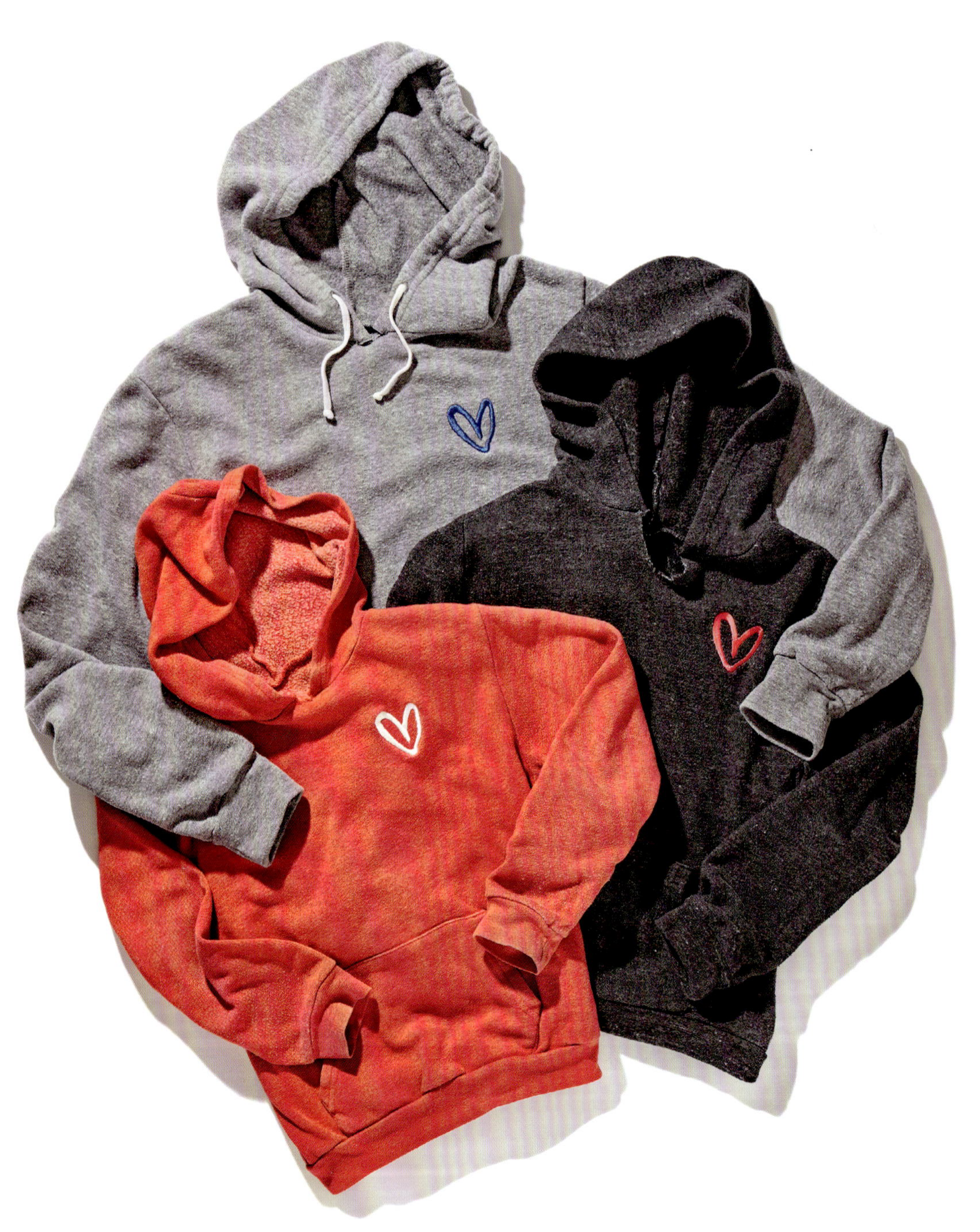

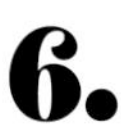

Shannon Buth | AUSTIN, TEXAS

Boys outnumber girls five to one at Shannon Buth's house. Her crew includes one high school sweetheart for a husband, a set of surprise twin boys, an oldest son, and a youngest son. It's all boys, all the time. Shannon wouldn't have it any other way. But she'll emphatically tell you she couldn't handle any of it without her community of strong, supportive women.

In 2014, one of those strong women, her friend Lindsey, popped by Shannon's house with a gift while Shannon's mother, Linda, was visiting. Linda had cancer and the treatments had recently stopped working. "We knew it would be her last visit," Shannon remembers. The gift was matching bracelets, one for Shannon, one for her mom. Both were engraved with the words "Live what you love."

"Those four simple words resonated with me so deeply," Shannon says. "My mom died a month later, and those words became my motto."

Overwhelmed with kids and grief, while also feeling the love and support from her community, Shannon wanted to bring some joy into the world. So, she gave birth again, this time to a business. It started with a soft, comfy sweatshirt embroidered with a heart.

"An imperfect heart," Shannon says, "stitched over your heart, as a daily reminder to live your passion, laugh every day, love deeply, and lift others up."

The plan was to donate $5 to a local women's shelter for each sale. The sweatshirts sold out immediately at a local holiday market, and later online. So, Shannon expanded to a more extensive line of apparel, appropriately naming it the Live What You Love collection. She launched the line—an array of T-shirts, hats, and sweatpants, all embroidered with a heart—just as the COVID-19 pandemic hit, just as many people were stuck at home in their sweatpants. She has never looked back.

Running an apparel business with a mission and big heart turned out to be a great fit for Shannon. She gets to utilize her past experience in the fashion industry, can run operations from home while caring for the boys, and gets to honor her mom every day.

"My mom had the biggest heart, and I think she is looking down, so damn proud of this mission and message. I know she is so happy that something so positive came from her passing."

At the time of publishing, Shannon has donated over $65,000 to women's organizations.

But perhaps Shannon's favorite success is the one she never expected.

"I'm proudest when I see my boys and husband wear my imperfect-heart apparel," she says. "I guess I thought that because a heart is considered more feminine that men wouldn't rock the heart. They surprised me in the best way—my kids' buddies now want heart sweatshirts, and my male friends wear my golf shirts. It's the biggest accomplishment of my life to be raising sensitive and caring men."

The story of Russ & Daughters begins, perhaps surprisingly, with no daughters. It was just Joel Russ . . . and a barrel of fish.

After his arrival in New York City in 1907, the hardworking Eastern European Jewish immigrant sold herring to make a living on the Lower East Side. Joel eventually saved enough money to open a storefront. And so, from behind a counter on East Houston Street, he served up a version of the American dream that, more than one hundred years later, would be considered a legend by many.

The bustling shop quickly became a neighborhood staple, so Russ put his three young daughters, Hattie, Ida, and Anne, to work. Even though they were just kids, they were expected to contribute to the family's livelihood from behind the counter. By 1935, they had spent a substantial part of their childhood and formative teen years in service to their father's store. That's when he changed its name.

Russ & Daughters became the first known business in the country to have "& Daughters" in its name.

Niki Russ Federman is the granddaughter of Joel's youngest, Anne Russ Federman, and is aware that her grandmother gave a huge part of her life to the store. "In her retirement, she once told me she was still trying to figure out what she wanted to do when she grew up," Niki says.

It wasn't until Anne was in her seventies, and living in Florida, that she discovered a personal sense of purpose for possibly the first time in her life. She began volunteering with an organization that helped recent immigrants improve their English by pairing them with local residents for casual conversation sessions. She was proud of her contributions and impact.

As Anne found her calling outside the family business, Niki found herself gravitating toward it. After graduating college with a degree in political science, she worked in the art world and tried business school. But in time, she says, she realized there was one place where all her interests and passions could collide. That place was Russ & Daughters.

"I realized the rare gift I had," Niki says. "To be part of a lineage where I could continue a one-hundred-year-plus-old tradition and be in metaphoric conversation with the past, while putting my own imprint on it and keeping it relevant today."

Niki is now a fourth-generation owner of Russ & Daughters, along with her cousin

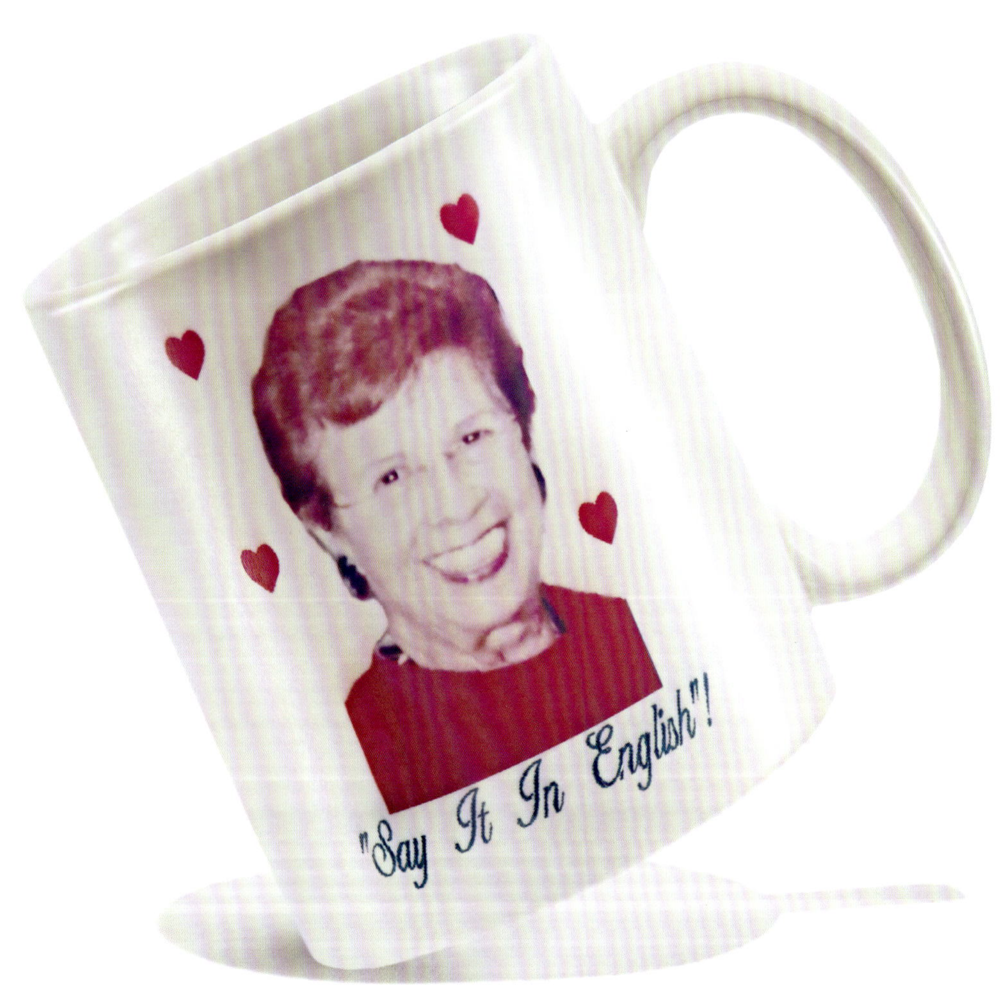
"Say It In English"!

Josh Russ Tupper. Even though the business is practically part of their DNA, they are both first-time restaurateurs.

Under the modern touch of Niki and Josh, the business survived the COVID-19 pandemic (it was actually the store's second pandemic—the first was the Spanish flu of 1918). They also expanded their nationwide shipping facility and opened a bakery. As a first in the 110-year-old legacy of the brand, they opened a restaurant space, aptly named Russ & Daughters Cafe. More expansion is planned, ensuring future generations get a taste of the Russ family legacy.

One of Niki's most cherished items from her grandmother is a mug that Anne gave her "students" that reads "Say It In English"! with her face on it. It is a sweet and funny testament to Anne's impact on and connection with them, and to Niki, a striking symbol of the first time Anne had known fulfillment on her own terms.

As Niki reflects on making the choice to run her family's legendary business, she says that choice—having one at all—is something she is incredibly appreciative of.

"My grandmother and her sisters did not have a choice. I did, and I chose to follow in their footsteps," Niki says. "I know it gave my grandma pride that I chose to become involved. I feel very proud to build on the contributions of three generations of my family, including my grandmother Anne's."

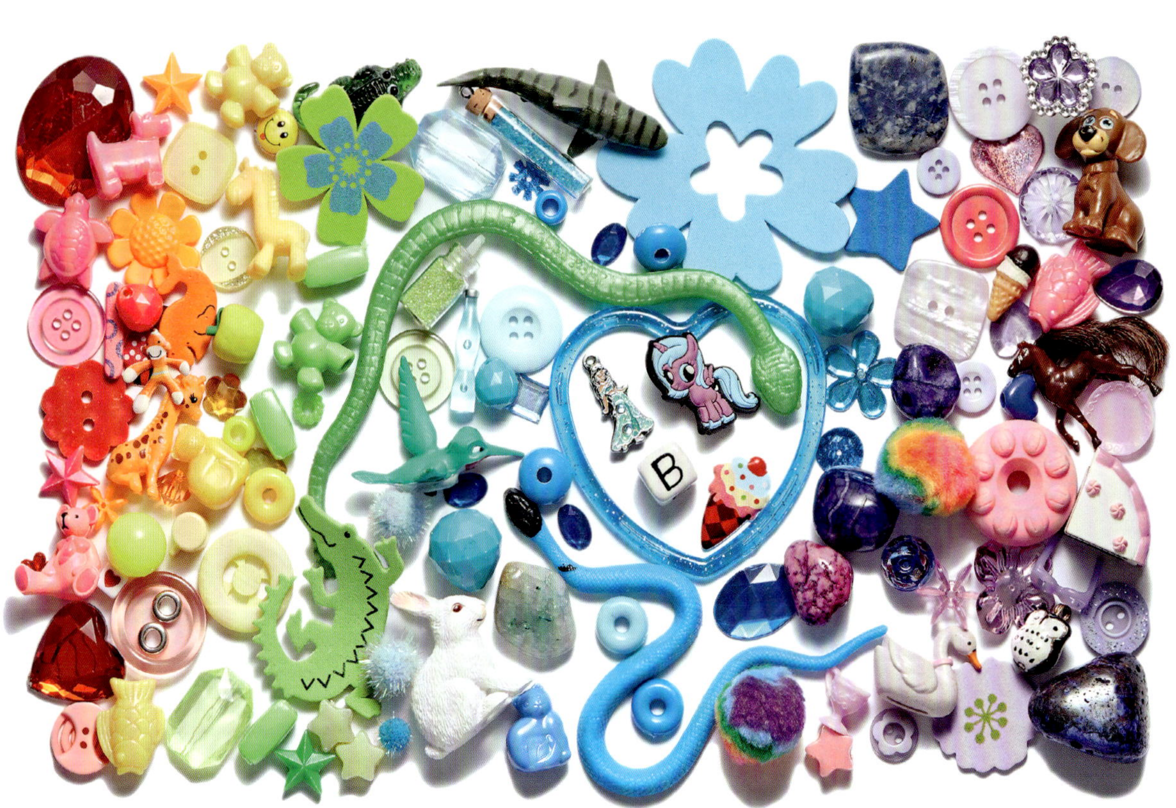
B

8. Katie Anne Lester | LEXINGTON, KENTUCKY

When Katie Anne Lester's daughter, Bennett, vomited one day, she figured it was a stomach bug. When Bennett experienced vision change, a doctor said she needed glasses. It was only after Katie Anne noticed Bennett's walk was off that the medical dots were connected. Within twenty-four hours, Bennett was diagnosed with a brain tumor and underwent surgery. She was two and a half.

The family moved from their Lexington, Kentucky, home to the Ronald McDonald House in Cincinnati, Ohio, while Bennett underwent two more brain surgeries, six rounds of chemotherapy, a bone-marrow transplant, and many other procedures at the Cincinnati Children's Hospital Medical Center. It was there that "the collection" began.

Bennett got a lot of gifts while she was in the hospital. She was especially drawn to any small parts that came along with them. "She *loved* little things and as soon as she got something little, she would tuck it away in her hospital bed table's drawer," Katie Anne says. "The year we spent Christmas in the hospital, she didn't want to open any gifts but instead woke up suggesting we play with her collection."

Katie Anne and her husband would often lay in bed with Bennett at the hospital and play together with all the tiny pieces she had amassed.

"During her chemo she was so weak. Picking up those little pieces was really all her body could do."

Despite everything the Lester family and medical staff did for Bennett, her tumor continued to grow rapidly, so they decided to stop her treatment. She would live the rest of her days at home, as loved and comfortable as possible.

"The next six months we lived life like most people will never get to experience. Nothing was held back. We went to Disney twice and stayed a month at the beach, which was her favorite place on the earth. Most of all, we loved on each other every single day like there was going to be no tomorrow," Katie Anne says.

Bennett passed away just shy of her fourth birthday in 2015. The "collection" lived in a metal lunchbox for a long time. All the little things were one big reminder of the family's loss.

"Ever since her passing, this collection has bothered me," Katie Anne says. "I cry every time I see it, am terrified of losing it, but felt an enormous sense of guilt keeping it locked up in a box." Deciding to have the collection photographed was an act of connecting to the light Bennett brought to the family.

"Seeing the collection bright and happy keeps her present," Katie Anne says. And in a testament to just how bright Bennett's light was, Katie Anne says that hundreds of thousands of people let the family know they were forever impacted by her short life. She received over ten thousand messages, mostly from social media, and two hundred thousand more through a CaringBridge website she set up to keep friends and family up-to-date on Bennett's treatments. She still gets messages to this day.

"I had tons of mothers write saying they were going to parent their children better and more intentionally because of Bennett," Katie Anne says. "Fights were forgiven, and families were kinder to each other because of a three-year-old girl. Her fight and spunk reminded people that life is short and you never know what tomorrow holds. Our story isn't a sad story—it's a love story."

Our story isn't a sad story—it's a love story.

—Katie Anne Lester

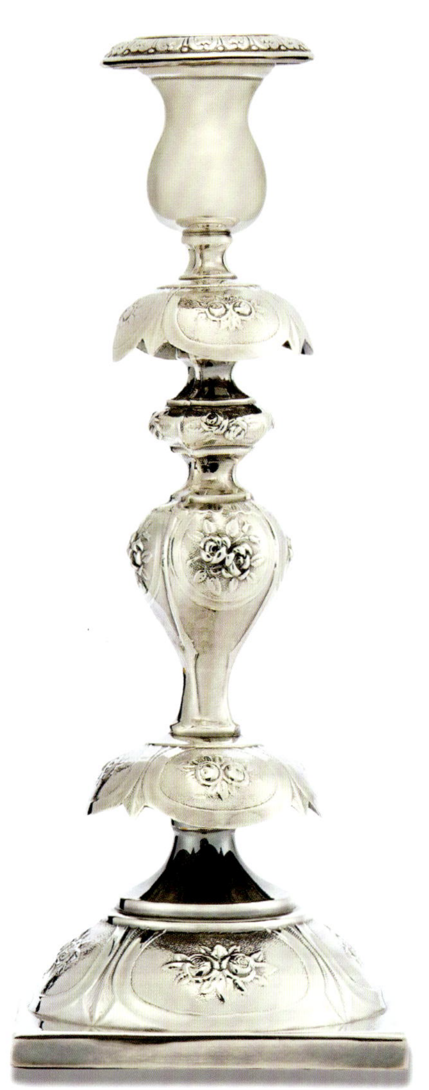
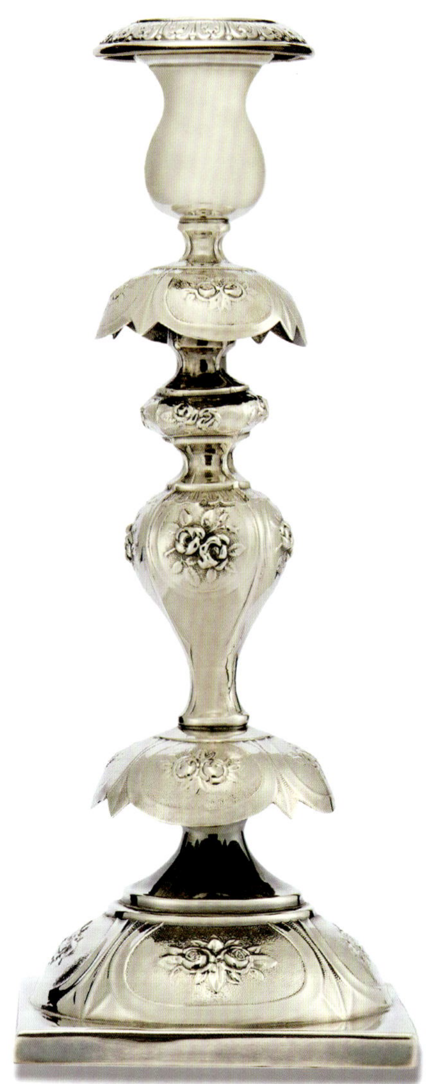

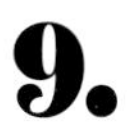

Hallie Abrams | CLEVELAND, OHIO

Immigrating to America in the early 1900s was a significant life event. But once Anna Bergson was aboard the boat, no one thought much of a woman and two little girls with a few loaves of bread. And that is exactly what she intended.

Six years prior, Anna's husband left her in Poland with their children so he could build a new life for them in America. As one of the few literate women left in her town, she kept busy by reading letters to other women whose husbands had also gone to America in search of better lives for their families.

Every Friday night, Anna managed to put a traditional meal on the table. A pair of silver candlesticks adorned the table, casting a hopeful light.

"I like to believe she was praying for the day she'd be reunited with her husband," Anna's great-granddaughter, Hallie Abrams, says.

In 1919, Anna's husband sent for her and the girls. She could bring few belongings, but she would not part with her candlesticks. Before boarding the boat, she baked each of them into a loaf of challah bread to keep them safely out of sight during the crossing to America.

The Bergson family, and their candlesticks, made it to Ellis Island safely. Anna settled with her husband in Cleveland, Ohio, where he had been working as a tailor. Together, they built their new life in a new land on a foundation of long-standing customs. Every Friday, Anna still put a traditional meal on the table, lit by the warm glow of the Shabbat candles.

Four generations later, the story of the family's candlesticks is still being written. Anna's great-granddaughter, Hallie, inherited them from her grandmother, Eileen. She uses them every Friday night on her own family's dinner table.

"This treasure is a direct connection to the generations that came before me. And when I light my candles on Friday night knowing that my grandma and great-grandma both did the same, it gives me a shiver and a smile."

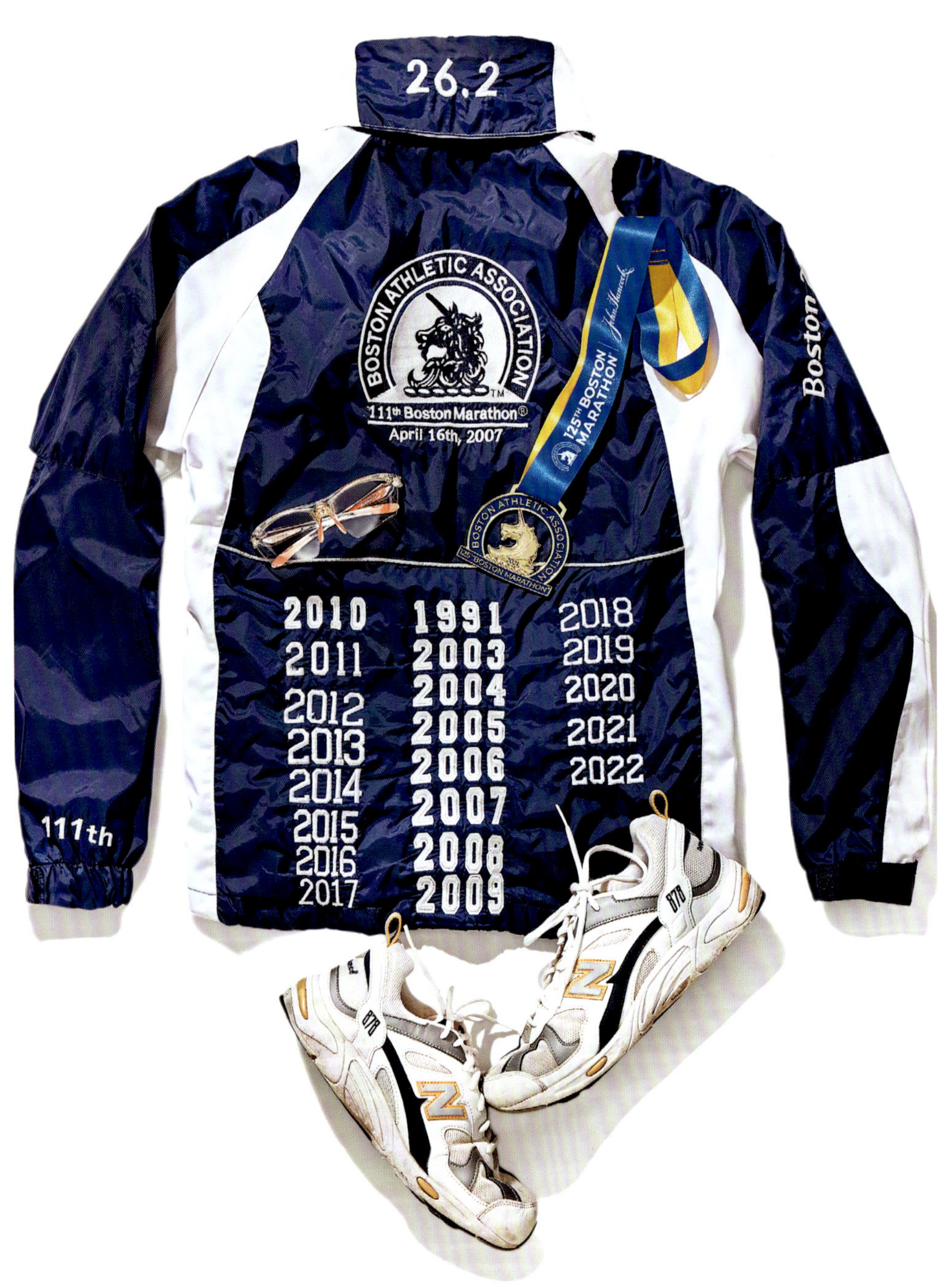

26.2
BOSTON ATHLETIC ASSOCIATION
111th Boston Marathon®
April 16th, 2007
125TH BOSTON MARATHON
BOSTON ATHLETIC ASSOCIATION
125TH BOSTON MARATHON
Boston
2010
2011
2012
2013
2014
2015
2016
2017
1991
2003
2004
2005
2006
2007
2008
2009
2018
2019
2020
2021
2022
111th
878
878

Just reading about the long road to Kenneth Williams's many accomplishments will make you tired. But his story will energize your soul.

Kenneth picked up the running habit in his thirties from a friend. Since then, he has run through 135 pairs of running shoes. He counts seventy-three marathons under his belt, including the Boston Marathon, which he has run every year for the last twenty years. In 2022, he tripped and fell at mile 21.5 of the Boston Marathon and broke his elbow and finger. He got up and finished third in his age division.

At eighty-three years old, he has run more than sixty thousand miles in his lifetime. Pictured is Kenneth's race-day jacket and favorite accessories.

In his hometown of Corinth, Mississippi, Kenneth is the CEO of Corinth Coca-Cola Bottling Group, a company run by his family since 1905. His love for fitness and his roots led him to make a very special contribution to both Corinth and the running community: In 1982, he started his own race and called it the Corinth Coca-Cola Classic 10K Run.

Runners from around the country come to Corinth on the first Saturday in May and wind through the streets of the town for what has become the largest 10K in Mississippi. Runners call the race "Miles of Smiles."

Liz Williams is Kenneth's granddaughter. She says seeing her grandfather run with such a contagious spirit taught her perseverance.

"Keep pursing your dreams, no matter your age," Liz says. This was one of her grandfather's most important lessons. Kenneth had a lesson for other kids too.

In 2004, Kenneth founded Step With It, an exercise awareness program for kids. Kenneth led by example. He ran four hundred miles from the Tennessee/Mississippi border all the way south to the Gulf of Mexico. It took thirty-five days. He stopped a few times—to speak with approximately ten thousand kids along the way about physical fitness. During his run, he raised $112,500 for Boys and Girls Club chapters throughout the state.

"This really speaks to his service and his heart for his community," Liz says. "He taught me so much about living life to the fullest. His heart runs deep."

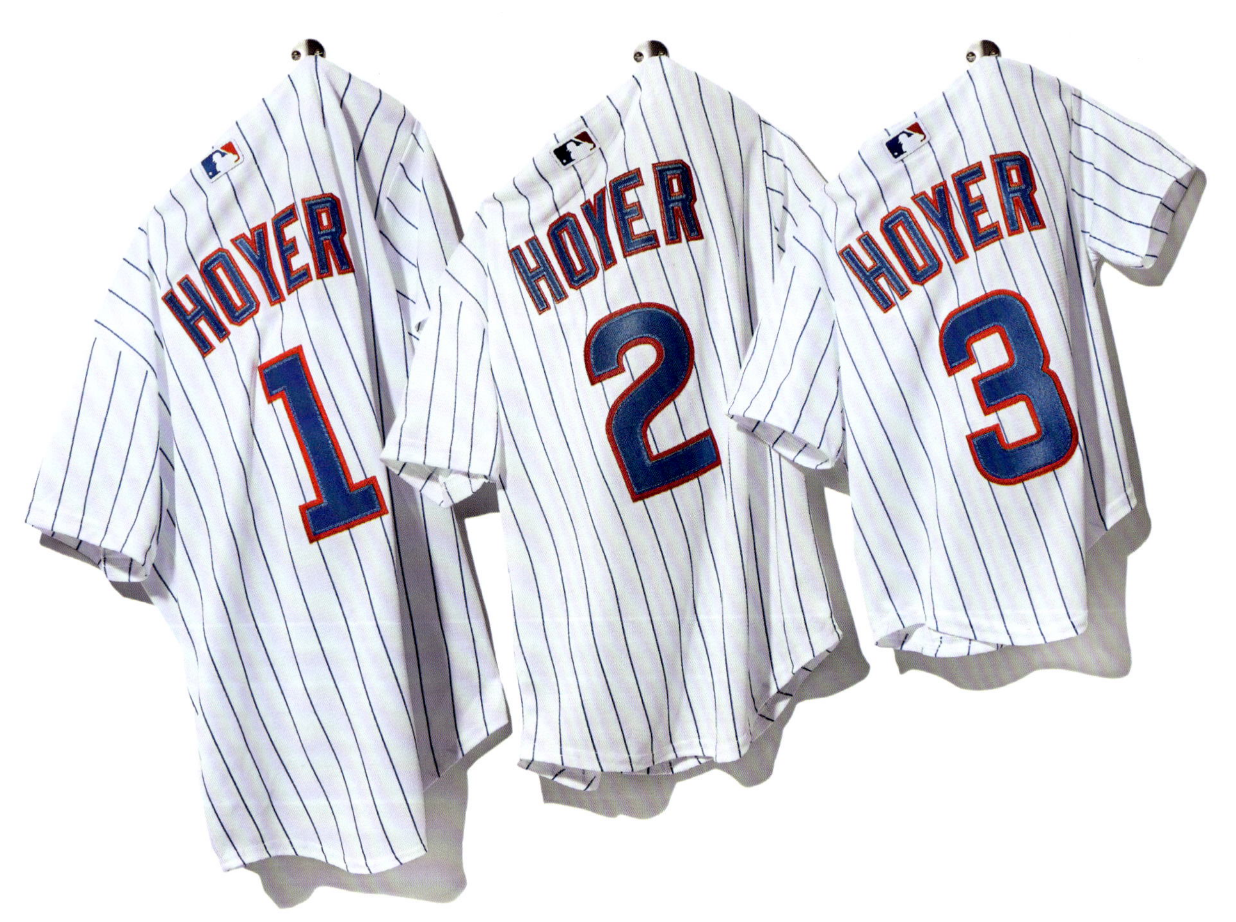
HOYER
1
HOYER
2
HOYER
3

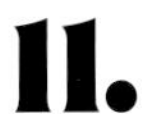

Merrill Hoyer | CHICAGO, ILLINOIS

"I live in a locker room," jokes Merrill Hoyer. With three boys, two dogs, and a baseball team executive husband under the same roof, life on the home front is constantly in some state of disarray. But a life full of little boys and big jobs is exactly how Merrill likes it. "We sort of have our own baseball team," she says.

In addition to acting as co-captain of Team Hoyer, Merrill's husband, Jed, is president of baseball operations for the Chicago Cubs. "Jed grew up watching games with his dad, poring over stats," Merrill says of her husband. "He has loved the game his entire life."

The Hoyer family thrives on sports and competition. In between Jed's major league games, the family can be found navigating their way to various practices and games for the kids. Merrill throws her racquets into the mix weekly as an accomplished squash and tennis player.

"'Go big or go home, but, of course, have fun with it all' is our family mantra," Merrill says.

When her youngest was born, a friend gave her three crisp white jerseys emblazoned with "Hoyer 1," "Hoyer 2," and "Hoyer 3" in honor of Merrill's now complete home team. She says the jerseys represent the competitive nature of their family but also the generational connection baseball brings to their lives.

"The boys play catch outside for hours and hours with their dad. It's their way of connecting."

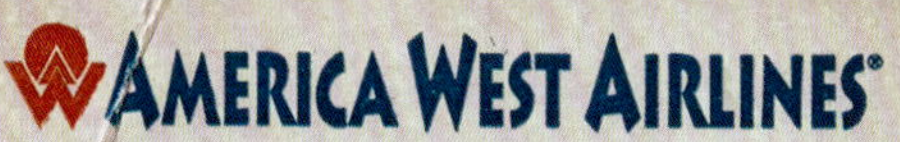

Name of Passenger

BEEMER/MARTHA

From

PHOENIX

To

WASHINGTON DULLES

Flight	Class	Date	Time
FLT. 855		16MAR	

Gate	Boarding time	Seat
	1230P	20D Aisle

12. Martha Palan | PROVIDENCE, RHODE ISLAND

Martha Beemer Palan was living in San Francisco when her mother passed away, giving her the feeling that it was time to move home to Washington, DC. So she packed her bags and boarded a flight.

On her connecting flight in Phoenix, headed for Washington Dulles International Airport, Martha settled into her aisle seat. She exhaled. She was headed home and feeling pretty good about the empty middle seat beside her.

Then one last passenger slipped through the door just as the flight attendant closed it.

"He came running onto the plane, a mess, with stuff falling out of his bag," she remembers of the passenger. He was headed for the seat next to her.

"Once he got settled, he apologized in advance for the big messy burrito that he was about to eat, and I told him not to worry about it as I had just inhaled a Whopper, and we laughed," Martha says. "And then we started chatting . . . all the way across the country."

The guy in the middle seat with the burrito was Andy, a major in the Marine Corps. He had just come off active duty so, like Martha, he too was starting a new chapter in Washington. They talked a lot about his service and the pending invasion of Iraq. He was honest about feeling some sadness about not being there . . . for his friends.

"I didn't know anyone who had been on active duty, so it was a new perspective for me," Martha remembers. "He was interesting."

When the plane landed, Martha and Andy walked to baggage claim together, said their good-byes, and split. Andy headed for a Hertz rental-car bus; Martha headed for the Avis bus.

"It was hard and weird to walk away from him," Martha says. "There was a lot of energy happening on that plane."

Just before Martha's bus pulled away, she spotted Andy running, business card in hand. Their first date was the following night.

Mr. and Mrs. Palan are now happily married and have a daughter. (In a delightful coincidence, Martha's mother and father also met on an airplane.)

Martha has always kept the boarding pass from her flight to DC. It's a reminder that you never know who will end up in the middle seat.

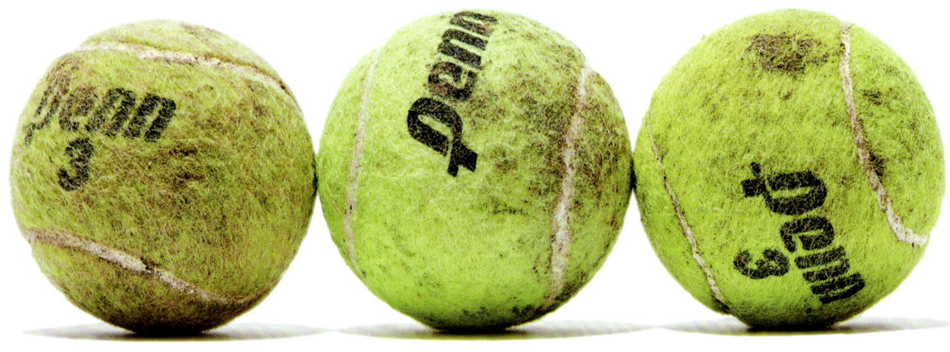
Penn
3
Penn
Penn
3

13. Whitney Whitmore | WILLIAMSBURG, VIRGINIA

Whitney Whitmore is an adult, but when a cousin gifted her a puppy, she got into big trouble with her mom. Then her mom and the puppy fell in love.

"Bailey was her reason to get out of bed most days," Whitney says. Her mom, Kitty, was battling breast cancer. While Kitty was braving a mastectomy and chemo, Bailey started sleeping at the end of Kitty's bed.

"He helped me navigate through the darkest time in my life," Kitty says. "He became the most loyal and steadfast best friend anyone could ask for."

There was only one thing Bailey loved more than Kitty, and that was tennis balls. "He wanted nothing more than to go outside and play ball on the golf course," Whitney says. "Playing ball with Bailey required not one, not two, but three tennis balls."

Every day for eleven years, when Whitney came home from work, they went straight to the golf course to play fetch. "It was our thing," she remembers. As Bailey grew older, the family watched him visibly slow down. And then, as happens in life, there would be no more fetch.

"The morning we said good-bye, I took him one last time out to his mound on the golf course and I threw the ball. He just watched it roll away," Whitney recalls. "At that moment, I knew he was tired and it was his time."

"Bail's tennis balls are old, dirty, faded, and have been slobbered on countless times, but they are his. They are my very favorite thing to see because I imagine our sweet boy sitting on top of his mound on the golf course, chasing all the balls his little heart desires."

Kitty remembers Bailey for his convincing spirit.

"He'd wedge his head between my nightstand and bed, those sweet brown eyes gently motioning, come on . . . we got this!" And "got this" she did—Kitty is now cancer-free.

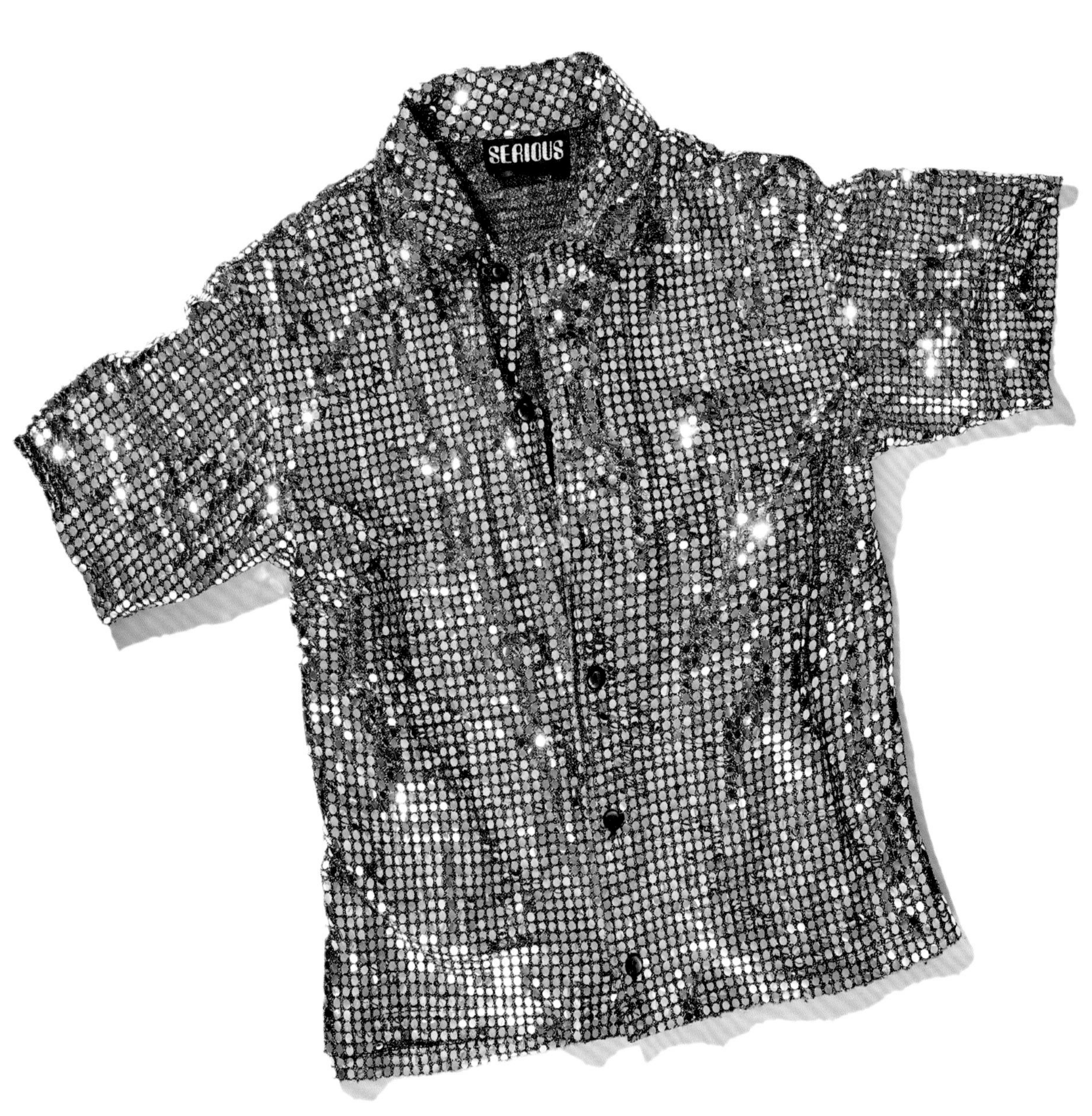
SERIOUS

14. Ben Aaron | NEW YORK, NEW YORK

Ben Aaron was making mixtapes at the age of nine. By the age of thirteen, he had landed his first gig as a DJ. By fourteen, his father, Mark, was driving him to New York City nightclubs so he could stand on the sidewalk outside to hear new music through the brick walls.

"There wasn't a fake ID strong enough to get me in," Ben joked. But his age didn't hold him back from his love of music, a love his father supported and encouraged.

Mark lugged his son's DJ gear to every gig and lugged Ben to the record store on the weekends, where they would spend hours perusing the merchandise. They even shopped for clothes together to make sure Ben had the appropriate attire for a DJ.

When a new store called Scream opened at the local mall, father and son went to check it out. The store stocked mostly rave gear, but among the plastic pants and fluorescent tank tops, Ben's dad dug up a sequined shirt.

"My dad lifted it up and said, half-jokingly, 'How 'bout this?'"

It was the coolest thing Ben had ever seen. It became his calling card.

As Ben's teenage DJ gigs gave way to the demands of adulthood, his prize DJ shirt was relegated to the Halloween-costume pile and, eventually, to a box at his dad's house.

In 2013, Ben married Ginger Zee, chief meteorologist for ABC News, and soon after, he became a father himself. He and Ginger now have two boys, Adrian and Miles. Ben remembers the boys first "meeting" the disco ball shirt by accident—his father had mailed it to him after years in storage. The boys were enamored upon first sight, just like Ben was when his dad found the shirt so many years ago.

"Adrian immediately wanted to try it on. Miles was all giggles," Ben says. Ben and the boys hold daily dance parties now—and someone always has the shirt on.

"We will spend a solid hour nonstop dancing to everything from Led Zeppelin to the *Electric Boogaloo* soundtrack. They get really into it."

Ben says his disco ball shirt has always been less of a shirt and more of a celebration.

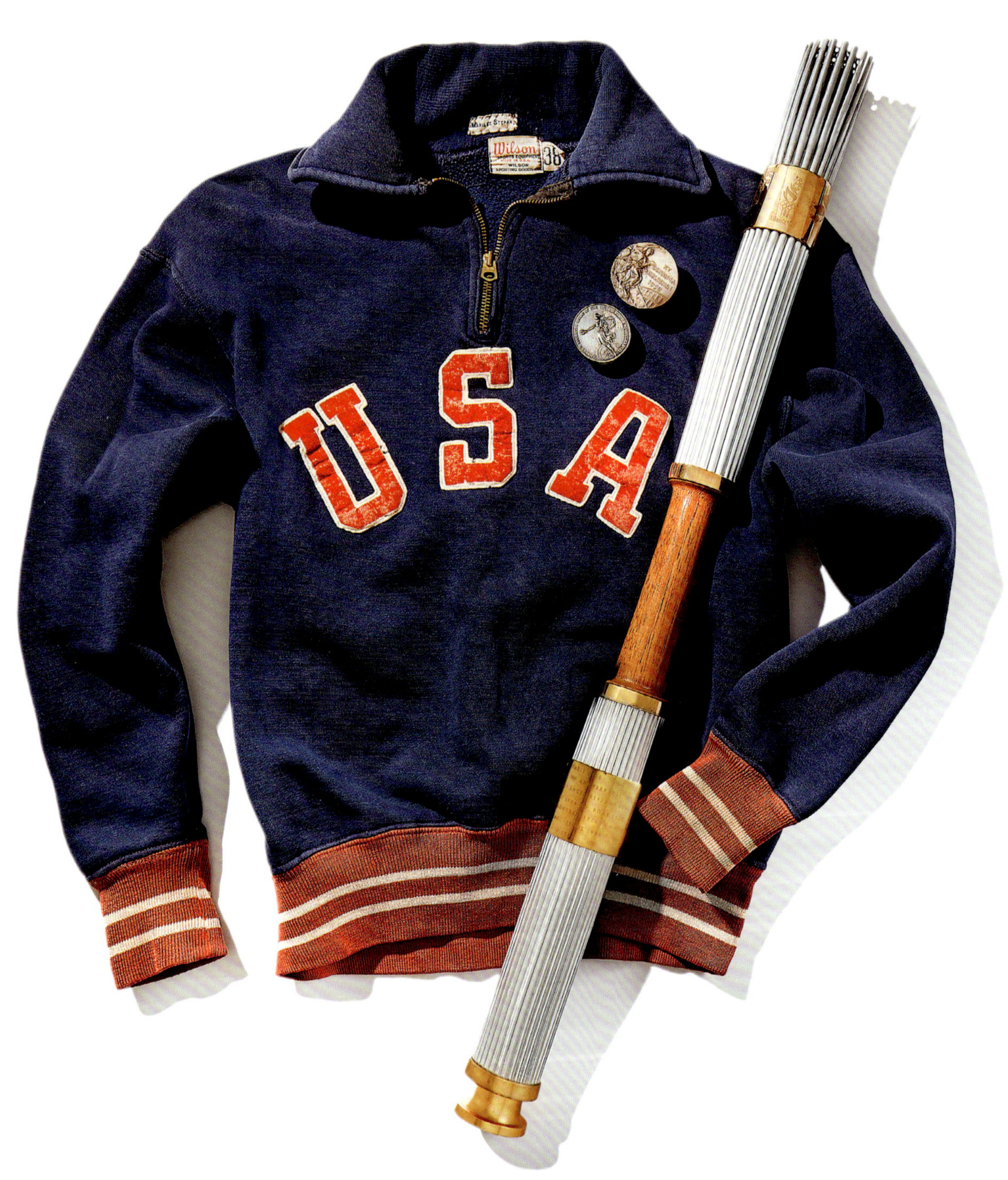
Wilson
USA

Family legend has it that Mary Lou Quinn Stepan, the 1929 Illinois state freestyle champion and nationally recognized swimmer, may have lovingly started her infant daughter on swim lessons in the bathtub. That daughter, Marilee Stepan Wehman, would go on to become an Olympian at the age of seventeen.

After her early bathtub lessons, Marilee formally learned to swim in Lake Michigan as a child. At age eighty-five, she could be found swimming fifty lengths a day at the country club pool. This is the story of the in-between.

Marilee became a nationally ranked swimmer in the two hundred–yard freestyle at age fifteen. This was impressive on its own, but even more so because her high school had no swimming program, no coach, and no pool. She practiced with the boys at Chicago's Lake Shore Athletic Club.

By age seventeen, her notable talent and work ethic had earned her a spot on the 1952 US Olympic team. She returned home from the games, held that year in Helsinki, with a bronze medal in the one hundred–meter freestyle relay. She was met in Winnetka, Illinois, with much fanfare in the press—and also a few realities of the times.

Erin Kiernan, Marilee's granddaughter, recalls the family Olympian famously being told by her father (whom she adored) that it was time to hang up her swimsuit and get married. "Which she did," Erin says. "But she was an ardent advocate for women in sports throughout her lifetime."

Marilee would go on to become one of the first women to serve as a board member of the US Olympic Committee and the Illinois Olympic Committee. She endowed a scholarship for underprivileged female athletes at the University of Chicago and served on behalf of countless other organizations throughout her lifetime.

But it seems the real benefactors of Marilee's spirit are those who got to call her wife, mom, grandma, and great-grandma. Of growing up with Marilee as a mom, Mary Louise Kiernan, the oldest of Marilee's daughters, perhaps says it best: "I always considered myself lucky to be from this gene pool." Marilee's granddaughter, Erin, felt her impact outside the pool.

"My grandmother inspired me to approach my ambitions with confidence, knowing that if I worked hard, I could do anything, including beating the boys!" says Erin.

Marilee's namesake granddaughter, Marilee Kiernan, may have gotten the most potent of the swimming genes. She swam for Yale University, and recently completed the triple crown of open-water marathon swimming: the English Channel, circumnavigating Manhattan, and the Catalina Channel in California.

"My Grammy was an early advocate of women and girl power," Marilee says. When she was younger, her grandmother started a secret club in her Palm Beach backyard exclusively for her granddaughters. "We affectionately called it the Secret Garden Club, a sacred place where we could share stories and empower each other," Marilee says. "As a women's health physician and advocate myself, I think those early experiences of us girls taking some time to support and see each other were extremely formative. They inspired the spirit in which I seek to create a safe space for and treat all of my patients, colleagues, friends, and family today," she says.

Outside of the Secret Garden Club, Marilee impacted the male members of her family just as much. Her grandson, Robert Kennedy, has a fitting and distinct memory of his grandma—her love for sportsmanship.

In 1996, with her Olympic medal–winning swim in the history books, Marilee Stepan was honored by the US Olympic Committee for her years of dedication to the games: She was selected to carry the Olympic torch through Illinois on its way to the Atlanta games. "She carried with dignity and grace the torch of honor and fair competition her whole life," says Karen Kennedy, her middle daughter. "It was the ultimate honor," Marilee's youngest, Alison McNally, says. "Mom, running with the eternal flame, family watching, lighting up the world. That's what she did. Mom was our flame."

Mom was our flame.

—Alison McNally

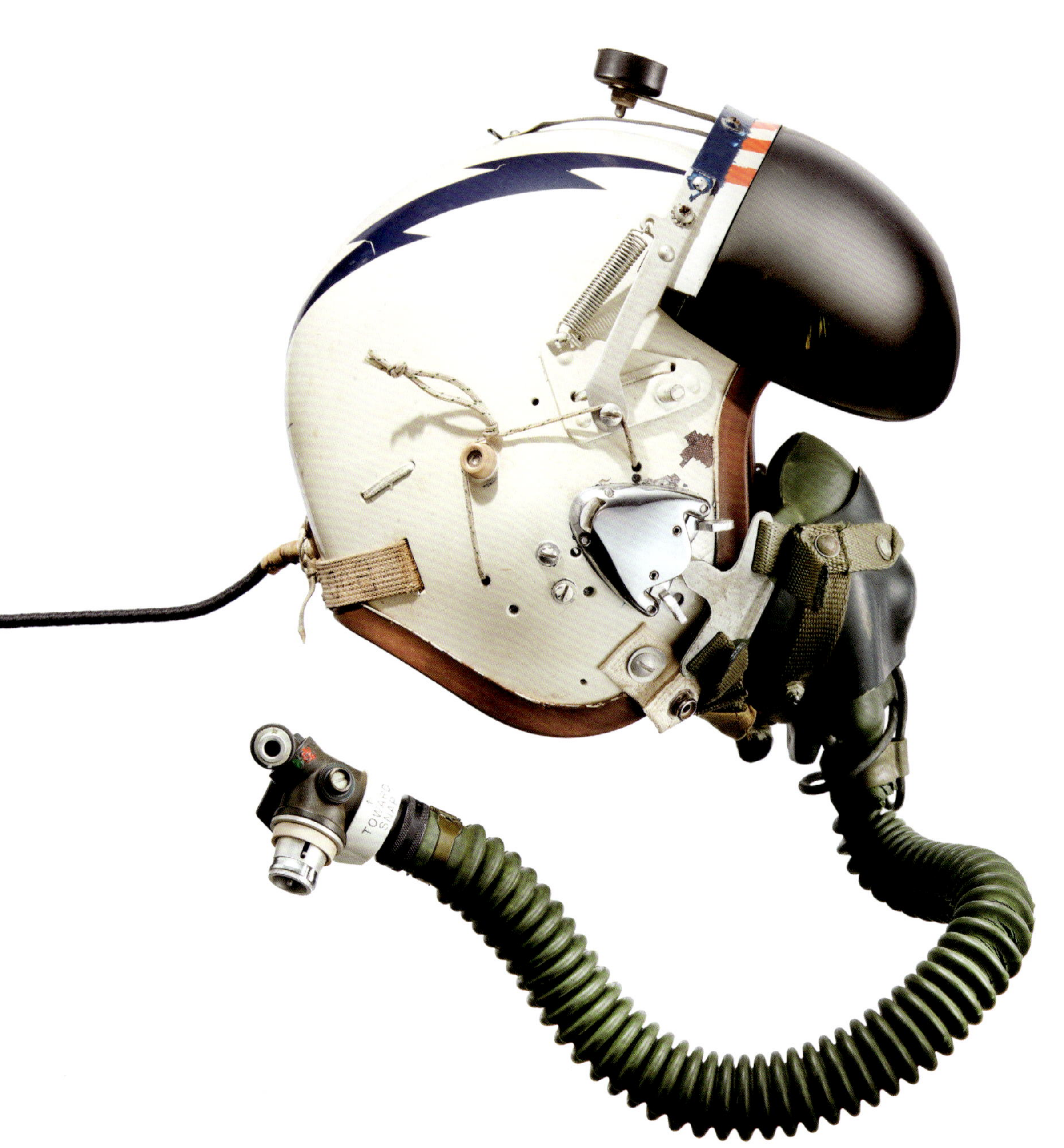
TOWARD
SNAP

16. Margi Young | WICHITA, KANSAS

When Margi Young was a kid, her father was always gone for work. And by work, we mean flying fighter jets. He accompanied Air Force One and President John F. Kennedy to a conference in Costa Rica in 1963 and participated in the military flyover at JFK's funeral later that year. He also served two tours and more than two hundred missions in Vietnam in 1972. Margi's father, Lt. Colonel Young, was a tactical fighter pilot in the US Air Force.

Her earliest memories of her dad are of missing him. He was a kind and larger-than-life figure who was always away in service to his country. She remembers growing older and, like so many other military kids, becoming proud of his service despite the sacrifice. She also keenly remembers that when he returned from his first tour in Vietnam, he had changed.

"He came back as a more distant father," Margi says. "It was a hard thing for a kid to understand."

In his later years, while Lt. Colonel Young remained somewhat distant, he could always be found tinkering in his beloved airplane hangar. His single-engine Myers 200 aircraft was his pride and joy. It was around this time that Margi found room in her heart to have compassion for how her father's service in the sky had affected him down on the ground. She made a true effort to stay connected to him as he got older.

"When I became a mom, I felt it was important that I connect with him so that my children would know him. He was their history," she says. He was hers too. She fondly remembers how kind he was to other veterans in his older years.

When her father passed away, Margi found things like scuba gear and spare airplane parts in his hangar. She also found his helmet from Vietnam tucked away in a closet.

"Time had taken its toll on the helmet, but it symbolized the rawness of his memory, his years of service, and his way of life," Margi says. "I think he'd want to be remembered as a decorated fighter pilot—but also as being the best man he could be."

Margie's brother, Mark, once a student of his father's, is now the steward of his father's beloved airplane. He flies it often in his honor.

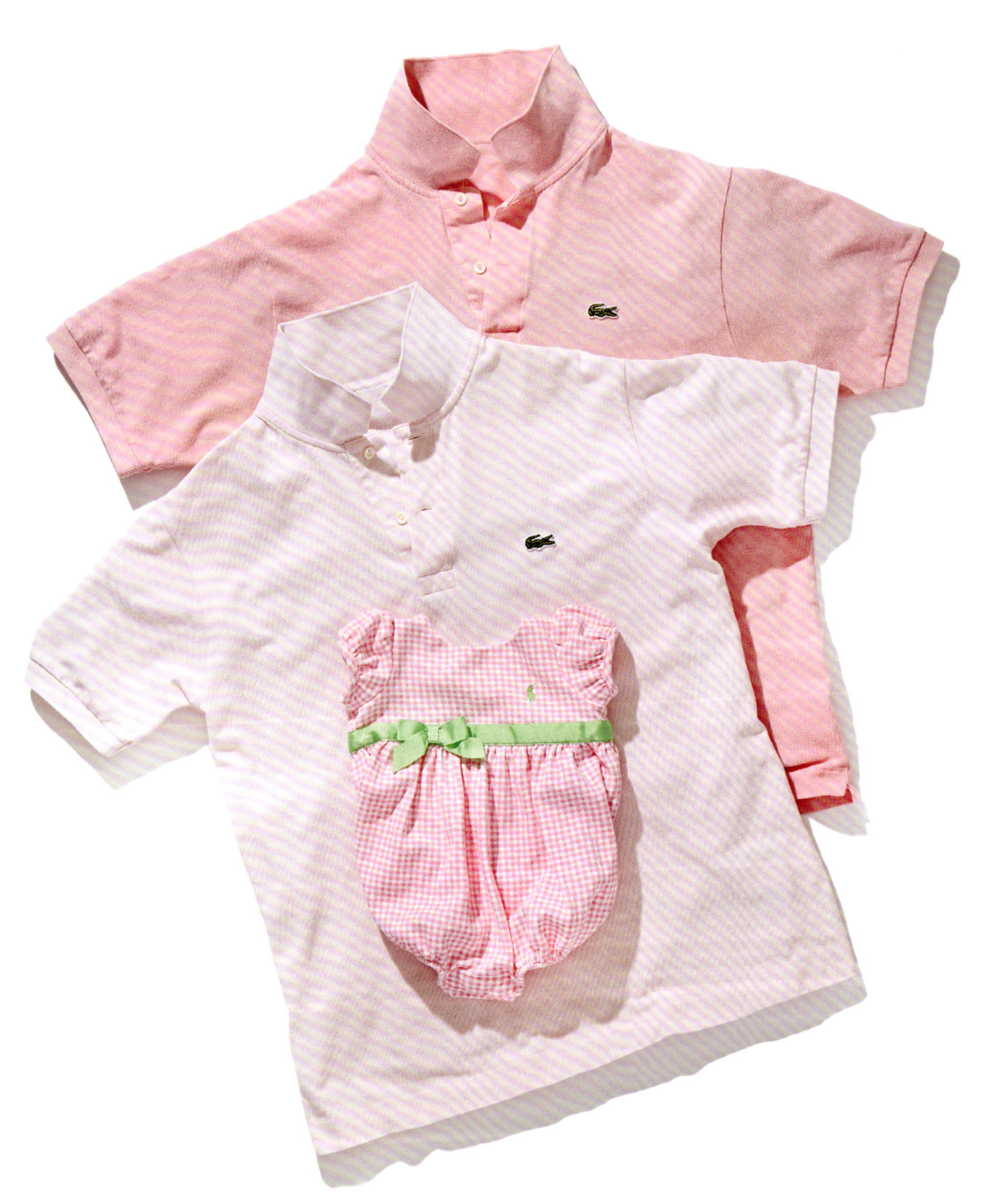

One night in 2002, Danny Cohn threw on a pair of jeans and an old sweater and headed out for what he figured would be another disappointing dinner date. But the minute he saw Andrew Miller's handsome, Kennedy-esque grin, he knew it was forever.

That night, on their first date, Danny and Andrew discovered they wanted many of the same things in life. A family was at the top of the list. For the next thirteen years, Danny and Andrew tried.

"The journey to having a child, for us, included parenting courses, required parenting tests, and visits to our home from social workers who came to determine if we were worthy of being parents," says Danny. During one visit, a social worker cited an air conditioner unit located unacceptably close to a bed. Danny couldn't help but think about all the kids out there who don't have beds, let alone air conditioners. Or families.

"We had to do a lot of proving ourselves," Danny says. The formalities and legalities often made it seem like society was not on their side. Yet everyone who knew them closely and loved them knew they were destined to be good fathers who were dedicated to their family. Andrew's grandparents generously set aside money for him to start a family. "Even ninety-year-olds, who could barely grasp two men getting married, were pushing for us to be dads," Danny says.

There were also the traditional challenges of starting a family, similar to those faced by so many others. "I think adopting is a lot like going through fertility treatments," Danny notes. "You take a lot of tests, you are told it's all a go, and then in the blink of an eye it doesn't happen, and everything is dashed after all the hoping and praying."

Finally, in 2015, with all the right papers filed, tests passed, and legalities buttoned up, they got the call. It was at the hospital, upon first meeting their daughter, Nora, that Danny finally exhaled. Their family was complete.

"All of the things we had to go through was just the universe leading us to her," Danny says.

The winter after Nora was born, Danny and Andrew got to do something they had wanted for so many years. They got to send out a family holiday card—the kind they had, up until now, only received from other families. Pictured are the outfits they wore for their photograph.

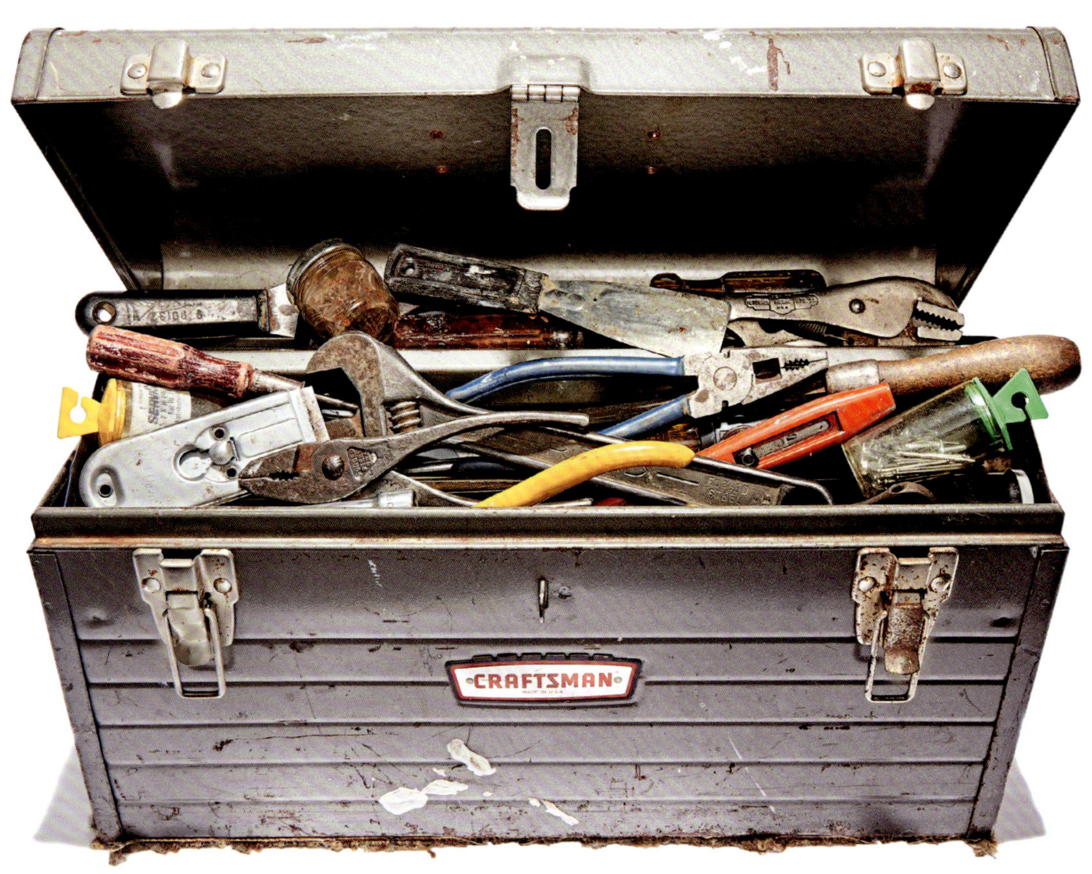
CRAFTSMAN

18. Denise Rubino | EAST HAMPTON, NEW YORK

When Leonard "John" Rubino and his wife, Kitty, first moved into their new home, she wanted a new kitchen. So, he tore the current one out and built her a new one—by himself. When she wanted a deck, he built her that too. And when he had no place to sit on the deck, he built himself a bench to enjoy while barbecuing.

John's daughter, Denise, says her father was famous for being a Mr. Fix It. He would spackle and paint any wall that needed it. He could figure out how to repair anything. And he could rewire just about anything and turn it into a lamp.

"Even neighbors would stop by to borrow a tool because they knew he'd have exactly what they needed," Denise says.

One of her favorite memories of her dad involved a stoplight. He found one while antiquing with his wife. They bought it and, once home, John rewired it. For most of Denise and her brother John's childhoods, the Rubino family had a working stoplight in their den.

John's spirit for the sport of fixing and improving was so strong it can still be felt, nearly thirty years after his death. In 1995, John crossed paths with something he couldn't fix—cancer. But Denise says her father's spirit of self-reliance and hard work is still very present in everything she does. And she means that literally—she has his toolbox, pictured, complete with every tool she remembers him tinkering with when she was a kid. She now tinkers around her own house, Dad's tools in tow.

"He is the reason I refuse to call an electrician or plumber until I try to fix the problem myself," Denise jokes. "He taught me to have confidence and to figure it out."

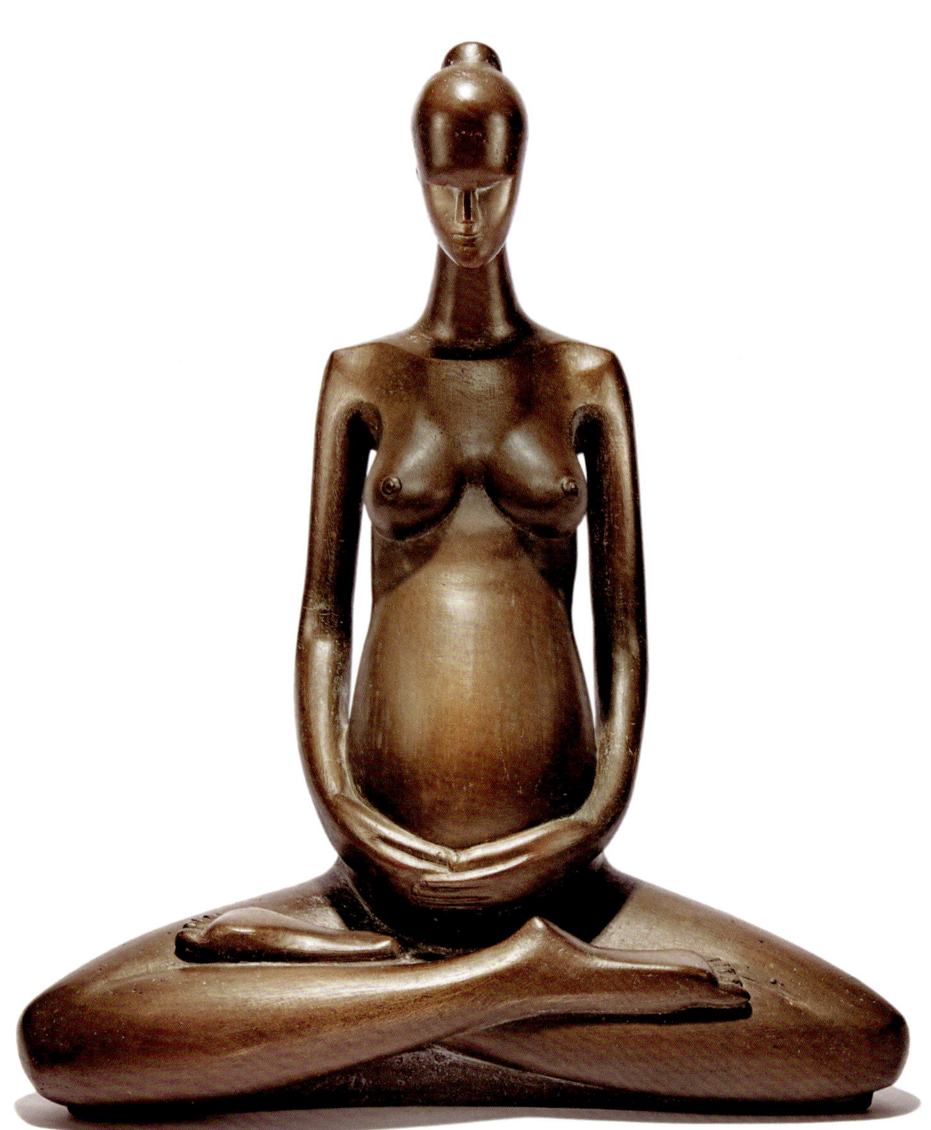

Christy Turlington Burns was a few months away from becoming a mother for the first time when a small art gallery on the ground floor of her New York City apartment building put this sculpture in their window display. The bronze casting, by artist Pham Ngoc Long, was a pregnant yogi, head bowed in prayer. It spoke a familiar language of empowerment to Christy each day when she passed it. As she inched closer to her due date, the statue disappeared. The power of its message did not.

Christy has proven herself to be a powerhouse in the modeling industry for decades, but she credits her yoga mat for her most important work.

"Yoga opened me to my power to make an impact, on myself and others," Christy says of her practice. "Yoga opened me to service." And so, like the sculpture sitting quietly in the gallery window, she used her practice to share empowerment with the greater good.

Christy has lent her voice to many humanitarian causes over the years, but the one dearest to her heart took shape in 2003, when her experience with postpartum complications inspired an idea.

"I had every resource I needed to get my daughter and me safely through," Christy says of her health scare. "It mainly got me thinking, 'What about the women who don't have access to quality, respectful maternity care?'"

Seven years later, Christy had founded Every Mother Counts, a nonprofit organization dedicated to making pregnancy and childbirth safe and equitable for every mother everywhere. Today, the organization has invested more than $30 million in community-led maternal health programs across ten countries: the United States, Haiti, Guatemala, Mexico, Tanzania, Kenya, India, Indonesia, Nepal, and Bangladesh.

She shared a story about a recent trip to Guatemala on behalf of her organization.

"It was our first visit since 2019 because of the pandemic. We celebrated the third class of graduates from the Corazón del Agua midwifery school who had to complete their curriculum remotely. These Indigenous women come from rural areas across the country and return to their communities with added skills and knowledge to provide compassionate and culturally congruent care to women and families. I am so proud to support their training and foster the mentorship needed to build the pipeline for this critical health care."

Christy's work abroad and at home makes her a working mother of epic proportions. Not only does she steer her two teenagers through life, but her organization also counts more than one million lives impacted worldwide.

She is also still empowered by the yogi mother sculpture she saw in the art gallery window so many years ago . . . because it now lives on her bookshelf. Her husband, actor Ed Burns, is the reason it disappeared—he bought it as a surprise gift for her.

Yoga opened me to service.

—Christy Turlington Burns

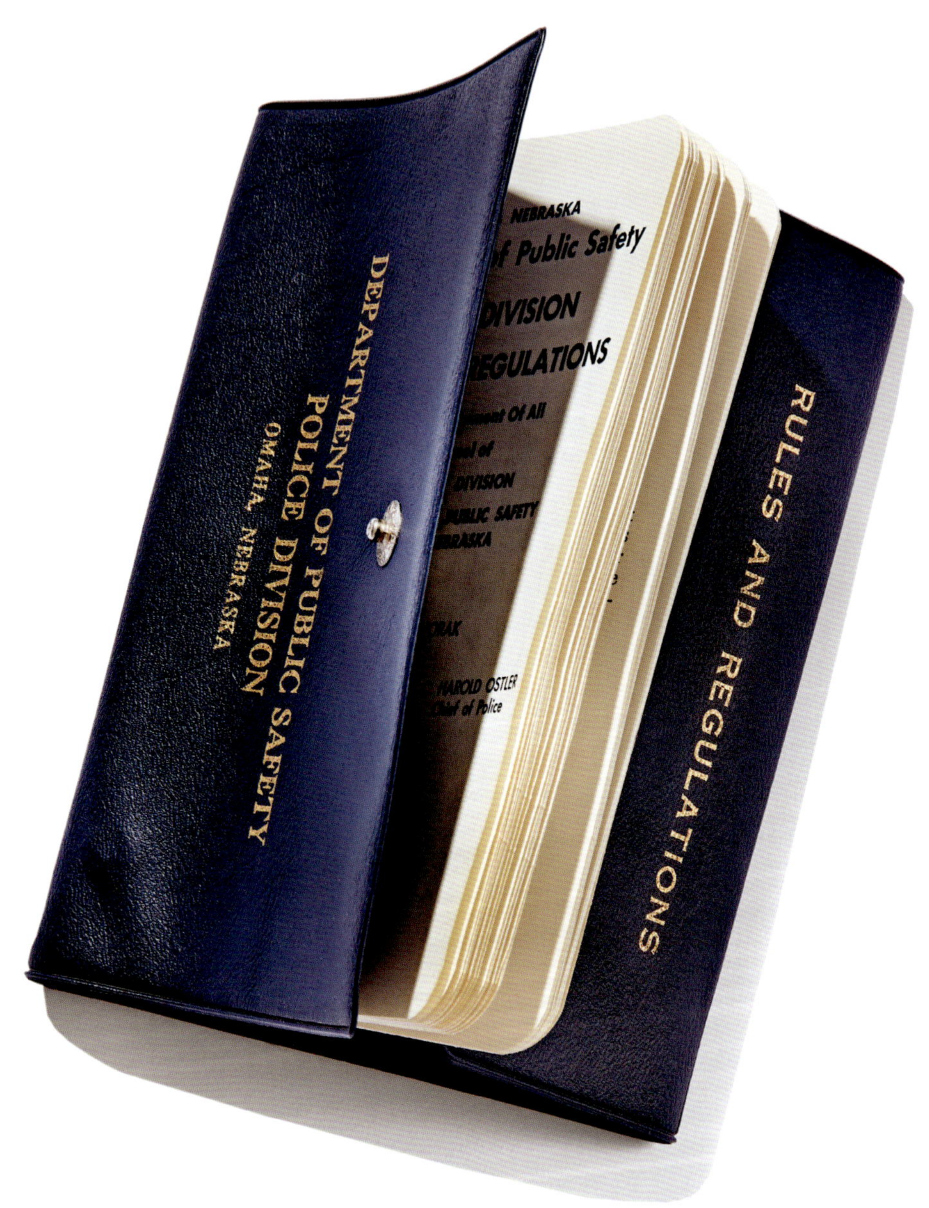
DEPARTMENT OF PUBLIC SAFETY
POLICE DIVISION
OMAHA, NEBRASKA
RULES AND REGULATIONS
NEBRASKA
HAROLD OSTLER
Chief of Police

Keeping the people of Omaha, Nebraska, safe has been a Friend family tradition for generations. Officer Anthony "Tony" Friend has served as an Omaha police officer for twenty-five years, and he's been with the sheriff's department for almost three years. He comes from a legacy of service—his great-grandfather, father, two uncles, and a handful of cousins were, and are, law-enforcement officers. Tony estimates that there are two hundred years of law enforcement among them.

Of all the experience and knowledge the Friend family holds, Tony says that some of his most powerful lessons came from his father, Bill. Tony credits his dad with instilling integrity and professionalism in him—a "by the book" approach to law enforcement. Tony still has his father's *Rules and Regulations*, pictured, as a reminder of his father's service.

"My dad was a true gentleman and professional. He always carried that book to quickly reference laws," Tony says. "It is very old, but the point does not change with time."

When Bill passed away, a retired cop friend of his shared a touching thought with Tony at Bill's funeral, something Tony knew to be very true: that his dad knew how to handle any situation.

"[My dad] passed on to me the value of fair treatment of everyone, no matter what differences," Tony says. "He always told me to stop and think. To not rush into anything. I believe that has given me the patience to adapt to any situation I encounter," he says.

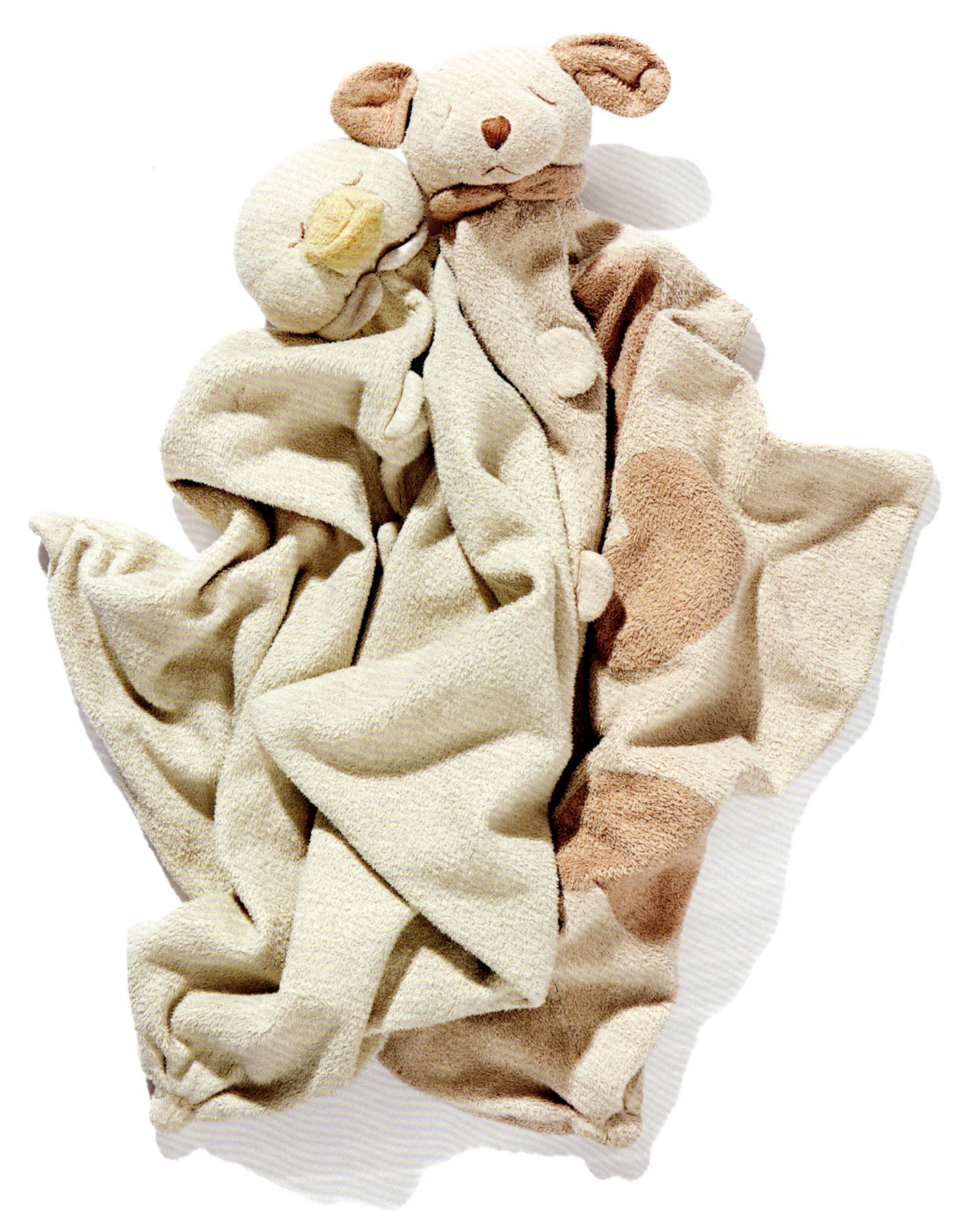

Sometimes, a broken heart can be a superpower.

Gretchen Holt Witt's son, Liam, was diagnosed with neuroblastoma at the age of two and a half. He would endure rounds of chemotherapy and other cancer treatments for four years. At first, Liam responded to the treatments—he was a lucky one—so Gretchen used the time to put her gratitude to work for other kids still fighting the disease.

She knew there was a new and powerful antibody treatment option in development. But she also knew from firsthand experience that there was an astonishing lack of research in the field of pediatric oncology and Gretchen wasn't having it. She set out to raise the money needed to get the treatment across the finish line so it could help kids like Liam as soon as possible.

She decided she'd raise the money by making a whole lot of cookies. Together with 250 volunteers, in a rented commercial kitchen space in New York City, she wound up baking 96,000 cookies. They raised $420,000, all of which went directly to the new antibody treatment.

In time, Liam's cancer returned. Although he fought hard, the life-saving treatments he needed were not yet available. Liam was just shy of his seventh birthday.

His beloved stuffed animals, pictured, were his constant companions during his battle and remain a connection for Gretchen. "Thick and thin, good times and bad, they were there," Gretchen says. "Liam rubbed them for comfort," she says of the many visible marks of time on the stuffed animals. "I would grab them if there was a fire," Gretchen says. "They are the most direct link I have to Liam and how hard he loved."

Liam's spirit and the impact of the first cookie sale drove Gretchen to keep moving forward after his passing. "He would want to see us doing exactly what we're doing—making it better for other kids," Gretchen says. She and her husband founded Cookies for Kids' Cancer in 2008 to inspire people to organize their own bake sales and to raise money for cancer research. Volunteers now bake in twenty-four countries, and all proceeds from the bake sales go directly to cancer research. To date, there have been more than fifteen thousand grassroots events, and Cookies for Kids' Cancer has granted $18 million to pediatric cancer researchers at leading hospitals. These grants have helped make twenty-five new treatments available, all of which have saved lives. A mother's love, embodied.

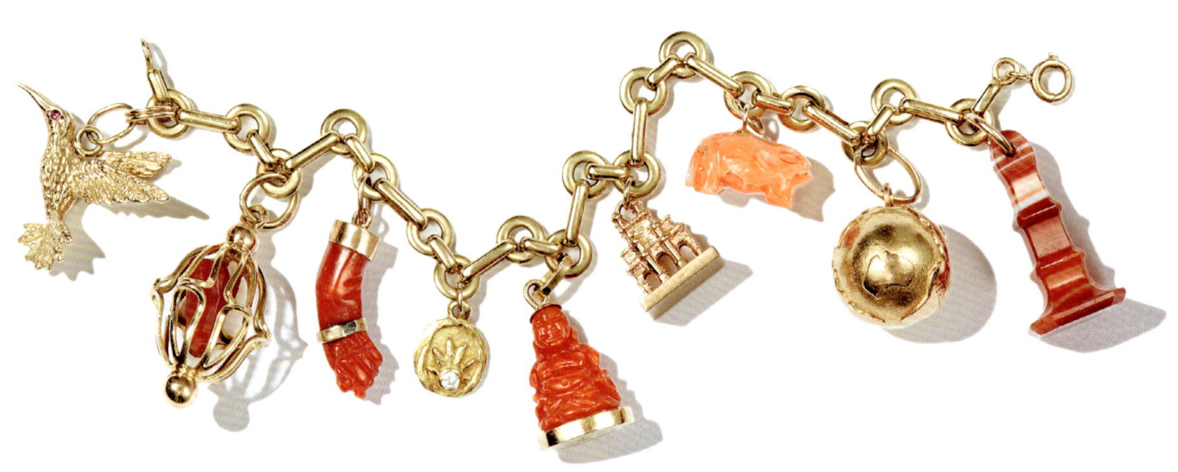

22. Nate Berkus | NEW YORK, NEW YORK

Nate Berkus credits two generations of women in his family for instilling in him the importance of individual style. His mother designed her own wedding ring and freely mixed denim with Chanel before it was cool. His grandmother was known for her trademark classic style—lots of navy blue and white. Their common thread was jewelry; every treasure held a story.

Growing up in a fashionable environment will leave its mark, and it shows in Nate's namesake design empire. But he also built another kind of empire based on individuality and personal style—a family. Together with his husband, Jeremiah Brent, Nate is now focused on making sure his stylish family traditions continue.

"Poppy already has her own stylish point of view," Nate says of his daughter. "She knows how to pile necklaces and 'stack' plastic bracelets. It's fascinating to me."

In support of Poppy's uncanny ability to accessorize, and inspired by all the stories his mom used to tell him about her own jewelry, Nate designed a charm bracelet for Poppy. Though Nate admits he fully creative-directed the palette—corals and agates mixed with gold—he and Jeremiah curated every charm to perfectly symbolize Poppy's spirit and story.

The hummingbird is a tribute to Jeremiah's grandmother—she loved hummingbirds and he saw them everywhere after she passed away. The birdcage reminds Poppy she will always be free to make her own choices. The bunny symbolizes the family's home in Montauk, where Poppy used to delight in watching them hop through the yard. The globe reminds Poppy of all the beautiful places she is destined to see in her life.

"Our daughter navigates situations with such awareness, sensitivity, kindness, and grace. It's something we wish we could take credit for, but the truth is, she is simply all these things both naturally and instinctively," Nate says. "I've always felt traditions remind us of where we come from and where we aspire to go—her charm bracelet is all of those things."

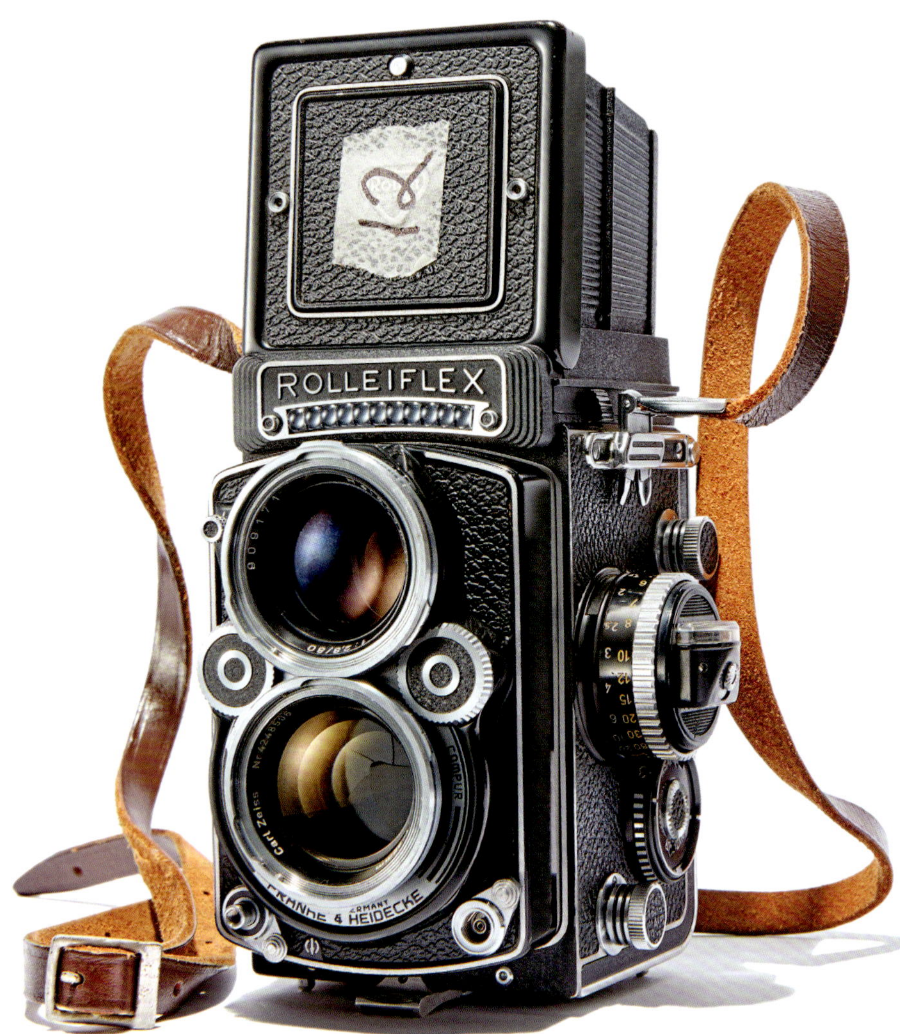
ROLLEIFLEX
Carl Zeiss
COMPUR
FRANKE & HEIDECKE

There's a very good chance that, over the years, you have looked at a picture made by this camera. Its owner, legendary fashion photographer Pamela Hanson, has created imagery for nearly every fashion brand or glossy magazine you could name.

"It has been everywhere with me for the last forty years," Pamela says of the vintage twin-lens reflex Rolleiflex. That includes Paris, where her fashion-forward documentary style put her on the map in the 1980s.

"I just loved recording life," she says humbly of her early days. By the 1990s, her eye for style and composition had established her as a force in an industry mostly dominated by men. But if you want to have a discussion about a woman's place in photography, Pamela isn't having it.

"Why does there have to be a distinction?" she says. "We are all just photographers."

It is her sharp focus on image-making, not societal constructs, that has taken her and her cameras around the world with the most creative photography crews and most talented models through the years. But, though she is an industry legend in her own right, Pamela, whose work is part of the Smithsonian collection, will tell you that her proudest accomplishment is her family.

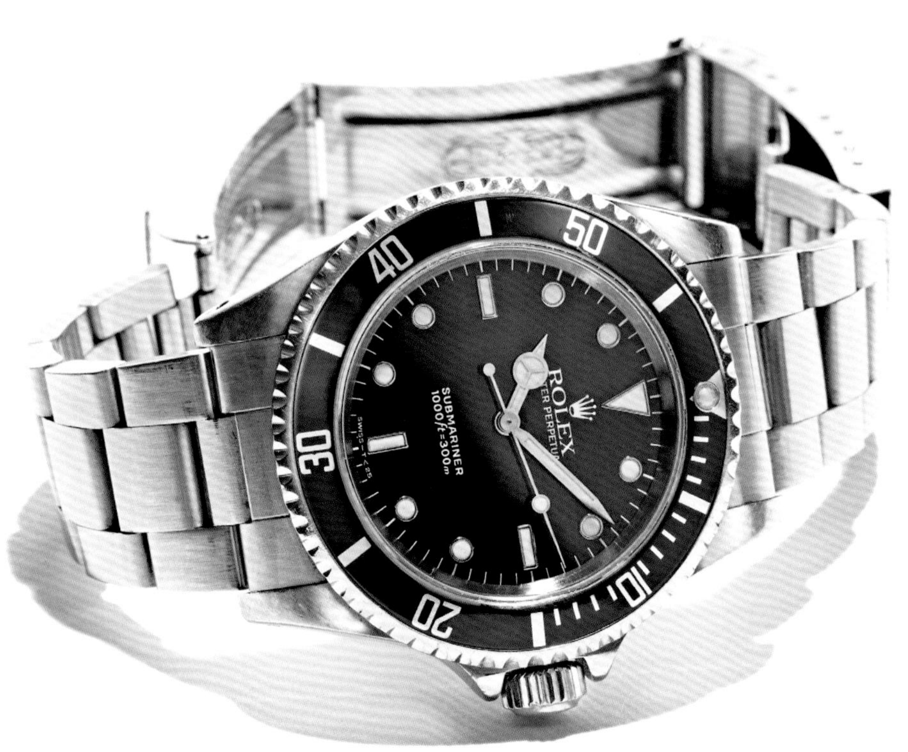
ROLEX
SUBMARINER
1000ft=300m

Steven Plofker was out for a drive one day, his arm leisurely hanging from the car window, when the engagement gift he received from his wife, a watch, slipped off his wrist without him noticing. The watch was priceless, but its value was not taken for granted—it was insured and replaced and remains a treasured gift from his wife of thirty-six years, cosmetics mogul Bobbi Brown.

That a symbol of their partnership was insured comes as no surprise—Steven and Bobbi are well known for making wise life decisions (cosmetics dynasties, boutique hotels, real estate development). They are also known for their dedication to each other. "Neither of us could have accomplished all the things we have without the support of the other," Bobbi says of her husband. Steven was integral to the launch of her namesake beauty company in 1990 and advised as it grew into an empire. Bobbi, in turn, has always been a creative force in Steven's urban-development projects. (Both agree their most rewarding project through the years is their three boys.)

"I feel so lucky that I get to do life with him; he really has helped make all my personal and professional dreams come true."

These days, the powerhouse decision making continues for Bobbi and Steven. Together, they opened a boutique hotel, The George, and Bobbi launched Jones Road Beauty, a new cosmetics collection free of harmful chemicals and designed for all skin tones and types. The brand is on track to be Bobbi's next empire.

For all of the many accomplishments the couple has seen over the years, both in business and with family, Steven's Rolex remains a stylish reminder that their partnership is a valued and timeless treasure.

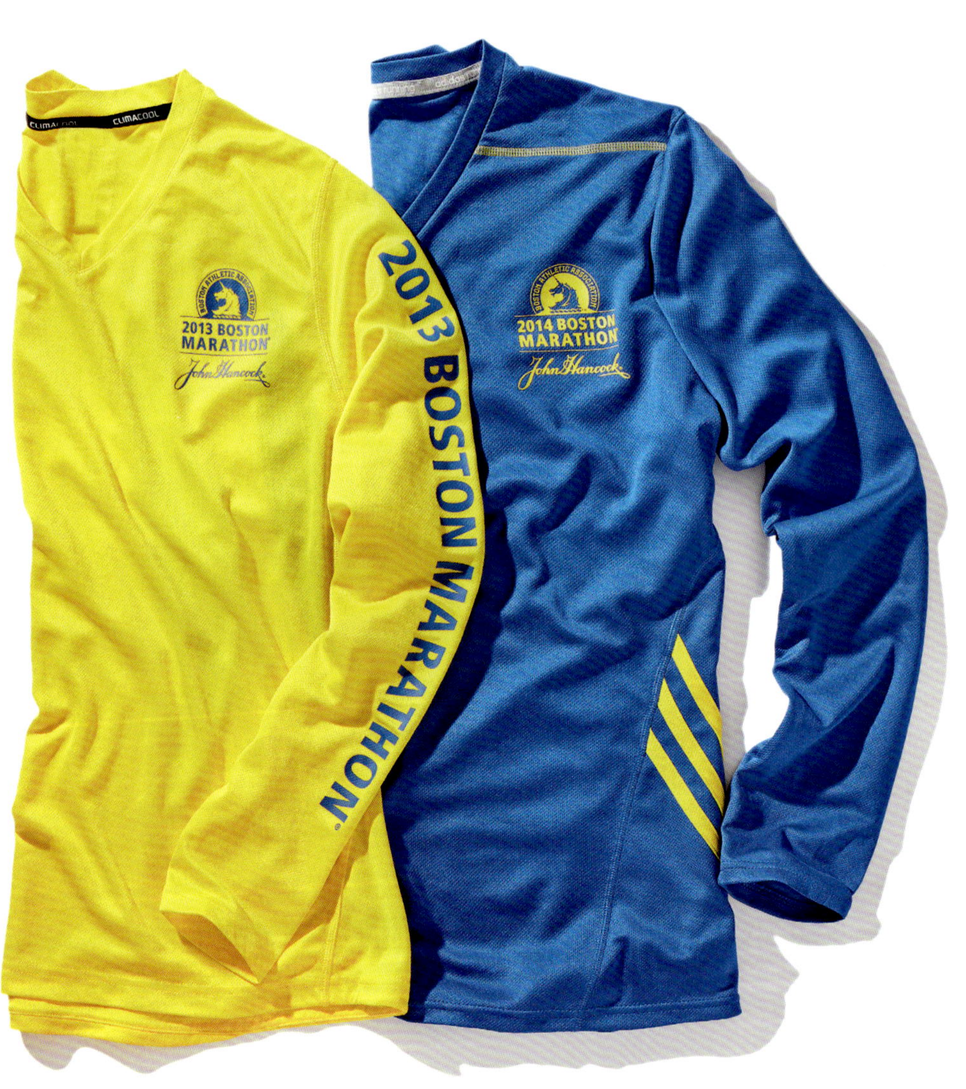
CLIMACOOL
BOSTON ATHLETIC ASSOCIATION
2013 BOSTON MARATHON
John Hancock
2013 BOSTON MARATHON
BOSTON ATHLETIC ASSOCIATION
2014 BOSTON MARATHON
John Hancock

25. Carey Socol | NEW YORK, NEW YORK

Carey Socol once set a goal for herself: to run a marathon in all fifty states in the United States before the age of fifty. She met this goal but didn't stop there—she just expanded her ambitions to one hundred. She has run the New York City Marathon fourteen times and has completed marathons in all fifty states.

This is the story of the one she couldn't finish.

In 2013, Carey was a little over a mile from the finish line of her twenty-seventh marathon, the Boston Marathon. That's when she started noticing something was off. The runners ahead of her had simply stopped running and police officers along the route were on their phones. Not just a few, Carey remembers. "Every single one of them."

"We waited for a while on the course," Carey said of her fellow runners. "We had no idea [of] the extent of the situation unfolding ahead of us," Carey says.

Soon the runners would learn: A bomb had been detonated at the finish line. Carey left the course immediately, winding through Boston's streets on foot, to find her family, who had been waiting for her along the course. (They were shaken up, but safe at her aunt's house.) Thousands of runners, some of whom had finished, some of whom had not, were also wandering around the city, dazed.

"Learning about what had unfolded rocked my world," Carey says. "The devastation and loss of life changed me." But one thing didn't change. Carey intended to cross the finish line.

Exactly one year later, she went back to Boston and completed the race. Pictured are her race shirts—one from her first try and the other from her successful finish.

"Digesting what this act of terror did to the city and to my beloved marathon community . . . I was determined more than ever to keep running, keep marathoning, and to return—no matter what—to Boston, to complete what I had started," Carey says.

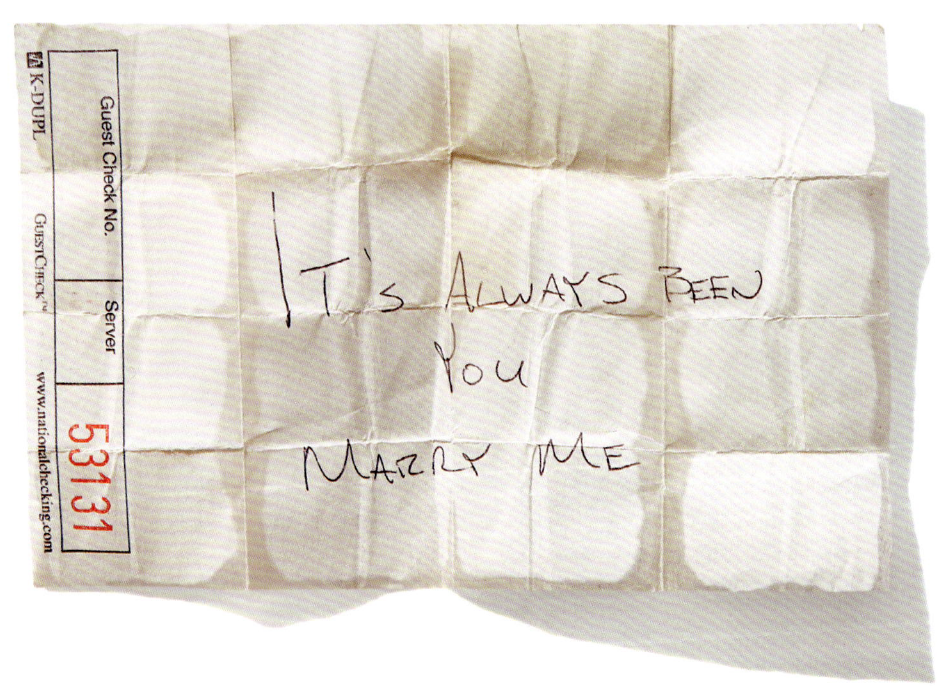
Guest Check No.
Server
53131
K-DUPL
GUESTCHECK
www.nationalchecking.com
IT'S ALWAYS BEEN
YOU
MARRY ME

26. Marissa Stephenson | PORTLAND, OREGON

Marissa and Kevin met in 2004 as journalism students at the University of Kansas. He fancied himself a writer, and she fancied herself an editor. A perfect match seemed written from the start, yet the two were always planted in the friend zone.

"I had a huge crush on him," she says. "But we struck up a friendship and it seemed that's all it would be."

Kevin moved home to Chicago after graduation, Marissa to New York City. They kept in touch, but by 2005 Marissa had moved past her crush and was dating someone. That's when Kevin planned a trip to New York City.

"Kev came out to the city in the spring of 2006 to interview for a music-writing job, and, unbeknownst to me, to share a declaration," Marissa jokes. They saw a band together one night and then talked for hours at a restaurant in the East Village. She recalls sensing the energy between them had somehow shifted.

Kevin walked her to the subway that night, and before walking away, he pressed a folded note into her hand:

"It's always been
you
Marry me"

"Looking at it on the subway platform, I did the thing you read about in books, see in movies—an immediate suck-in-the-air gasp," Marissa says. The note was written on the server's notepad from the restaurant. "A rush of old, buried feelings hit," she recalls.

The next morning, Marissa had to break the news to Kevin—she was dating someone. It was back to the friend zone. They didn't speak for months.

As fate would have it, Kevin got the music-writing gig and moved to New York. Marissa eventually ended it with the other guy. The two agreed to meet for a drink one night and have been together ever since.

"The rapport and chemistry we have—it was all there from the first night to the good-bye in the subway," Marissa says. "Eighteen years and two children later, for me, it has always been him too."

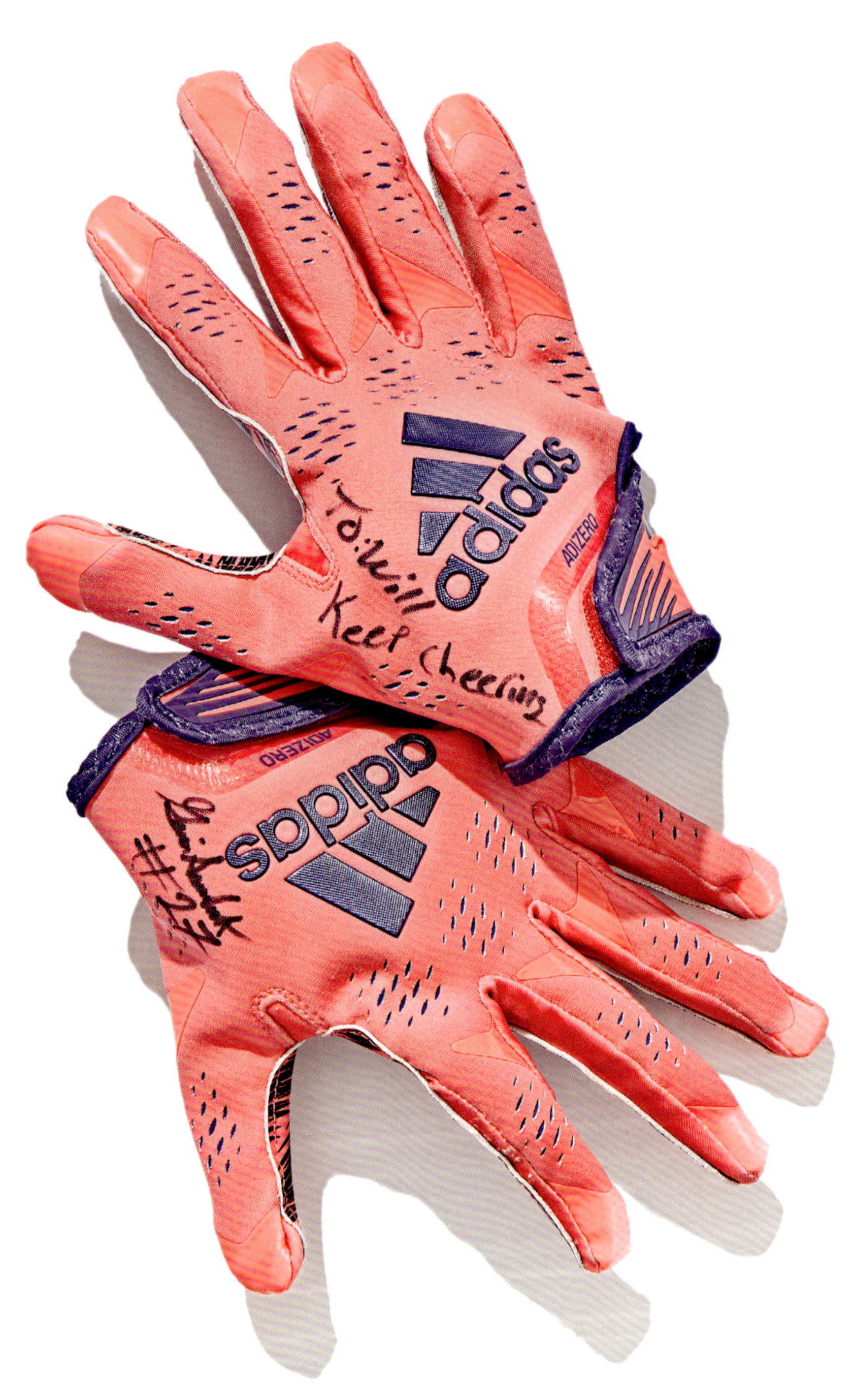
adidas
ADIZERO
To: Will
Keep Cheering
adidas
ADIZERO

27. Sarah Brock Edson | DENVER, COLORADO

"He's just a fourteen-year-old boy," Sarah Brock Edson humbly says of her son, Will. "But people gravitate to him wherever we go."

Will was born with Down syndrome. Sarah freely admits the shock and uncertainty of his diagnosis was terrifying at first. She will also tell you that a few months after his diagnosis, a peace set in. "He was an easy baby," she says. "And really stinking cute." Her charming, joyful boy was just getting started.

Will is now a teenager, and though he comes face-to-face with adversity daily, he does have a happy place, and that place is anywhere sports happen. Swim team, golf, and cross-country running are where he shines, and it shows. A runner from Will's cross-country team made a special request to the coach to be his running mate last season. A fellow swimmer on Will's team wrote his college essay about Will's optimism and willingness to push through adversity. Most recently, Will's classmates elected him to the homecoming royalty court. "His classmates see his determination and zest for life. They are always impressed with how Will just keeps going, even though things are tough for him," Sarah says.

Sarah is a high school teacher in Denver and brings Will to her school's Friday-night football games often because putting him in proximity to athletics fills him—and everyone around him—with joy. At one of these games, Will started a phenomenon that grew into a school tradition. The team's players enter the football field through a tunnel below where the crowd is seated. That day, Will leaned over the fence to cheer the players, and his outstretched hand was met from below with a high five from a player passing through. And then another. Now, kids from the stands all gather in the same spot at every game—leaning over from above the tunnel, waiting for rounds of spirited, rowdy high fives from the home team.

"His ability to open minds and hearts is astounding," Sarah says.

Pictured is a pair of signed football gloves a player from Sarah's school gave to Will. "Keep Cheering," the player wrote on the gloves.

"To Will, they're a reminder that's he's part of the gang, so to speak, and part of the team. As his mother, the gloves remind me my son has value and purpose and is able to contribute to something larger than himself."

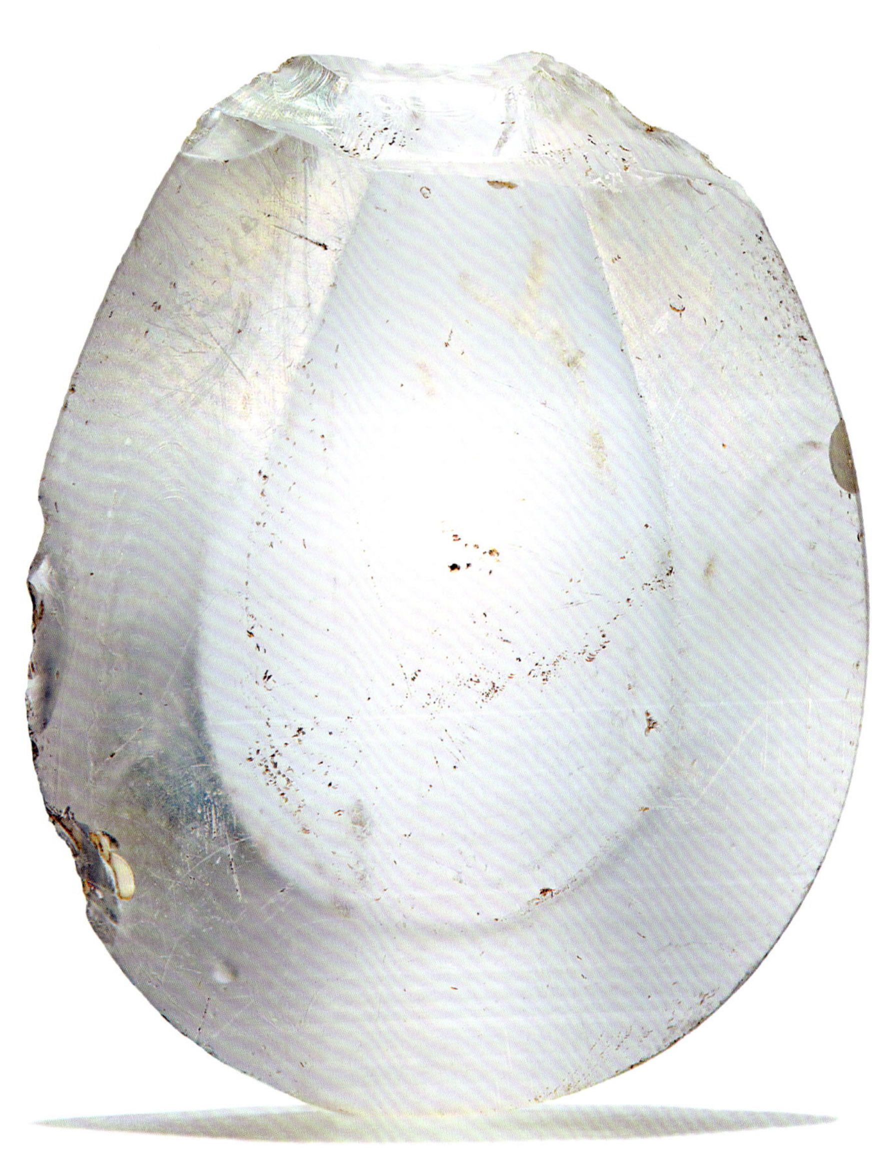

Josh Kilmer-Purcell and Dr. Brent Ridge were two big-city guys looking for adventure in Upstate New York when they crossed paths with a looted, derelict mansion built in 1802. It was perfect. They bought it.

The property was the onetime dream home of William Beekman, a local merchant, judge, and senator who, according to history books, lived a grand lifestyle. Beekman loved his home so much, he and his entire family are buried on the property.

Josh and Brent had plans to restore the property to its rightful grandeur when, in the financial crisis of 2008, they both lost their jobs. That's when the real adventure started. They had recently lent the property's barn to a local goat farmer who needed a home for his herd. Farmer John taught Josh and Brent how to milk the goats. Next, a neighbor taught them how to make goat's milk soap. Jobless, but armed with a new skill, Josh and Brent dug in.

What started with humble days of soap-making in their old barn became Beekman 1802, a skin care company named for the very farm they almost lost, and founded on the principles of kindness and community. Their neighbors still work for the company to this day. The company has since sold sixteen million bars of goat's milk soap and expanded to an entire line of products based on the benefits of goat's milk and other natural ingredients.

"We didn't start because we wanted to own a fun, creative company," Brent says. "We started because we had to pay the mortgage on our farm. We couldn't have done it without our community."

Just like their vibrant and bustling skin care business, the farm, located in Sharon Springs, New York, now enjoys endless days of beautification. Recently, and by accident, Brent dug up the glass prism shown here while adding flowers to the garden. There have been no other owners of the property—it must have belonged to a light fixture in the Beekmans' home.

"This is a little reminder that our home was once his castle. And that you'll find beauty if you dig deep."

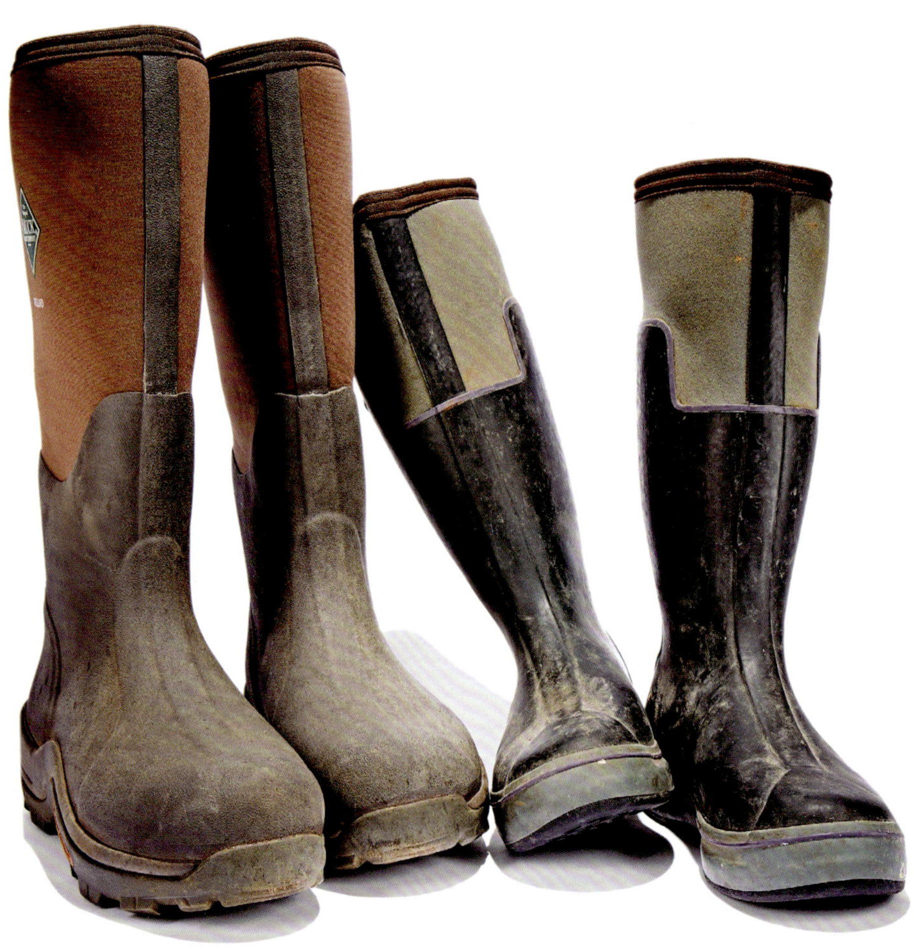

29. Bruce and Charlotte Sasso | AMAGANSETT, NEW YORK

Montauk, New York, is a remote fishing town on the easternmost tip of Long Island referred to by locals as "The End." But for Bruce and Charlotte Sasso, Montauk was the beginning.

Charlotte spent idyllic summers by the ocean there as a kid. Bruce grew up in Massachusetts but was drawn to Montauk by his love of fishing. Their worlds collided one summer on the town docks.

Bruce ran a shellfish business at the time, visiting the docks daily to sell clams and oysters to a distributor. There, he would see Charlotte at work on the cash register—her summer job. She studied political science at New York University, but that summer, she learned something unexpected: The seafood industry interested her more than politics.

"Sparks flew," Charlotte remembers of first meeting Bruce. "And then we did everything backwards—got a dog, a house, and then got married."

Bruce's seafood distribution business, on the other hand, was in fast-forward. He was running a pickup truck full of fresh catches from the docks to a local processing facility every day. The pickup, Charlotte recalls, eventually turned into a van, then grew to a box truck, and, eventually, a fleet. That's when the then owners of the processing facility offered to sell it to Bruce and Charlotte.

"We leapt at the opportunity," Charlotte says. The purchase came with a bonus, a jewel-box-size market space. In 1997, the Sassos became the new custodians of Stuart's Seafood Market, originally founded in 1955 by Stuart Vorpahl Sr. as a distribution center for local baymen to send off their catches to the Fulton Fish Market in New York City.

Bruce's extensive knowledge of the local seafood industry breathed fresh energy into Stuart's, but it was Charlotte who brought the market to a whole new level. A completely self-taught cook, she stocked the market cases with homemade salads, soups, and sauces. Everything that came out of Charlotte's kitchen was designed to complement everything that came out of the local waters.

"I learned from reading Julia Child's cookbooks," she says. "And making Bruce taste everything."

Bruce and Charlotte's partnership in life and in business would turn Stuart's Seafood Market into a legendary one-stop shop for coastal culinary traditions, where the line for a lobster roll, or anything else Charlotte created, could snake into the parking lot on any given summer afternoon.

They made lifetime friends out of customers. Their son's school would visit on field trips to learn about the local fishing industry. Even their two dogs became legends for greeting customers in the parking lot. The Sasso tradition served the community for twenty-five years.

There were highs over the years—Charlotte once made the national news and was interviewed on the *Today* show when they caught a rare blue lobster. "We named him Frank, for Old Blue Eyes," she joked. And there were lows. She recalls unloading lobsters at 11 p.m. many nights—even once on Bruce's birthday.

Recently, the many years of hard work led Bruce and Charlotte to "hang up their boots," pictured. Stewart's is under new ownership. Looking back on what she and her husband built together, she reflects, "All of the hard work and sacrifice was worth it. We love our community—and we still love each other! Still partners in life as well as business."

All of the hard work and sacrifice was worth it.

—Charlotte Sasso

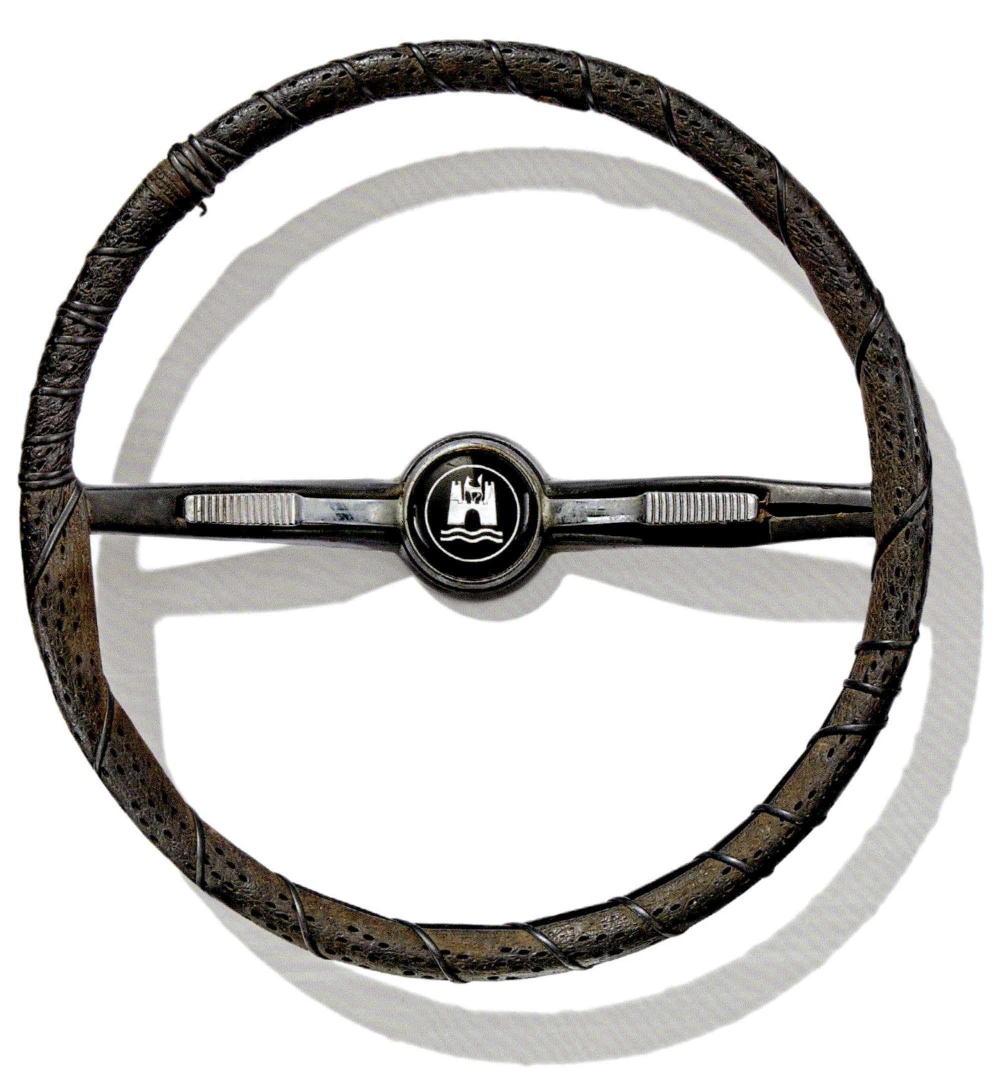

Five generations of the Freccia family have run Freccia Brothers Garage since 1922. When Guinevere Freccia stepped in to help with her family's business, she found this past to be very present. Everywhere she looked, there were heirlooms—dusty hubcaps and steering wheels, old carbon copy paperwork and business cards, and even a working rotary phone.

"The first thing I changed was the rotary phone. There wasn't even voicemail," Guinevere, who goes by Guin, says.

Although the shop's name pays homage to the family's male members, it was Guin's great-great-aunt, Emily Freccia, a Columbia Business School grad, who opened the shop with her brothers more than one hundred years ago. At the time of its founding, the family business was painting carriages.

By the 1960s, a Volkswagen dealership had opened across the street from the family's garage, so they learned the inner workings of Volkswagen car models. Today, the years of highly honed skills have earned the shop a reputation for being one of the most coveted destinations for Beetle restoration.

"No other car has ever been restored and passed down, generation to generation, like the Beetle," Guin says. "We work with a lot of heirlooms." Recently, she says, a customer shipped their family car all the way from England to be restored.

Guin's grandfather passed away in 2018, leaving her to steer this legendary local business in a modern direction.

"Part of the magic of the shop is marrying new technology with nostalgia. The guys in the garage, my father, Frank Freccia III, and husband, David D'Andrea Jr., can tune a car by ear—no computer needed. These cars are known for nostalgia, so I think that using technology where we can, and keeping the other things the same, is part of our success," she says.

Guin will get her hands dirty with the best of them. She grew up around the shop and knows her way around an oil change or tire rotation like no one's business. Her father is teaching her all aspects of VW restoration.

"My dad can smell a VW and know the year," Guin says.

Looking to the future, Guin has her eyes firmly planted on the road ahead. "We're still waiting on the technology, but the goal is to start offering electric conversions."

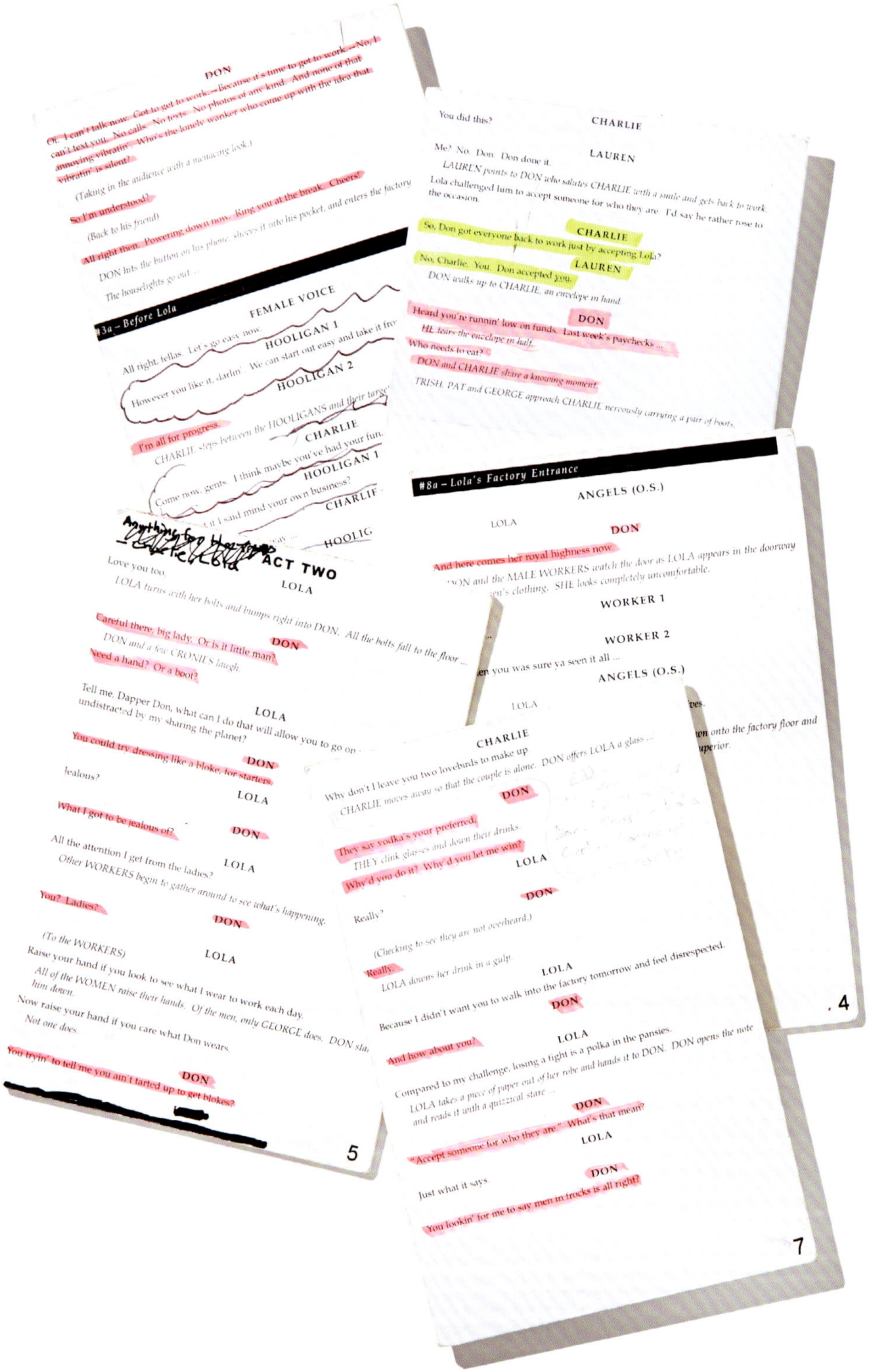

DON

Oi. I can't talk now. Got to get to work.—Because it's time to get to work.—No, I can't text you. No calls. No texts. No photos of any kind. And none of that annoying vibratin'. Who's the lonely wanker who come up with the idea that vibratin' is silent?

(Taking in the audience with a menacing look)

So I'm understood?

(Back to his friend)

All right then. Powering down now. Ring you at the break. Cheers!

DON hits the button on his phone, shoves it into his pocket, and enters the factory ...

The houselights go out ...

#3a – Before Lola

FEMALE VOICE

All right, fellas. Let's go easy now.

HOOLIGAN 1

However you like it, darlin'. We can start out easy and take it fro...

HOOLIGAN 2

I'm all for progress.

CHARLIE steps between the HOOLIGANS and their targe...

CHARLIE

Come now, gents. I think maybe you've had your fun.

HOOLIGAN 1

...t I said mind your own business?

CHARLIE

HOOLIG...

You did this?

CHARLIE

Me? No. Don. Don done it.

LAUREN

LAUREN points to DON who salutes CHARLIE with a smile and gets back to work.

Lola challenged him to accept someone for who they are. I'd say he rather rose to the occasion.

CHARLIE

So, Don got everyone back to work just by accepting Lola?

LAUREN

No, Charlie. You. Don accepted you.

DON walks up to CHARLIE, an envelope in hand.

DON

Heard you're runnin' low on funds. Last week's paychecks ...

HE tears the envelope in half.

Who needs to eat?

DON and CHARLIE share a knowing moment.

TRISH, PAT and GEORGE approach CHARLIE nervously carrying a pair of boots.

#8a – Lola's Factory Entrance

ANGELS (O.S.)

LOLA

DON

And here comes her royal highness now.

...DON and the MALE WORKERS watch the door as LOLA appears in the doorway ...en's clothing. SHE looks completely uncomfortable.

WORKER 1

WORKER 2

...en you was sure ya seen it all ...

ANGELS (O.S.)

LOLA

...ves.

...wn onto the factory floor and ...uperior.

. 4

Anything for Happiness
– Charlie & Lola

ACT TWO

Love you too.

LOLA

LOLA turns with her bolts and bumps right into DON. All the bolts fall to the floor ...

DON

Careful there, big lady. Or is it little man?

DON and a few CRONIES laugh.

Need a hand? Or a boot?

LOLA

Tell me, Dapper Don, what can I do that will allow you to go on ... undistracted by my sharing the planet?

DON

You could try dressing like a bloke, for starters.

LOLA

Jealous?

DON

What I got to be jealous of?

LOLA

All the attention I get from the ladies?

Other WORKERS begin to gather around to see what's happening.

DON

You? Ladies?

LOLA

(To the WORKERS)

Raise your hand if you look to see what I wear to work each day.

All of the WOMEN raise their hands. Of the men, only GEORGE does. DON sla... him down.

Now raise your hand if you care what Don wears.

Not one does.

DON

You tryin' to tell me you ain't tarted up to get blokes?

5

CHARLIE

Why don't I leave you two lovebirds to make up.

CHARLIE moves away so that the couple is alone. DON offers LOLA a glass ...

DON

They say vodka's your preferred.

THEY clink glasses and down their drinks.

Why'd you let me win?

LOLA

Why'd you do it?

DON

Really?

(Checking to see they are not overheard.)

Really.

LOLA downs her drink in a gulp.

LOLA

Because I didn't want you to walk into the factory tomorrow and feel disrespected.

DON

And how about you?

LOLA

Compared to my challenge, losing a fight is a polka in the pansies.

LOLA takes a piece of paper out of her robe and hands it to DON. DON opens the note and reads it with a quizzical stare ...

DON

"Accept someone for who they are." What's that mean?

LOLA

Just what it says.

DON

You lookin' for me to say men in frocks is all right?

7

31. Neil Kumar | PLAINVIEW, NEW YORK

Neil Kumar spent much of high school jamming with friends in bands. He loved punk and rock music and played the drums and bass guitar. But everyone knew he had a record-deal-worthy voice.

Over the years, a friend tried to convince Neil to audition for their high school's musical productions. One year, he finally agreed to audition for *Grease* and got a part. During the production, Neil brought the house down with his charming and decidedly un-punk-rock rendition of "Beauty School Dropout."

After the show, he was told the owner of a local theater company was in the school's lobby, hoping to meet him.

"I was intimidated. I didn't go," Neil says. "And it has haunted me ever since." He went back to jamming with his friends throughout college and early adulthood, but he always wondered if he could have taken his musical talents to larger stages.

In 2015, Neil was diagnosed with Hodgkin's lymphoma. He would fight it for the next three years. "I stopped singing, I stopped playing guitar; it just wasn't a part of my life anymore," he says. "I got used to not being creative or musical. I worked, I raised my kids, and that was it."

Neil was successfully living cancer-free and joyfully expecting his second child when the COVID-19 pandemic hit. One night, wide awake in bed, a familiar push made Neil search the web for the local theater-company owner who had wanted to meet him back in high school. His theater still existed. They were casting for a musical.

In 2022, Neil pushed past his internal roadblocks and auditioned at the local theater company for the Broadway hit musical *Kinky Boots,* which, ironically, is about taking risks and operating out of your comfort zone. He was cast as Don, the main character. Pictured are his cue cards.

"After the last performance, in the lobby of the theater, I was saying hello to all the wonderful people in my life who came to see me dance around in eight-inch stiletto-heeled boots, when someone tapped me on the shoulder. It was the owner of the theater, the one from high school, taking the time to come over and tell me how much he enjoyed my performance and [he] thanked me for being a part of the production," Neil says. "It was twenty years later that I finally got to talk to him, but man, that felt good."

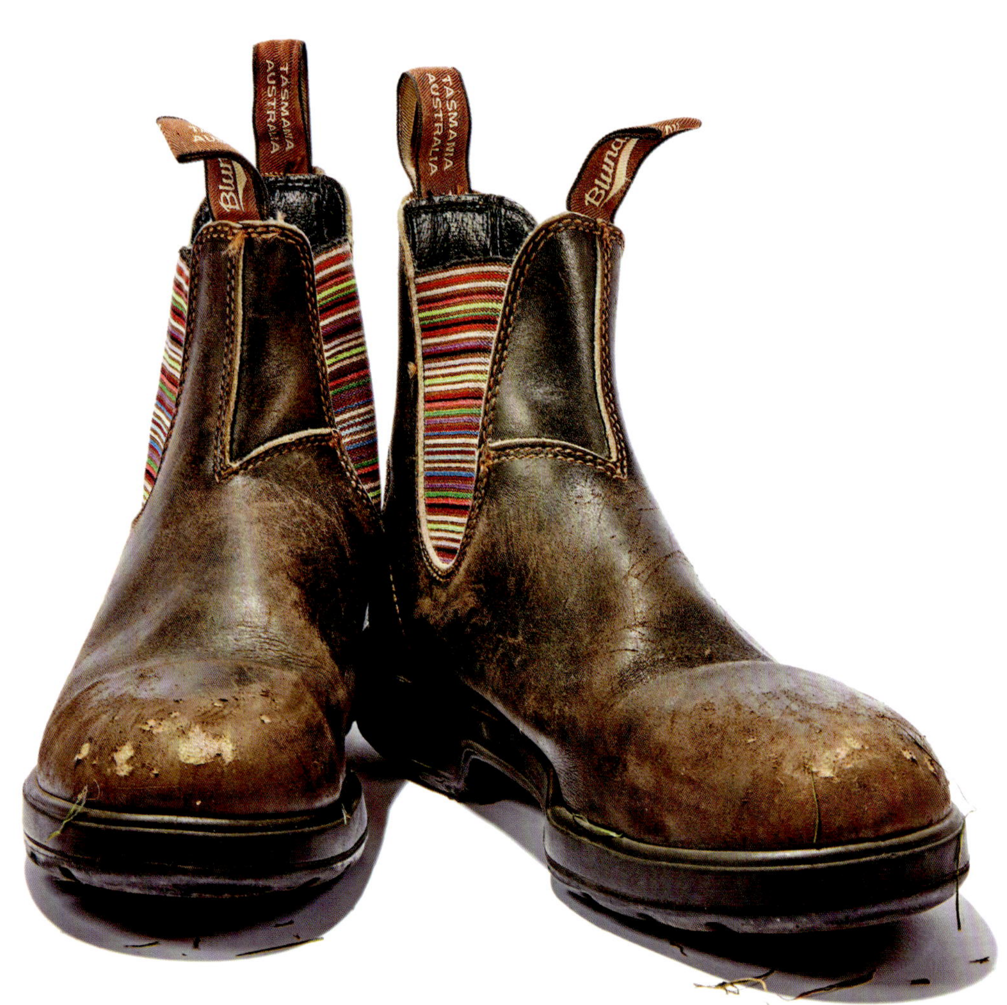
TASMANIA
AUSTRALIA
TASMANIA
AUSTRALIA

32. Libby DeLana | NEWBURYPORT, MASSACHUSETTS

Whirling around in an orbit filled with conference calls, to-do lists, and high-level client meetings, Libby DeLana gracefully walked the line of creativity and commerce for years. She served as design director for the legendary advertising agency MullenLowe and, eventually, cofounded her own agency, Mechanica. She formed a reputation along the way for being a brilliant creative mind. But her mind was not immune to the demands of life's realities. A disconnect—to herself and to nature—had settled into her psyche. And so, one day in 2011, she went outside and took a walk.

Since then, she has gone for a walk every day for thirteen years.

"My walk became a meditation practice, a playground for creativity, my best friend, a doctor, coach, and therapist," Libby says. It became a symbolic way to manage many of life's challenges—one foot in front of the other. "It's so simple," Libby says. But there was nothing simple about the deep reward her daily practice brought her.

"I go every single day. No matter what," Libby reflects. "It is on the days I don't 'want' to go that I often have the most meaningful and insightful walks." Eventually, Libby's no-matter-what attitude would turn out to be the most fulfilling part of her practice.

And she isn't just strolling around in the sunshine. Cold weather or extreme humidity only eggs her on. Windy beaches and overgrown forest trails strengthen her resolve.

"It's about commitment," Libby says. "Following through on commitment is self-love."

These days, Libby is the force behind a growing movement called This Morning Walk, and she is the author of *Do Walk*. The movement and the book both address the importance of caring for your soul and the deep-reaching mind-and-body benefits of taking a simple step—whether it's twenty minutes before your busy day or a few hours in a quiet forest.

Since her practice began, she has walked over twenty-five thousand miles, as evidenced by this pair of old but beloved walking boots, which are pictured, complete with years of battle scars. That's equal to the circumference of the earth. But she will tell you it's not about how far she has walked. Rather, it's about how far she has come.

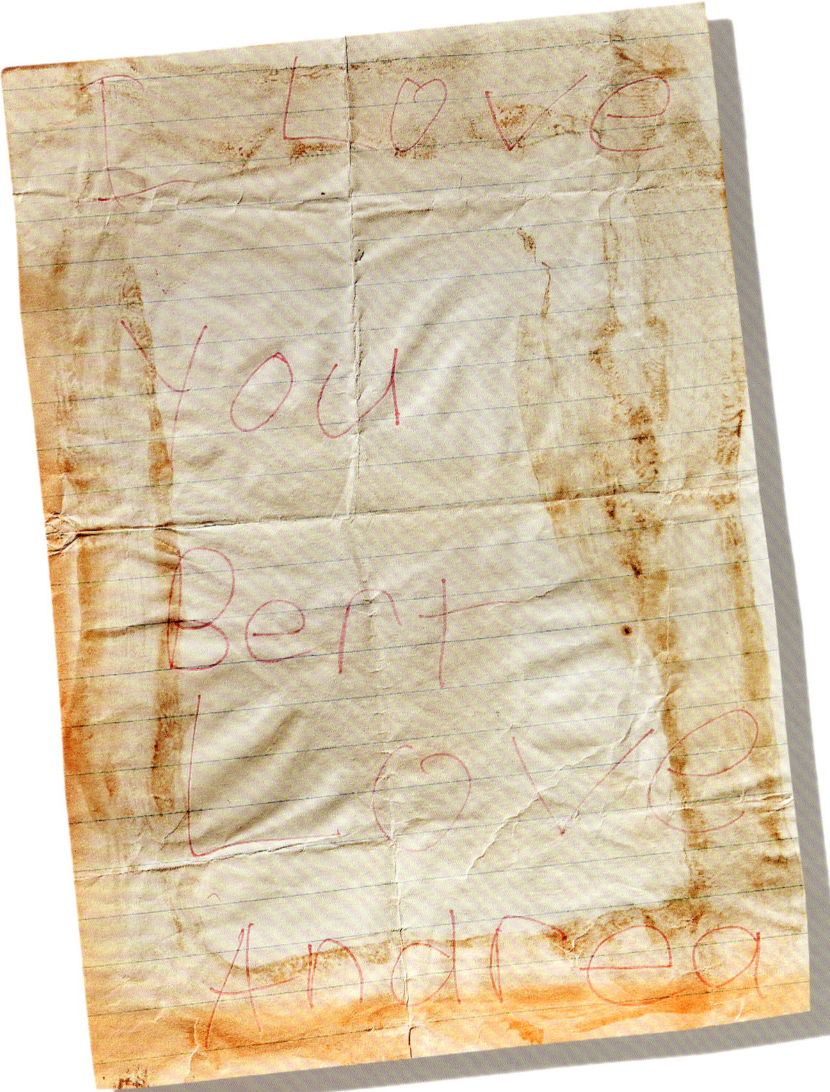

I Love
You
Bert
Love
Andrea

33. Andrea Worthing | FULSHEAR, TEXAS

Andrea Worthing had a bit of a reputation in first grade. She was known for slipping notes to her classmates through the metal slots in their hallway lockers.

This one, pictured, was for Bert. Bert's name was actually Bart, but the misspelling didn't stop him from bringing the note home to his mother. And it didn't stop his mother from tucking the note into his childhood scrapbook.

Andrea and Bart grew up together in the community of Wharton, Texas. They seemed a match from the minute they met in elementary school. They dated throughout high school and college. Both settled in Houston after graduating. The time had come for next steps and big decisions.

"We've always been best friends," Andrea says. "I take things much too seriously, and he is the one to keep us laughing at all times," she jokes. They were soon engaged. But when they announced their plans to marry, Bart's mother had some big news of her own: She showed them the love note she had kept all those years.

"We were just giddy," Andrea recalls. "I mean, what are the chances that this was the one note she decided to keep for thirty years?"

The note was framed and displayed on the welcome table at their wedding, an ode to a love that was written long ago. They have been married for thirteen years and have three children.

During their wedding ceremony, the pastor called Bart "Bert," an accidental touching tribute to the way their love had started back in the first grade.

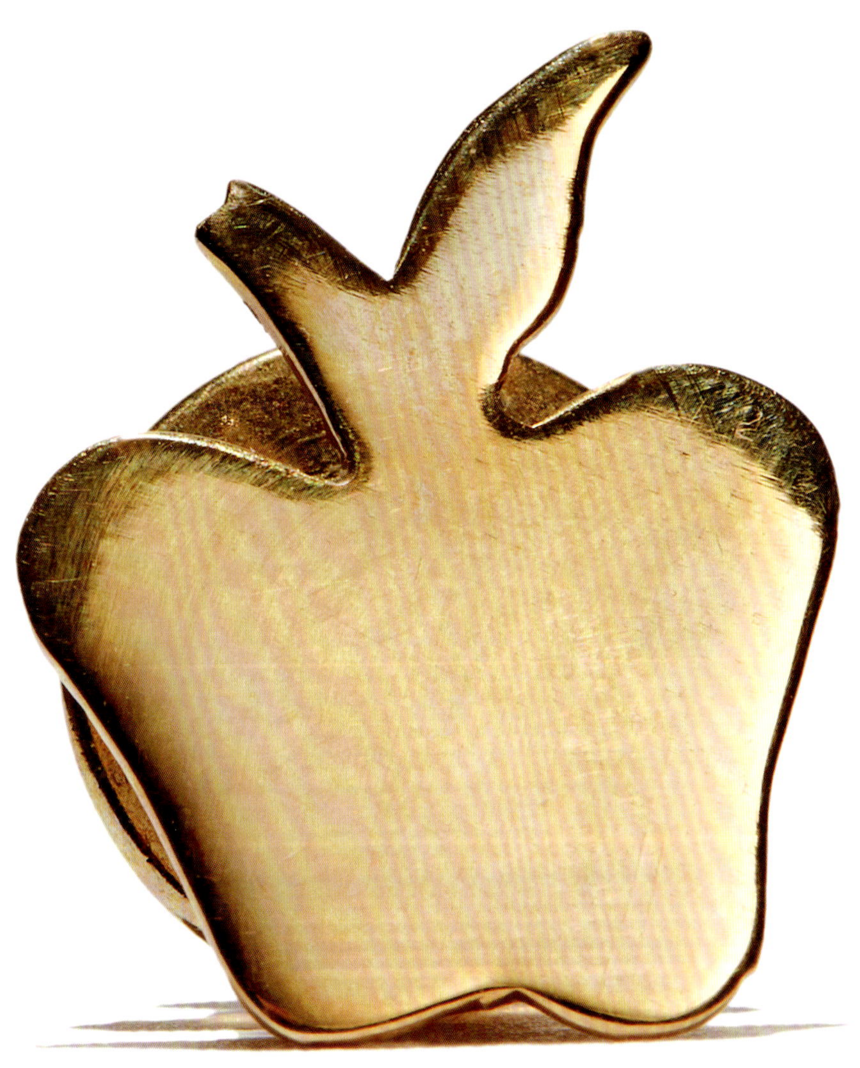

34. Jack Klein | NEW YORK, NEW YORK

Despite New York City's rough reputation in the 1970s, Jack Klein remained a proud New Yorker to his core for his entire life.

The Brooklyn native and World War II vet became an accountant after the war and lived an abundant life full of friends, family, and travel.

Jack's son, Justin, says that somewhere along the way, his dad bought a supply of "Big Apple" pins, pictured, and joyfully distributed them over the years to acquaintances and comrades alike—a token of friendship and hometown pride. Jack wore one himself every day.

Jack passed away in 1985 but the pins remain—and a handful of friends and family still have them.

"He was selfless and giving," Justin remembers of his dad. "The kind of guy that would make friends with everyone around him. The kind of guy that would sit down and make friends with the bartender."

Twenty years after his father's passing, Justin took his family to Florence, Italy, where his oldest daughter was studying abroad at the time. His father loved Florence and traveled there often. One night, Justin took the family to the American Bar at Harry's Bar, his father's favorite local spot. It was to be an adventure and a tribute to the far-reaching spirit of his dad.

When the family entered the bar, the bartender, Leo, was wearing one of Jack's apple pins.

"Leo told us how much he appreciated that my dad would take so much time to engage with him and the waiters at the bar," Justin said. Leo showed the family Jack's favorite seat and then did what he knows best: He made the family some drinks.

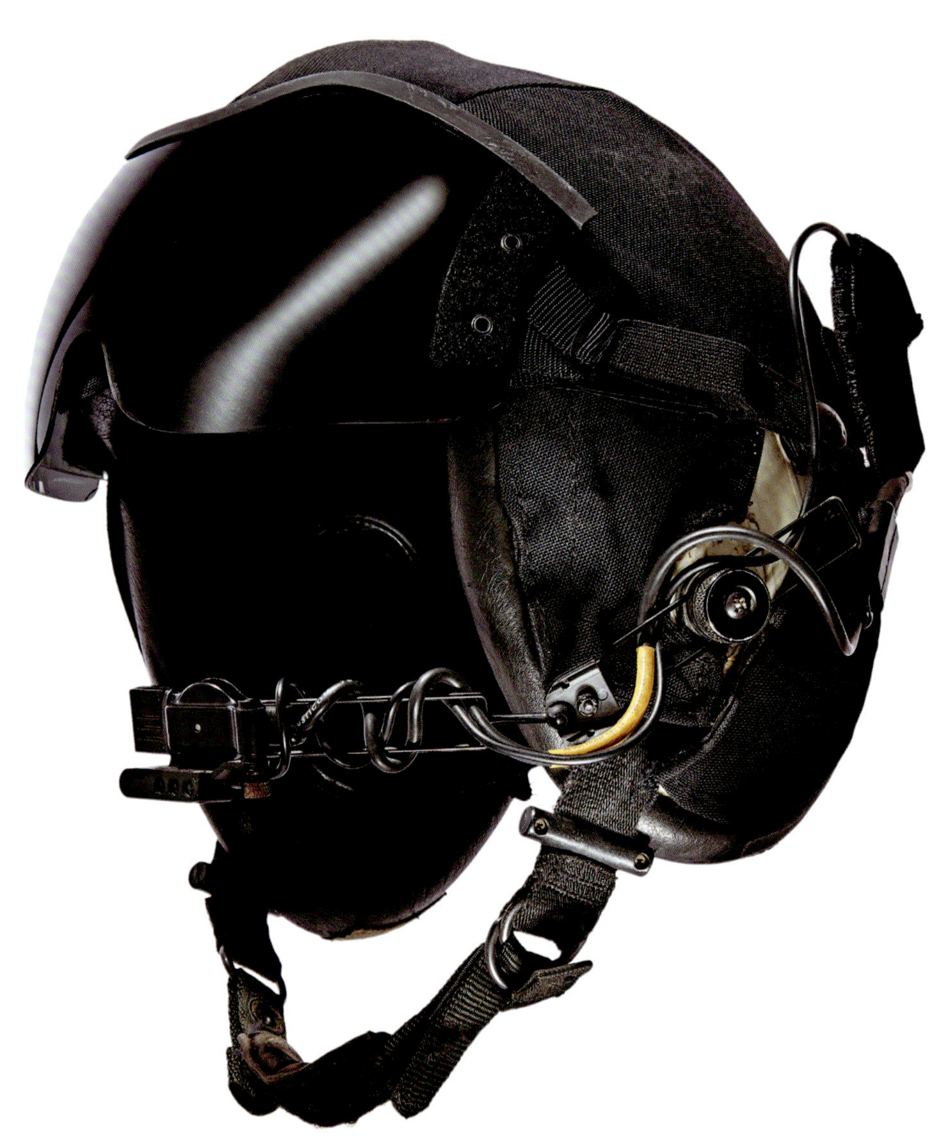

35. Andrew Turner | NORFOLK, VIRGINIA

A Huey helicopter carrying Colonel Andrew Turner and three other Marines crashed during the 2003 invasion of Iraq. Andrew remembers nothing of the crash. He woke up on the USNS *Comfort* with a concussion and a broken ankle. He was the only survivor.

By 2004, Andrew was back in the skies above Iraq providing support for Marines on the ground in An Najaf. The Marines were in town to keep the peace. Militias had been terrorizing the local population, hoping to draw American troops into a fight. Unfortunately, it was working.

On August 5, 2004, Marines were engaged with the militia and in need of air support to identify and deliver fire against targets on the ground. Andrew says the Huey and Cobra helicopters that responded were able to deliver a heavy mix of rockets and gunfire against the enemy. But it was a single shot from somewhere below that pierced Andrew's Huey. A bullet entered the pilot's eye and exited through his temple. Not knowing if his pilot was even alive, Andrew took the controls. The helicopter was already in a free fall, headed for dangerous territory.

"This can't be happening again," Andrew remembers thinking. He crash-landed the helicopter in the middle of An Najaf with enemy forces in proximity. He remembers thinking it was over, even though everyone survived the impact.

That's when Andrew noticed an ambulance parked near the crash site—and a red crescent painted on the wall next to an adjacent building. He had crash-landed in front of a hospital.

He recalls bursting through the doors of the hospital in full flight gear—helmet on, visor down, with his M16 at the ready. Despite the entrance—and the language barrier—hospital personnel rushed to help Andrew and his crew. The Marines soon arrived and secured the area—the same Marines the crew had been protecting from the air had found them. But there was one simple thing that had protected Andrew all along: his helmet.

Andrew and his crew made it home. He now lives in Norfolk, Virginia, with his wife, Kate, and their two Labrador retrievers. These days, Andrew jokes, he flies a desk.

The helmet is packed away, but Andrew says he'd reach for it in a second if called upon again to serve in the air.

"It could have been much worse for me if the helmet didn't do its job."

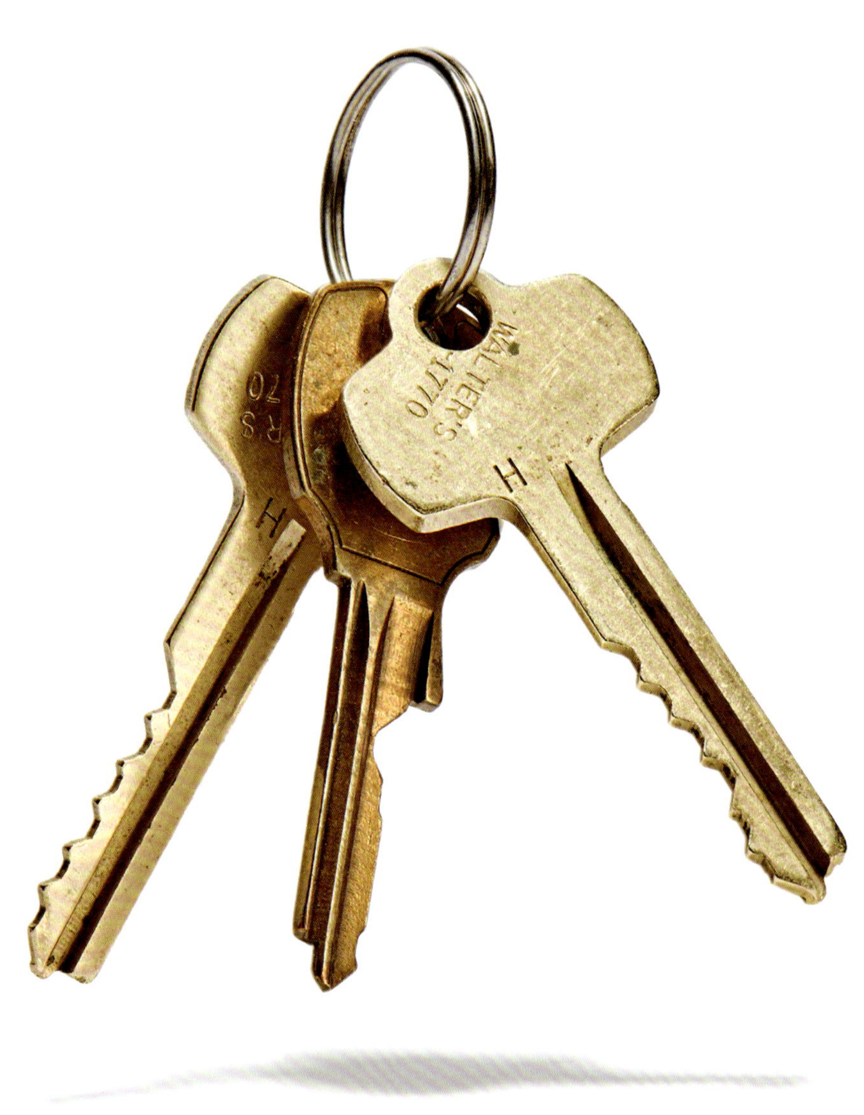
WALTER'S
H

36. Beth McLaughlin | SHARON, MASSACHUSETTS

It is a proven fact that if you put a bunch of twenty-year-olds in an apartment building in the middle of a vibrant city, and tell them the roof is off-limits, they will throw parties on it.

"I was on my own for the first time," Beth McLaughlin recalls of her beloved first apartment in the Beacon Hill neighborhood of Boston. "In the mid-1990s, Boston was just fun and slightly gritty."

Beth was a recent grad with an art history degree and had landed a job with an art consulting firm. But in her free time, Beth and her roommate were professional rooftop-party throwers.

Beth recalls every detail of one particular party, when a memorable guest arrived.

"He was wearing a polo shirt, pleated khaki shorts, and white sneakers. I was wearing a black T-shirt dress, and I'm certain my eyebrows were plucked within an inch of their lives, being the nineties and all," she jokes.

That night, at her illegal rooftop party, she met Chris, the guy in the khaki shorts, who would go on to become her husband. They have been married for almost twenty-five years.

Beth can't remember why, but she never gave the keys to the building back to the landlord when she moved out of that apartment. One day, she was in the neighborhood and tried the lock just for fun and the keys worked. So, Beth and Chris made a tradition of going back to the building together over the years. They would go with Champagne in tow and head directly for the roof.

The couple now has two kids, and they recently took them back to the old neighborhood where it all started.

"We thought it would be fun to show them where Mom and Dad first met," says Beth. They all went to the apartment and tried the lock but, finally, after all those years, it had been changed.

"The end of an era, I suppose," Beth says. "But I feel blessed to have made those memories on that rooftop." She still has the keys to remind her.

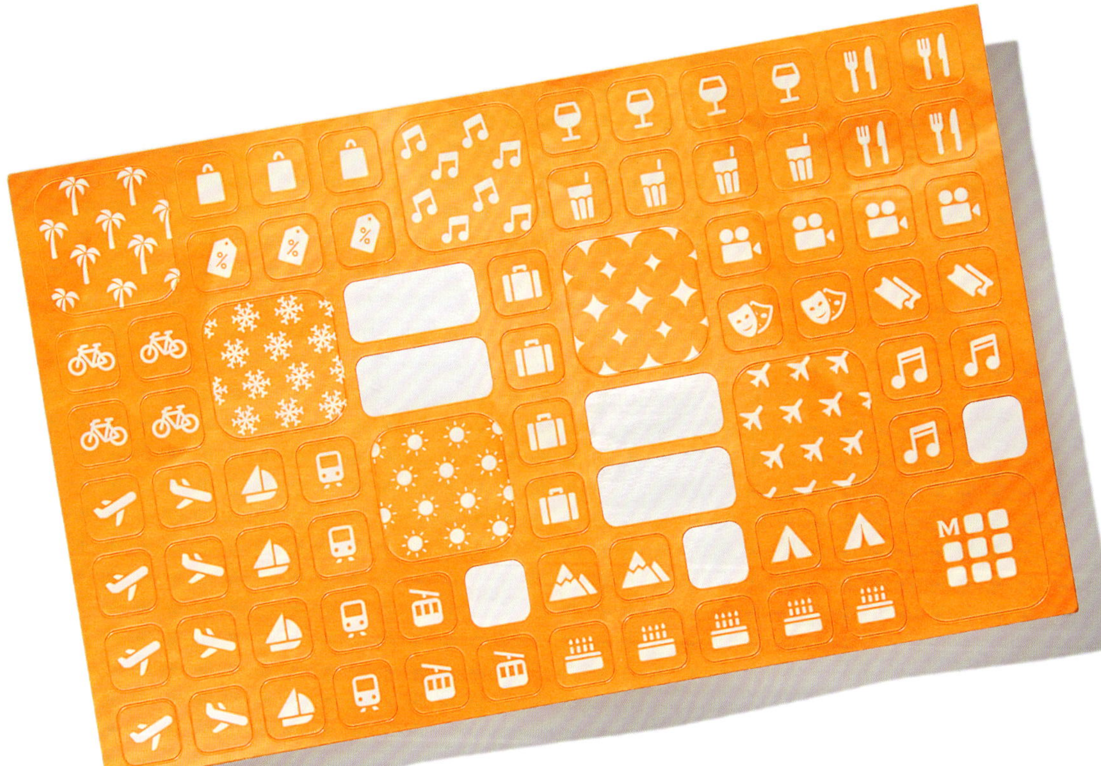

37. Ali Sherman | OMAHA, NEBRASKA

Ali Sherman had just finished dinner at her parents' house and was headed for her car, which was parked in their driveway, when she noticed an orange sticker stuck to the driver's side window. It was bewildering. It happened again a week later, this time in a parking lot. She suspected her brother, David. They saw each other often around town, and he was known for being a first-class prankster. But he denied it.

"He had this sideways grin," Ali says. "When he flashed it, you knew he was up to something."

The sideways grin, dubbed by the entire family as "The Sherman Grin," is actually genetic—both of Ali's sons have it and so does David's son, Aaron.

"David once convinced Aaron that my car had a button in it that prevented his car from speeding past me on the street," she says. "He loved to prank the people he loved most."

Yet despite The Sherman Grin and Ali's suspicions, David denied involvement in the sticker mystery to the end. He maintained the stickers on Ali's car had to be some kind of manufacturer warning she had never noticed.

When more stickers showed up weeks later, Ali began to plan revenge on her brother, even though she was still not 100 percent certain what was going on. "I was secretly plotting a glitter bomb for his Jeep," she jokes. "But he seriously loved this car so, for some reason, I held off." That's when David was diagnosed with a fast-moving cancer. He was gone within weeks.

After her brother's death, Ali and her mother set about the solemn task of sorting through David's belongings. One day, while they were looking for the title to his car, they found this sheet of stickers. They were the stickers Ali kept finding on her car.

"We were laughing and crying," Ali says of the moment. "We found the thing we were looking for, and then it was as though he gave us an extra wink."

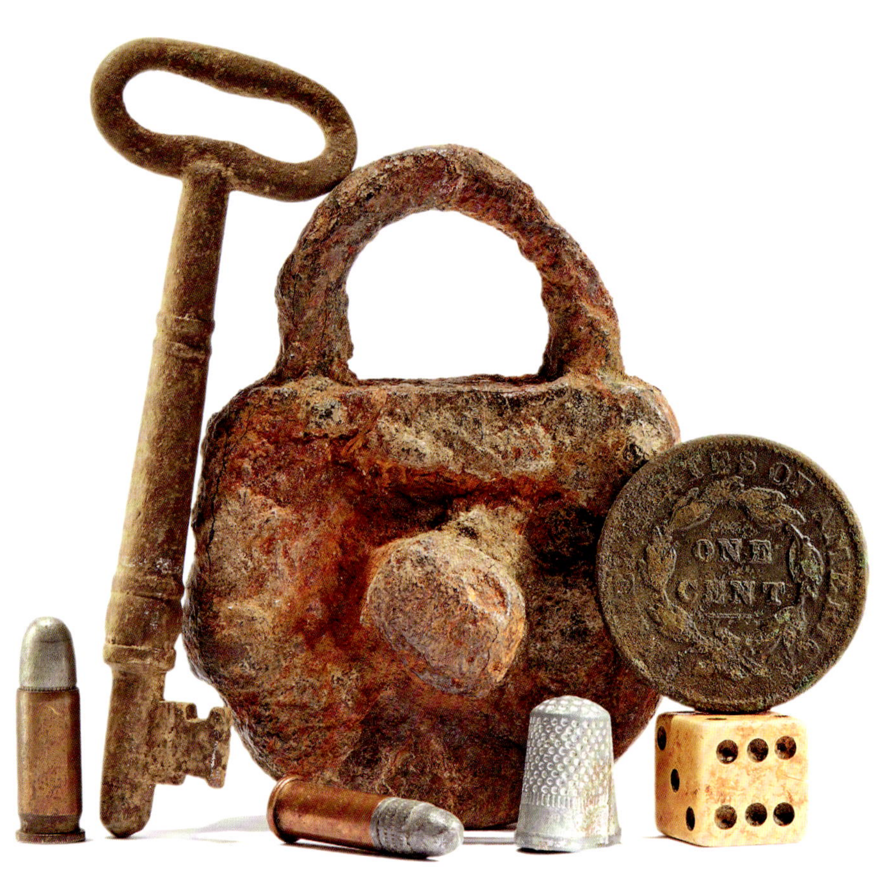
ONE
CENT

Maryclare and Garvin Roos fell in love at first sight . . . with a 285-year-old house.

"We never agree on anything right away," she jokes. "But when we pulled into the driveway and got out of the car, we knew." They made an offer on the house and were immediately outbid—five times. They were heartbroken. But in less than a week, a real estate miracle happened. All five offers fell through, and the house was theirs.

"I wholeheartedly believe this house picked us," Maryclare says.

This wasn't just any house, though. The Peter Thorp House in Weston, Connecticut, was built in 1739 and has been extraordinarily preserved ever since. Every nail is hand-forged, every beam hand-cut. Even one of the home's original hearth room fireplace mantels is said to be made from an American chestnut tree that grew in the front yard. The Roos intend to continue the preservation.

"We take such pride in preserving the touches of those who came before us," Maryclare says. "You can feel the love and attention that went into this house radiate through the halls."

One reason it's so easy to feel the magic of Thorp House is that the house has been actively revealing historical treasures to Maryclare ever since her family arrived. While she was cleaning one day, she found twelve unspent bullets tucked into the seams of the fireplace mantel. (She suspects they are from the nineteenth century when the house was a tavern.) She also finds rusted skeleton keys in far-flung corners of the property and makes a sport of going around to the pocket doors in the house to see if the keys fit. They often do.

Maryclare recently upped her treasure-hunting game and bought a metal detector. Wandering around with it in the yard is one of her favorite things to do.

"People drive by and honk," she jokes. Her finds are extensive and wondrous—coins, pottery, silverware, jewelry, a thimble. Pictured are some of her favorite finds. Now, even her kids, George, Charlie, and Madeleine, are in on the fun and join her for digs.

"We love finding things that allow us a peek into what life was like at various points in history. We live in such a time of disposable everything and instant gratification. I want the kids to learn that there is beauty in taking your time to create something beautiful—something that will withstand the test of time."

Though living amid so much history makes it easy for Maryclare to dwell in the past, so to speak, she still very much believes in the power of being present and planning for the future.

"I hope our story encourages other homeowners to dig into their property's history and preserve its beauty and character. There are still many tales to be told."

39. Jessica Diaz | BOSTON, MASSACHUSETTS

Get up. Get the kids ready for school. Go to work. Have a stroke. That's how it went for Jessica Diaz one day in 2013. Not only is she alive to talk about it, but she has also made it her business to tell as many people as possible.

"The day of my stroke started like any other day," Jessica says. After teaching two barre classes, she returned home to shower. That's when a shocking pain shot down the left side of her body. Her left arm went numb, then her left leg. A strange and terrible headache developed.

"I had no clue what it was I was experiencing. A stroke never crossed my mind," she says. Both Jessica's husband, Charles, and a nurse practitioner had to convince her to go to the hospital. Upon arrival, her symptoms got her admitted immediately. Tests revealed a blood clot in her brain.

"I was devastated. Never in a million years did I think it was possible for me to have a stroke. I didn't even know I was old enough to have one," she says. She was thirty-six years old.

The next morning, due to the quick treatment she received, and thanks to her excellent physical health, the feeling returned to the left side of her body. The doctors thought she would be in recovery for five weeks. She went home in five days.

At home, she says, an unexpected side effect of the stroke set in—anxiety that it could happen again. But instead of letting the anxiety take over, Jessica took it to the Massachusetts State House.

Jessica found out soon after her stroke that it was caused by a genetic blood-clotting condition called Factor V Leiden. Also known as factor five, it happens to be terribly dangerous when combined with birth-control pills, which Jessica's doctors had been prescribing her for years.

"I was mad," Jessica says. "A doctor will freely acknowledge they cannot prescribe birth control for a woman who has factor five. Yet they don't support testing before prescribing," she says. "It doesn't make sense."

In 2019, Jessica enlisted the help of an elected official and filed papers to introduce a bill in the state of Massachusetts that would require testing. A factor five test could save a life for roughly forty dollars. A bill's journey to law winds through layers and years of legal review and committee hearings. Once her bill made it all the way to a committee hearing, she wore

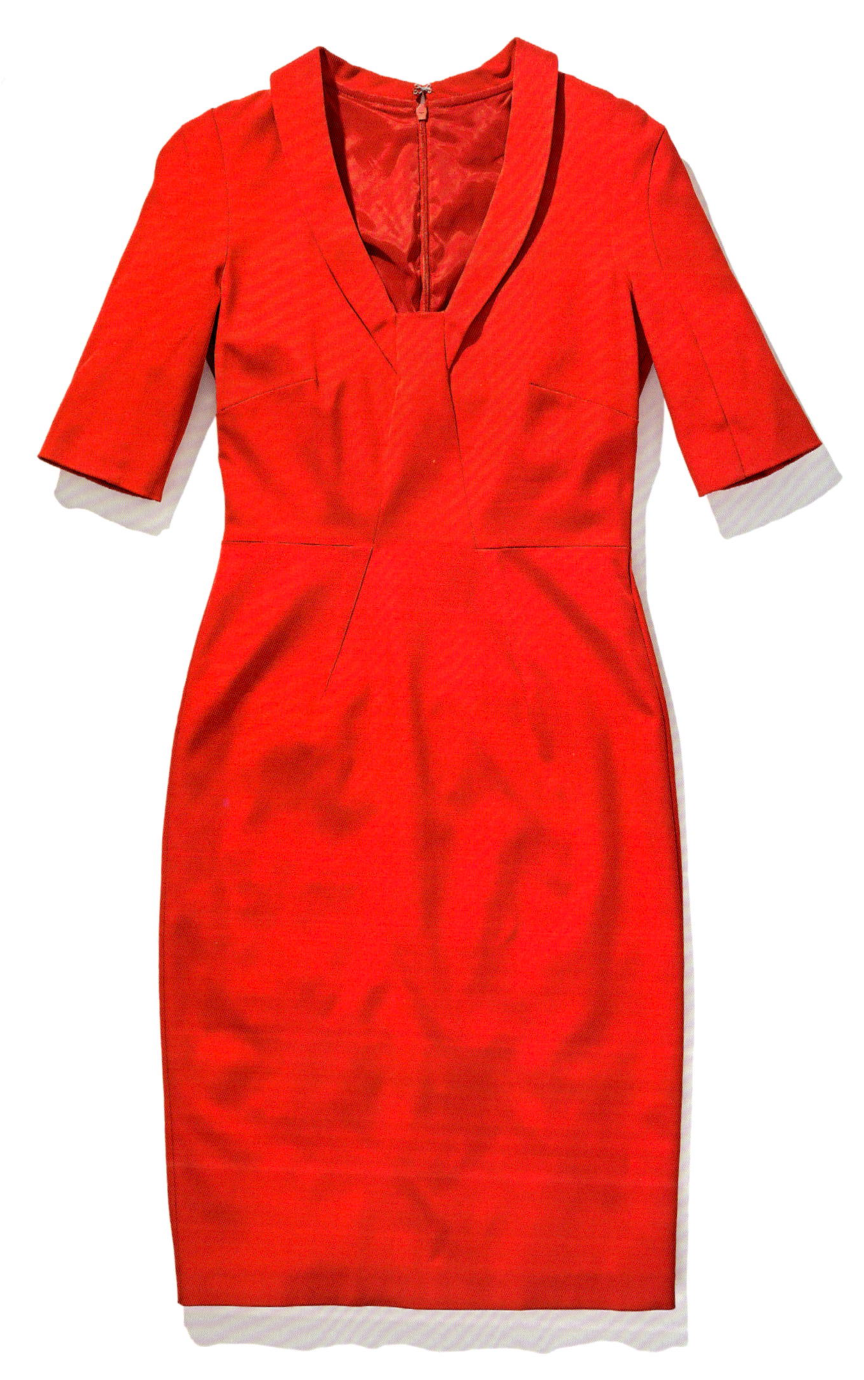

this red dress (wearing red showed her support of the American Heart Association [AHA]; the American Stroke Association is a division of the AHA) to testify on behalf of herself and all the lives she hoped to impact.

Unfortunately, her voice was met with silence—no one from the medical community would speak in support, and lobbyists came to her hearing to oppose her. The total lack of support from the medical community was astonishing. The bill went nowhere. She refiled it in 2021 and continues to wait.

Waiting doesn't seem to be a word in Jessica's vocabulary, however. She now works daily to raise awareness on her own terms. She is a speaker and Go Red ambassador for the American Heart Association, and for the American Stroke Association, and founder of Jessica Diaz Wellness—a company focused on stroke prevention and the principles of becoming the healthiest version of yourself.

Even though the fate of Jessica's legislation is still to be determined, she has created an entire community of voices for awareness and counts three major wins under her belt. Their names are Mary, Chloe, and Chase—Jessica's sister, daughter, and son, respectively—who discovered they have factor five through the genetic-test company 23andMe, which, thanks to a spike in awareness, now tests for it.

"I am sorry they have it but knowing is the first big step in preventing them from having a stroke or blood clot," she says.

How powerful to think that one determined woman in a red dress will likely end up saving more lives than legislation stuck behind red tape.

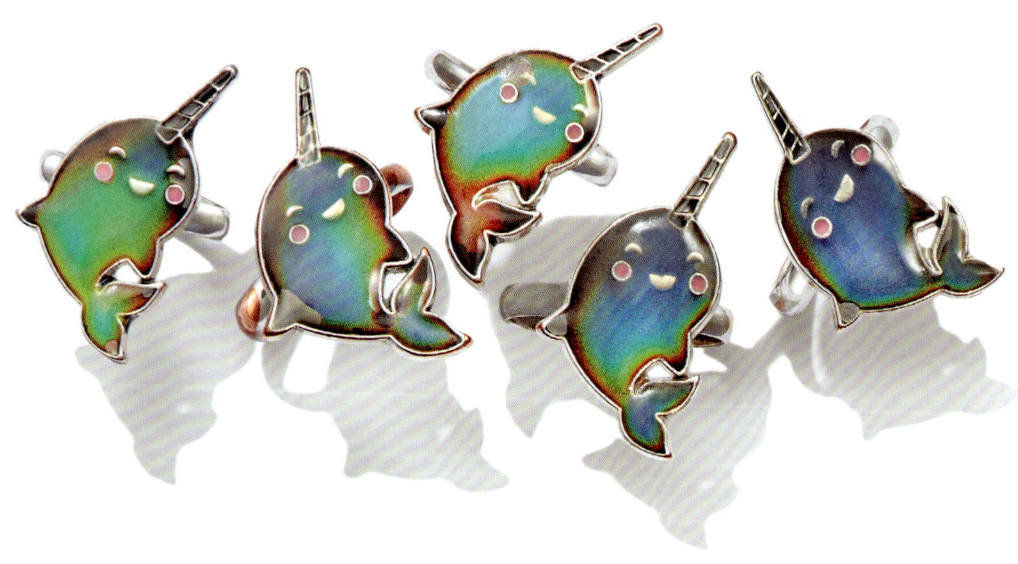

40. The Simms-Rosenthal Family | CLEVELAND, OHIO

In 2018, Bronwyn Simms and Noah Rosenthal did what a lot of people traditionally do when they fall in love: They moved in together. But their arrangement had a modern twist—their three children, all from previous relationships, moved in too.

"At the time, our kids were four, eight, and fourteen," says Bronwyn. "The decision to buy a house and merge our families wasn't made lightly. It was a commitment made with five people in mind."

"There were plenty of challenges that came along with a blended family," Bronwyn admits of the decision to move in together. But the Brady Bunch vibes were strong. "We are a tight-knit unit."

Even though their family unit looked different from other families, it didn't matter. Living together worked for them. And Bronwyn was used to "different"—it's one of the things she liked best about Noah from the beginning.

"He was unlike anyone I had ever met," she says. "He savors life. He is the guy that makes even the most mundane things fun and special, all the time." Little did she know that Noah was about to up his game.

That Christmas Eve, Noah went out with Bronwyn's oldest daughter to enact a plan. He was going to propose to Bronwyn and needed her daughter's approval and wanted her involvement. She gave her blessing. Off they went to buy a ring—not one ring, but five.

"How do you ask one person to marry you, but involve the kids so they become participants and not bystanders?" Noah asks. "I had a vision of how it could be inclusive."

That evening, around the Christmas dinner table, Noah proposed—to everyone—with these five narwhal-shaped mood rings. Symbolically, they were identical (and adjustable for even the smallest kid fingers).

"He was asking me, but also all of us, if we were willing to share in a commitment to become one family," Bronwyn says. "Everyone said yes!"

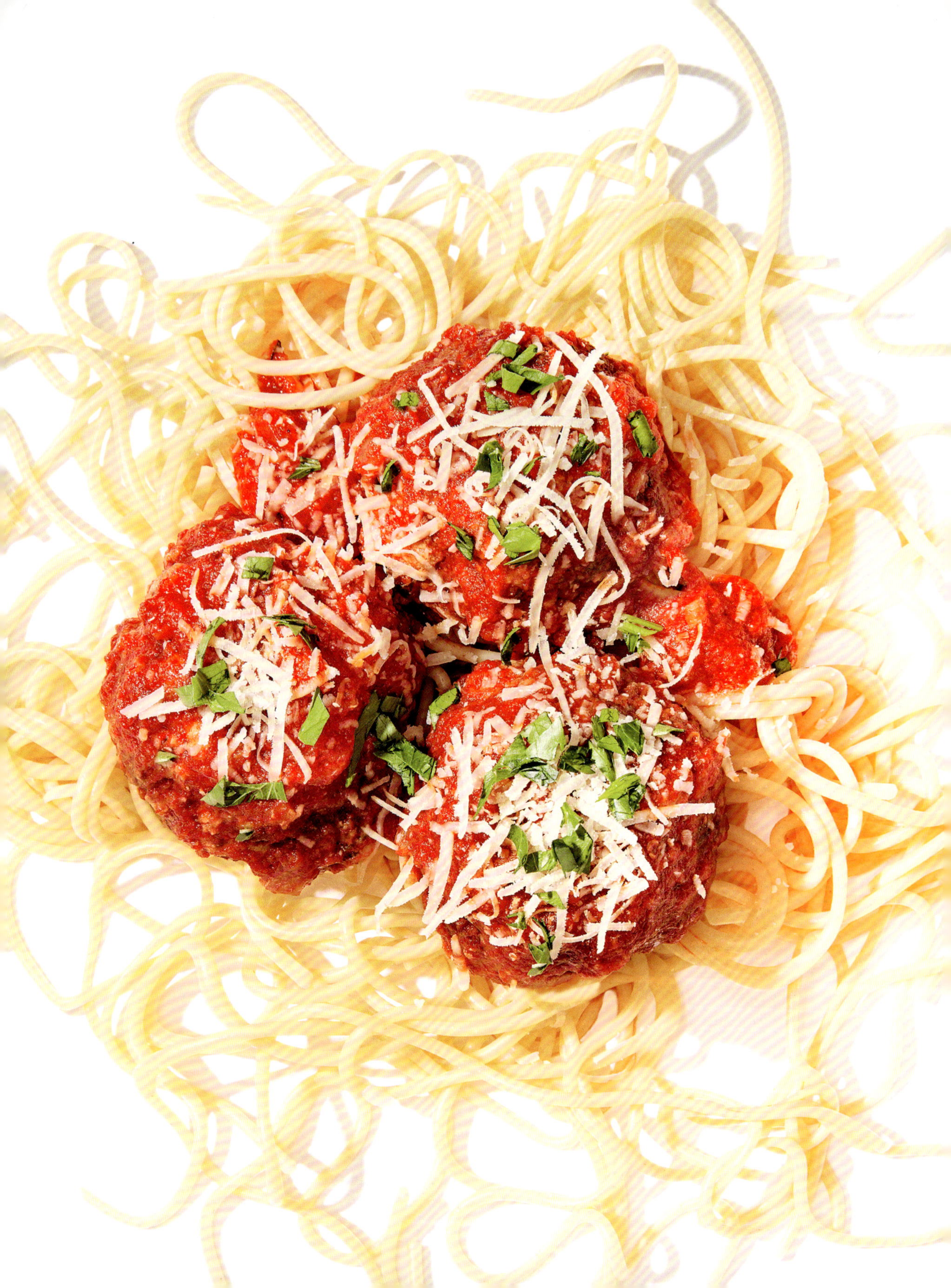

41. Laura Silverman | WESTPORT, CONNECTICUT

There's something in the air come fall in Westport, Connecticut. It's not pumpkin spice or crunchy fallen leaves. It's the smell of Laura Silverman's sauce on the stove. The self-described "mostly" vegetarian makes an exception every year when the weather turns cool and declares it "meatball season." Her recipe for spaghetti and meatballs also happens to be Laura's most treasured family heirloom.

"My family has always sworn by my great-aunt Rosa's recipe, but since I am not Aunt Rosa, it never came out right," Laura says.

"I used to ask her about the kind of canned tomatoes she used, thinking that could make the difference," she says. But Aunt Rosa held her (recipe) card tightly. "She would sweetly say, 'Oh, I don't know, maybe Hunt's?'" The secret to the sauce all along, Laura now knows, was that Aunt Rosa made it.

Laura owns that mindset in the kitchen these days. She has been working for years to adapt a spaghetti-and-meatballs recipe she found in *Gourmet* magazine. The goal is to lovingly and deliciously feed her own family—with a dash of tradition but in her own way.

Laura has been navigating family and tradition in her own way since she was a kid. She lost both of her parents when she was thirteen years old. It's a grief she carries every day, but she will also tell you it can be a gift at times.

"I've learned to let go of the noise and focus on what's really important—take the time to listen to your children, look them in the eye, and be truly present."

Thinking about family and heirlooms stirred up some feelings for her. Sometimes, she says, old family belongings just feel empty. "I held my mother's recipe box in my hands and actually said out loud, 'Was any of it ever even real?'"

With a vibrant spirit and a side of pure grit, Laura managed to define family "heirloom" on her terms. For her, it's the meatballs. A celebration of her past but firmly planted in the present—and future.

"My son says I make the best meatballs in the world, and that makes me feel like I created our own family memory. In the end, that's what we will have."

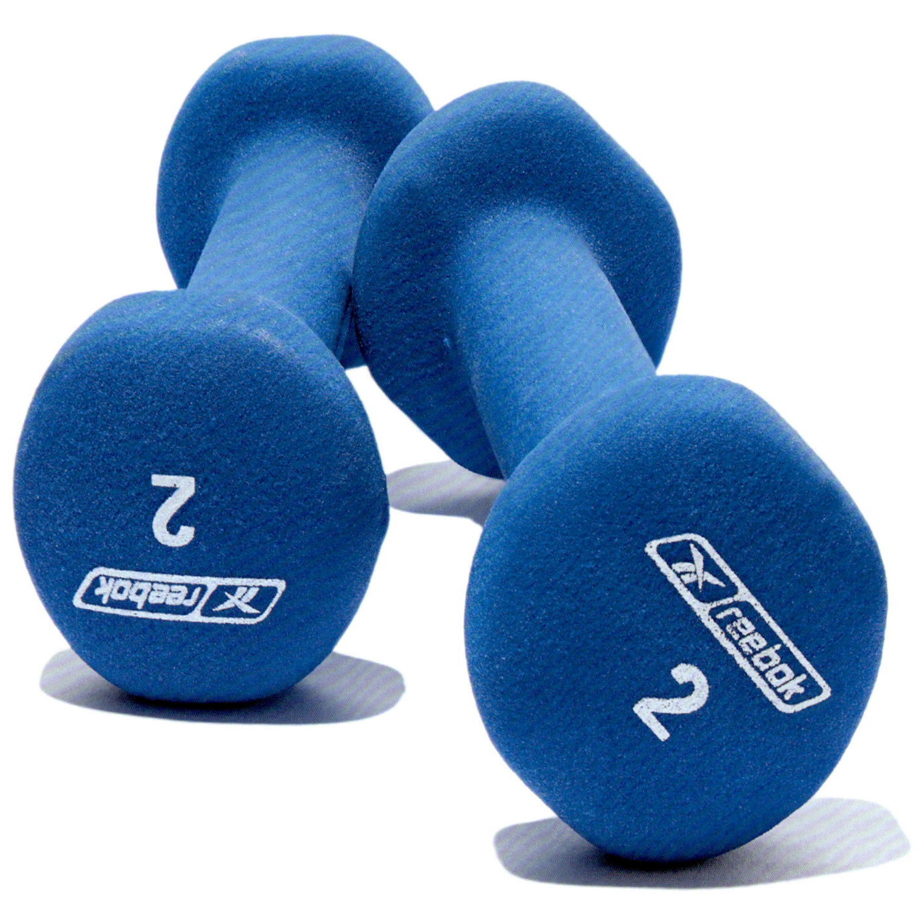
2
reebok
reebok
2

42. Vicki Perlmeter | OMAHA, NEBRASKA

In 1971, Roie Meyers went to her local library to read up on two strange health issues her daughter, Vicki, was experiencing—numbness and double vision. Vicki had seen several doctors, but at the time, MRI machines didn't exist and neither did a sophisticated test to explain her symptoms. She was told to go home and take it easy.

Roie used the information she learned at the library to diagnose Vicki with multiple sclerosis (MS). A doctor would later confirm what Roie already knew.

Of her early years of living with MS, Vicki says her symptoms would come and go and were generally manageable. She taught preschool and raised two daughters. She put down roots in a tight-knit community and became a fixture within her group of friends.

In time, Vicki's MS became more pronounced. Her preschoolers first noticed her cane. She gradually moved on to using a walker. She openly admits the deterioration of her body was impossible to accept. Yet, willfully, she says, "I am still here."

Vicki has now been living with MS for fifty-three years. She no longer walks but gets around in a van that has been retrofitted to accommodate her motorized scooter. Errands as simple as buying holiday cards often require assistance. She has watched her children grow up, her grandchildren be born, and endured the passing of not one but two significant others. Even her doctor has now retired.

"I am still here," she'll tell you again.

Much of Vicki's strength comes from her indomitable spirit. She also acknowledges a great group of friends and community who have supported her from the beginning. The third factor is MSForward, a gym in Omaha dedicated to serving individuals with physical challenges.

Twenty years ago, owner Daryl Kucera had just opened a traditional-style gym when he was diagnosed with MS himself. He pivoted and redesigned the space for the needs of those struggling with neurological challenges. Vicki remembers visiting the gym with an MS support group when it first opened. She remembers saying to herself, *I'm not going there.*

Vicki has been going to the gym twice a week for twenty years.

"It's the one place in my life where I have control," she says. She lifts weights (her favorites are pictured) and works with local physical therapy students to stay flexible.

While a lot of the members come with helpers, Vicki is quick to point out the thing that might just be the most satisfying for her about the gym: "I do everything there by myself."

For all the determination Vicki has to stay strong, she will be the first to say she struggles with anger over the hand she was dealt. But she practices acceptance every day. She keeps a note on her bathroom mirror, a quote from Theodore Roosevelt.

"I live by it," she says. "It reads, 'Do what you can, with what you've got, where you are.' Does it work every time? No. But I say it out loud. It gets me through."

I am still here.

—Vicki Perlmeter

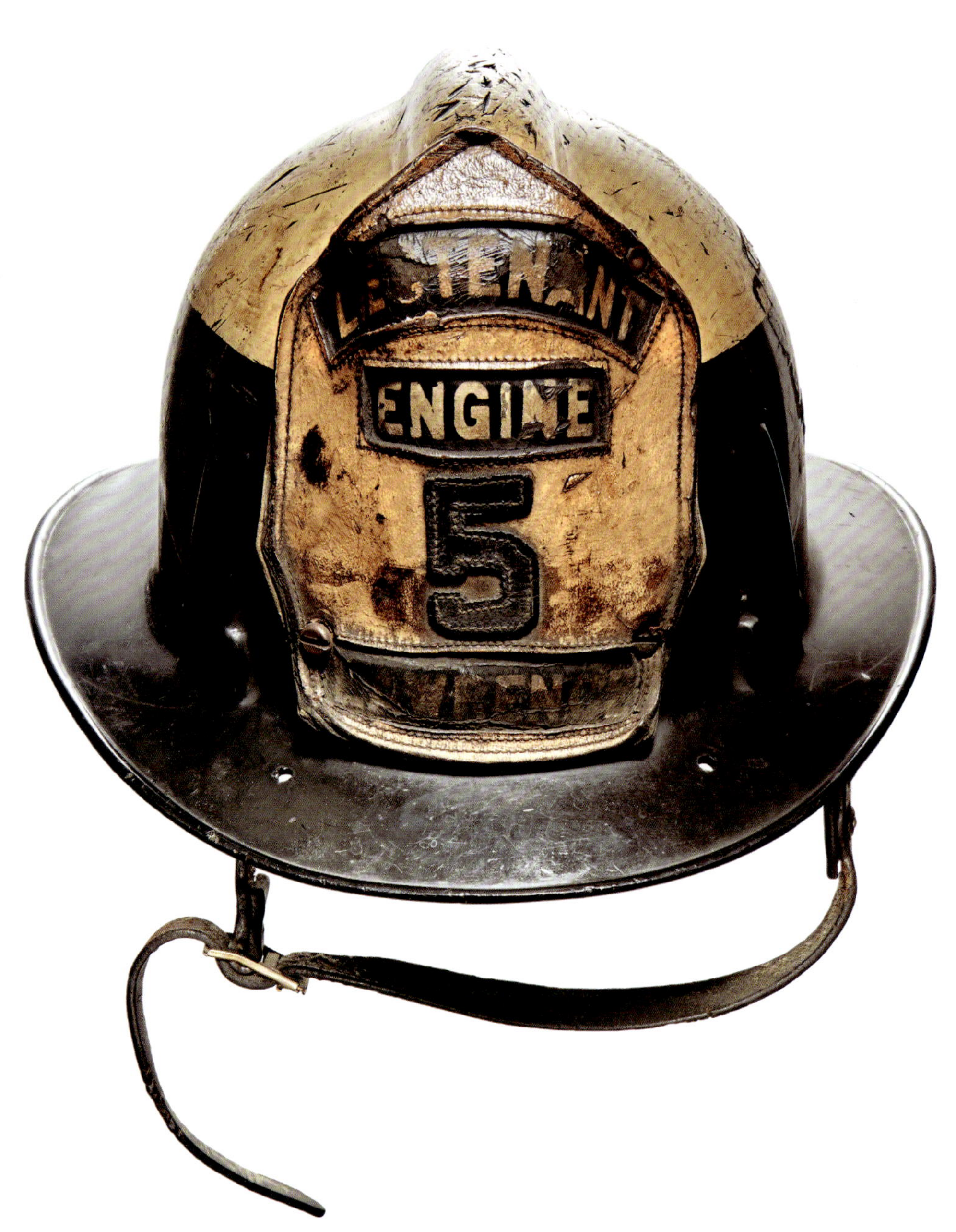
ENGINE
5

43. John "Jack" Burton | LAWRENCE, MASSACHUSETTS

Lieutenant John "Jack" Burton served as a third-generation firefighter in the town of Lawrence, Massachusetts, for over thirty years. He was a member of the Coast Guard and the Arson Task Force, and he served on various ambulance, engine, and ladder and rescue companies throughout his career. His service earned him the title of Firefighter of the Year not once, but twice.

Once, while responding to a residential fire, Jack caught a toddler who fell from a burning building. As he bent over to put the child down, a falling baby landed on Jack's back. The chance encounter broke the baby's fall and saved its life. It also earned him another title, this time in the press: the "human safety net."

While the human safety net could charge into burning buildings without a second thought, he was equally dedicated to his family. His son, Paul, says his father firmly believed that working hard was his best chance of keeping his wife, Jeanne, and their three children happy and safe.

There was one thing, Jack's family notes, that brought out another side of the hero. "He softened up when his grandchildren were born and loved watching them and his great-grandchild grow," Paul says.

This is Jack's helmet—a tough layer of protection for the man with a soft spot for his family.

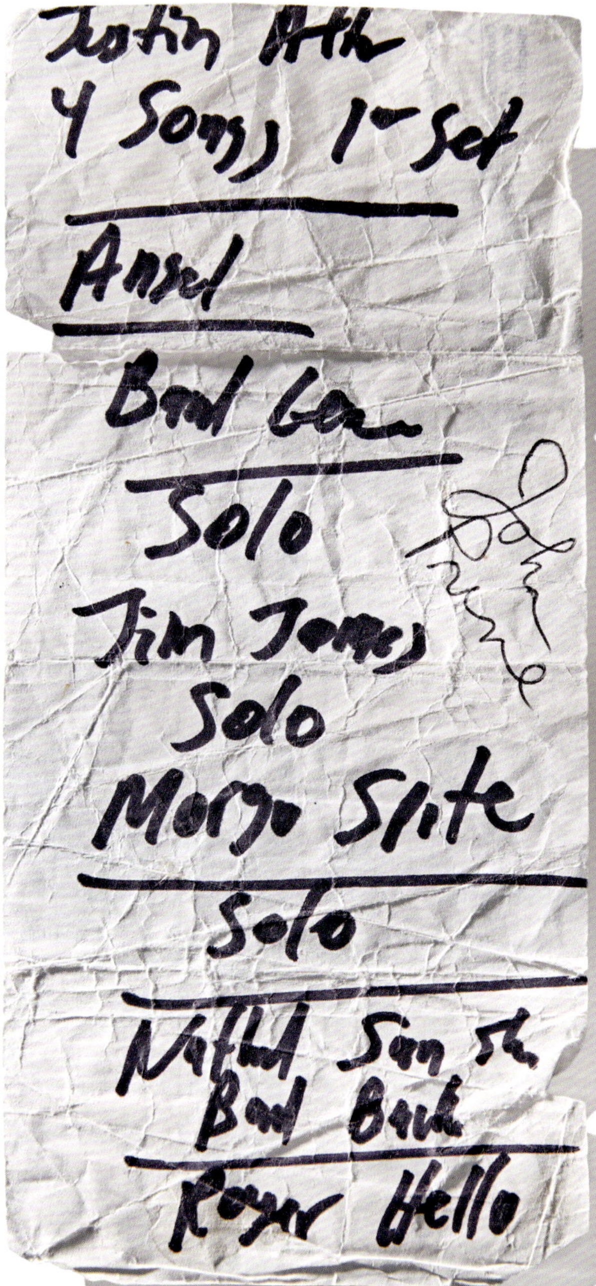

Justin Atk
4 Songs 1st Set

Angel

Bad Gea

Solo
Jim James
Solo
Margo Slite

Solo

Nathaniel Sun Sh
Bad Back

Roger Hello

John Prine

Jay Sweet took the reins as executive producer of the historic Newport Folk Festival in 2008. He had big shoes to fill. Founded in 1959, the festival is home to legendary moments in music—artists including Joni Mitchell, Bob Dylan, Odetta, Dolly Parton, Johnny Cash, Mavis Staples, James Taylor, Paul Simon, and countless others have made history there. Jay set out to maintain that historical relevance, but he knew he'd need to usher the festival into a new era to keep it viable. He did this by inviting the next generation of musicians to play with—often right beside—the legends. This set the stage for once-in-a-lifetime collaborations that stuck around in people's hearts long after the show had ended. Jay's mix of generational musical alchemy proved to be a hit. The festival has been selling out in advance since 2014—before any of the lineup is even announced.

"The uniqueness of Newport is that the moments that happen here don't happen anywhere else," Jay says. "Our job isn't to sell the most tickets, bring the biggest artists, or throw the wildest party. It's to help manifest these moments of hope through the power of music and community."

In 2017, the festival lineup included legendary singer-songwriter John Prine, known for his many lasting impacts on the music community, one of which, and perhaps the most well known, is his song "Angel from Montgomery." John wasn't in the best of health that year, but he sent his trademark humor-laced, melancholy music into the crowd nonetheless. John was family to Jay. "He supported me from the minute I got the keys to Newport and always made me laugh, even at the low points," Jay says. As Jay walked him off the stage that night, John pushed a crumpled piece of paper into Jay's hand. It was the set list from his guest-laden performance, which included Jim James, Justin Vernon, Margo Price, Nathaniel Rateliff, Lucius, and Roger Waters. "Thanks for having me as always, that was a ton of fun," John told him. John knew Jay would somehow use the set list for a greater good—and trusted him to wield its power accordingly.

"It was John's way of giving back," Jay says. "He understood that it was important to give on stage, but also to give to others—to take the opportunity and make the most and pay it forward." The world lost John Prine to COVID-19 in 2020. Shortly after his death, Jay and the Prine family decided on how he was going to pay it forward in honor of

John—he was going to make a record out of this set list.

Jay is also the executive director of the Newport Festivals Foundation, a nonprofit that raises money for music curricula in schools, musicians in need, and related community programs.

Jay and his team made a vinyl record from the soundtrack of John's 2017 set. He used the proceeds from the sale of the record, along with money John left the festival when he died, for music education and to establish the John Prine Songwriter Fellowship. The scholarship provides resources for an underprivileged and underrepresented musician to play a set at Newport each summer—and pays them for their set.

"John comes from a line of people giving others a chance, so it made sense to celebrate his generosity this way," Jay says.

For all of Jay's reverence for those who came before him, and for those he hopes to nurture in the future, the present is where Jay wholeheartedly believes the true magic comes from. His granular memories from festivals over the years are astounding.

One such memory is from the summer of 2022. Brandi Carlile had just surprised the crowd by bringing her idol, Joni Mitchell, back to the Newport stage for the first time since 1969. It was Joni's first performance since a brain aneurysm in 2015 forced her to relearn how to walk and sing. But there she was, making history. People everywhere openly wept.

"While Joni was making her triumphant return, I watched a child in the crowd take its first steps," Jay recalls. "It filled me with, well, hope. The real magic is in the smallest moments."

The real magic is in the smallest moments.

—Jay Sweet

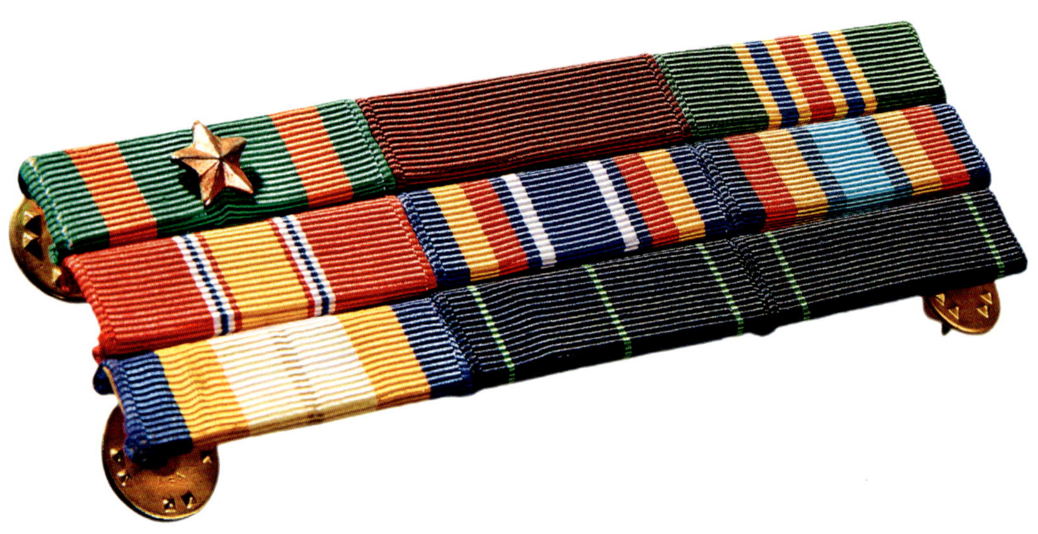

As a naval officer aboard the USS *John L. Hall*, Russell Ledet learned a lot of things. But one lesson really stuck: If he could be trusted to operate multimillion-dollar machinery, he could do anything.

This lesson inspired him to leave the military. He didn't leave because he was turning his back on serving. He just wanted to serve on behalf of a cause that called to his heart. He left the military as a decorated E-6 Petty Officer First Class, and received a Naval Ceremonial Duty Ribbon, pictured, that's awarded to only a few thousand service members.

"What do I need to do to be a productive person in the world?" Russell constantly asked himself as he plotted his next course. He answered this question by educating himself—extensively. First with undergraduate degrees in biology and chemistry from Southern University. Next came a master's degree in biomedical science and a doctorate of philosophy focusing on molecular oncology and tumor immunology from the New York University School of Medicine. Rounding out his accomplishments are an MBA and an MD from Tulane. And he was only getting started.

Russell is now the first African American in the Indiana University Health system to pursue a triple board residency working in the areas of pediatrics, adult psychiatry, and child and adolescent psychiatry. His new mission does not involve aircraft carriers and national defense, but it's just as integral to humanity: mental health for kids. And like any other mission, there are challenges to face down.

Russell says that when he walks into a treatment room, he is often met with surprise from his patients. "'You're the doctor?' the kids often ask. It's the first time they've seen a doctor who looks like me," he says.

"It's hard for a Black man," Russell admits of working within the institutional medical environment. But working with kids and mental health is just the type of service he was destined for, he believes.

"People rarely talk to kids about their mental health. Now, I can open their minds to the idea that the brain is just as important as the rest of the body. This is a chance for me to be effective for the next generation," he says.

Russell's dedication to future generations doesn't stop when he leaves the treatment room. In 2019, along with Dr. Sydney Labat and Dr. Rachel Turner, he cofounded The 15 White Coats, a nonprofit organization focused on empowering minorities to pursue medical careers. The organization funds medical school scholarships and provides mentoring. Russell says it is rare for minority students to receive such support in the medical field. This was his reason for taking action.

He put the organization on the map when he brought medical students—fifteen of them, all in white lab coats—to the Louisiana plantation where his ancestors were enslaved. A photograph from that day went viral, receiving more than two hundred million views on various social media platforms. "We did it to make sure people see Black doctors," Russell says. "So no one has an excuse to be surprised by it." The image was also a statement on progress, resilience, and determination—a subject Russell knows very well.

This is a chance for me to be effective for the next generation.

—Dr. Russell Ledet

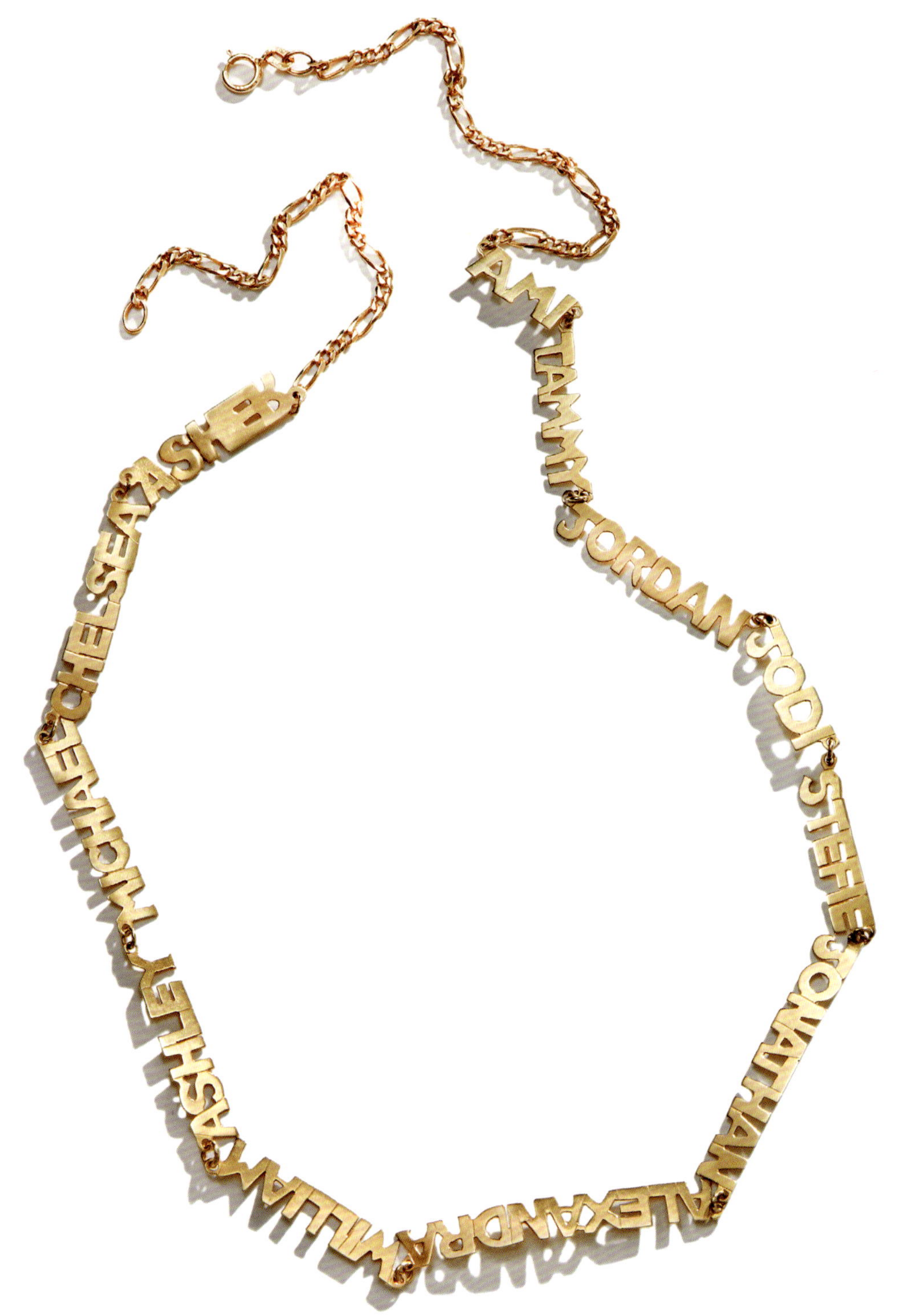
AMI
TAMMY
JORDAN
JODI
STEFIE
JONATHAN
ALEXANDRA
WILLIAM
ASHLEY
MICHAEL
CHELSEA

Next time you're traveling and want to buy someone a souvenir, make it count—it might become an heirloom. Wendy Kantor brought a necklace home from a trip to Jerusalem as a gift for her mother-in-law, Hana. It was a thoughtful gesture, heartfelt, but not extravagant. Yet to Hana, it was a strand of precious jewels. The necklace was strung with the names of her grandchildren—a celebration of life and family for a woman who came very close to not having either.

Hana and two of her sisters were the only members of her family to survive the Holocaust. She was a teenager when she was sent by the Nazis into forced labor. Liberation came in the spring of 1945. Just weeks later, Hana met Anschel Kantor, also a survivor. They would marry and move to America to rebuild their lives. There, what was stolen from them—community, tradition, and, most all, family—was reclaimed.

Hana's son, Harry, recalls that despite what she had been through, his mom was a happy person in spirit. She thrived on being surrounded by family, and she loved talking to anyone about anything, always leaving them charmed.

"America was a dream to her," he says. "She celebrated. Nothing held her back. This was her personality."

As the Kantor family reclaimed tradition and religious rituals in their new world, they ended up creating a few new ones of their own. The one tradition still ardently observed to this day is the Sunday-morning family gathering for bagels and lox. Appreciating a good meal as a family was a simple act of celebration and perseverance. It was the perfect opportunity for Hana to surround herself with her legacy.

The guest list grew significantly over the years. Hana's first grandchild, Jodi, was born almost thirty years to the day of her liberation. As represented by this necklace, eleven more followed. At present, there are twenty-four great-grandchildren, and counting.

For Hana, wearing the names of those who will continue her legacy was a symbol of pride and triumph and a way to keep the ones she loved close to her heart. She rarely took the necklace off. She passed away in 2023 at the age of ninety-nine.

"They were her life," Harry says of the kids, grandkids, and great-grandchildren. "Every child was a jewel to her."

In a moment of raw certainty, perhaps Wendy says it best. "The Nazis didn't win."

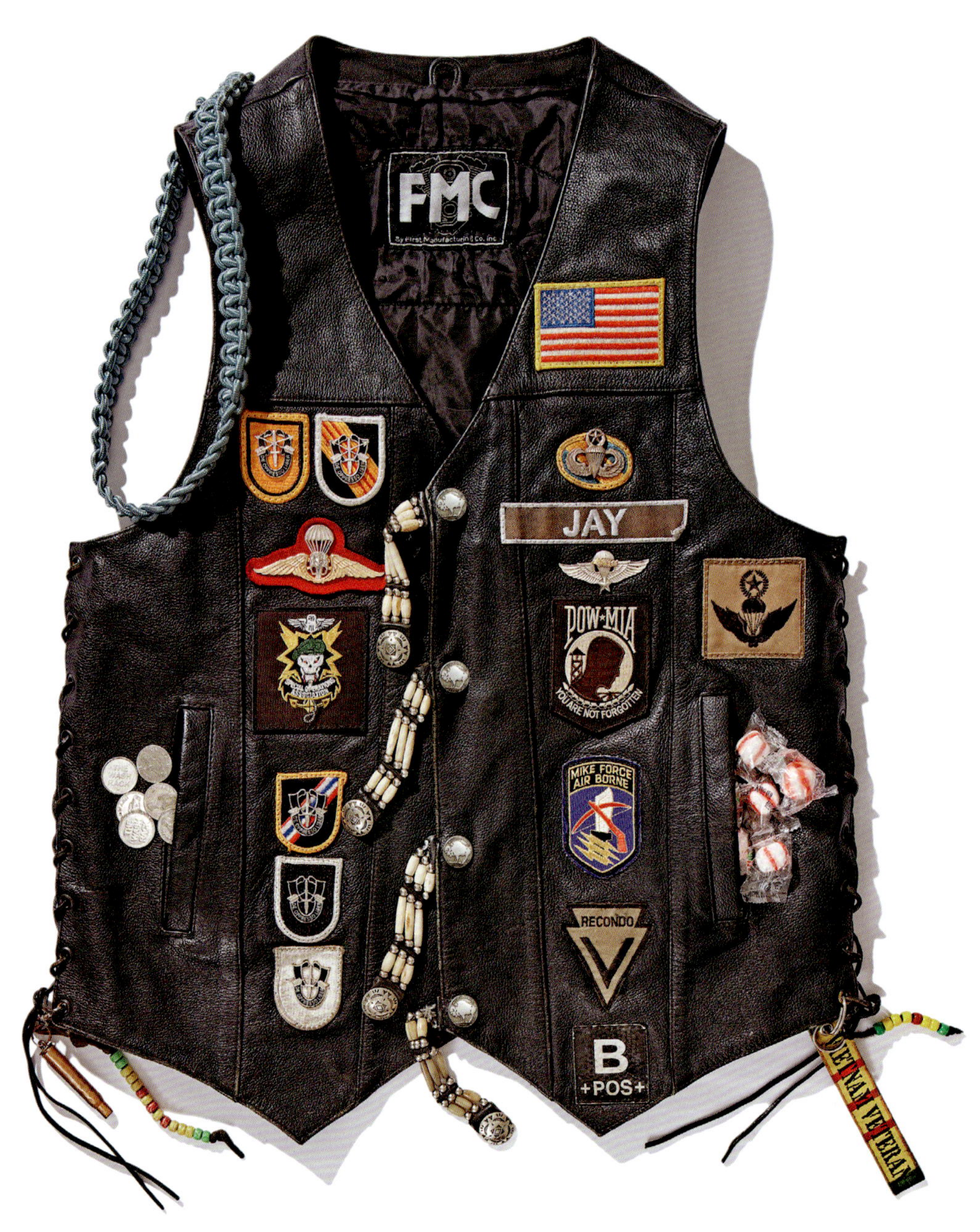
FMC
JAY
POW★MIA
YOU ARE NOT FORGOTTEN
MIKE FORCE
AIR BORNE
RECONDO
B
+POS+
VIETNAM VETERAN

Jay Massey lived more than a few legacy-worthy chapters of life. He paid his own high school tuition by selling metal hangers door to door and skipped graduation to enlist in the army. He became a Green Beret and spent three tours in Vietnam behind enemy lines gathering intelligence for the Military Assistance Command Vietnam, Studies and Observations Group (MACV-SOG). He was so good at his work, the military hired him to teach it to the next generation.

As a retired master sergeant, Jay became a well-regarded Dallas-area real estate appraiser. He was born a member of the Chickasaw Nation and remained an active and proud member his entire life. But perhaps Jay's most important role was the one within his own tribe—as a father.

"Pops had a fierce integrity and was eternally proud of his contributions to his people and his country," Jay's son, Alan, says. Alan remembers his dad as remarkably patient and grounded, considering the amount of time he spent at war.

"He cared the most about us getting a good education—we'd get in bigger trouble for getting a C in class than for getting in fights at school," Alan jokes.

Jay was exposed to Agent Orange in Vietnam. The resulting neuropathy seizures and pulmonary fibrosis would eventually lead to his death. "He had always lived by determination getting you where you need to be," Alan says. "So, when the doctor said his time was done, it was impossible for him to accept."

When they received the news, Alan and his then fiancée, Callie, moved their upcoming wedding to an earlier date so Jay could attend. Callie surprised the entire family by booking the rescheduled wedding at one of Jay's favorite restaurants, Campisi's Egyptian Restaurant. (Despite its name, Campisi's is a legendary Italian restaurant chain.)

"It was the only place Pops would wait around for," Alan jokes. The wedding was special for all the right reasons. But Jay still had not exactly accepted his fate—he would go on to outlive Callie and Alan's original wedding date. He outlived doctors' original predictions by sixteen years.

In the end, Alan says, his dad finally started accepting the inevitable. "He'd always made his own way," Alan says. "He had never been able to just allow things to happen. My dad had never given up in his entire life. But he never flinched. He was never bitter, ever the patriot."

At Jay's funeral, the chapters of his life came together, spilling out of the chapel and onto the sidewalk. His motorcycle vest, pictured, reflects his lifetime of diverse connections. In attendance were biker friends, military personnel, and a strong Chickasaw presence. Jay Massey received a traditional twenty-one-gun salute and also a sacred tribal smudging with sage and a bald eagle feather.

Pops had a fierce integrity and was eternally proud of his contributions to his people and his country.

—Alan Massey

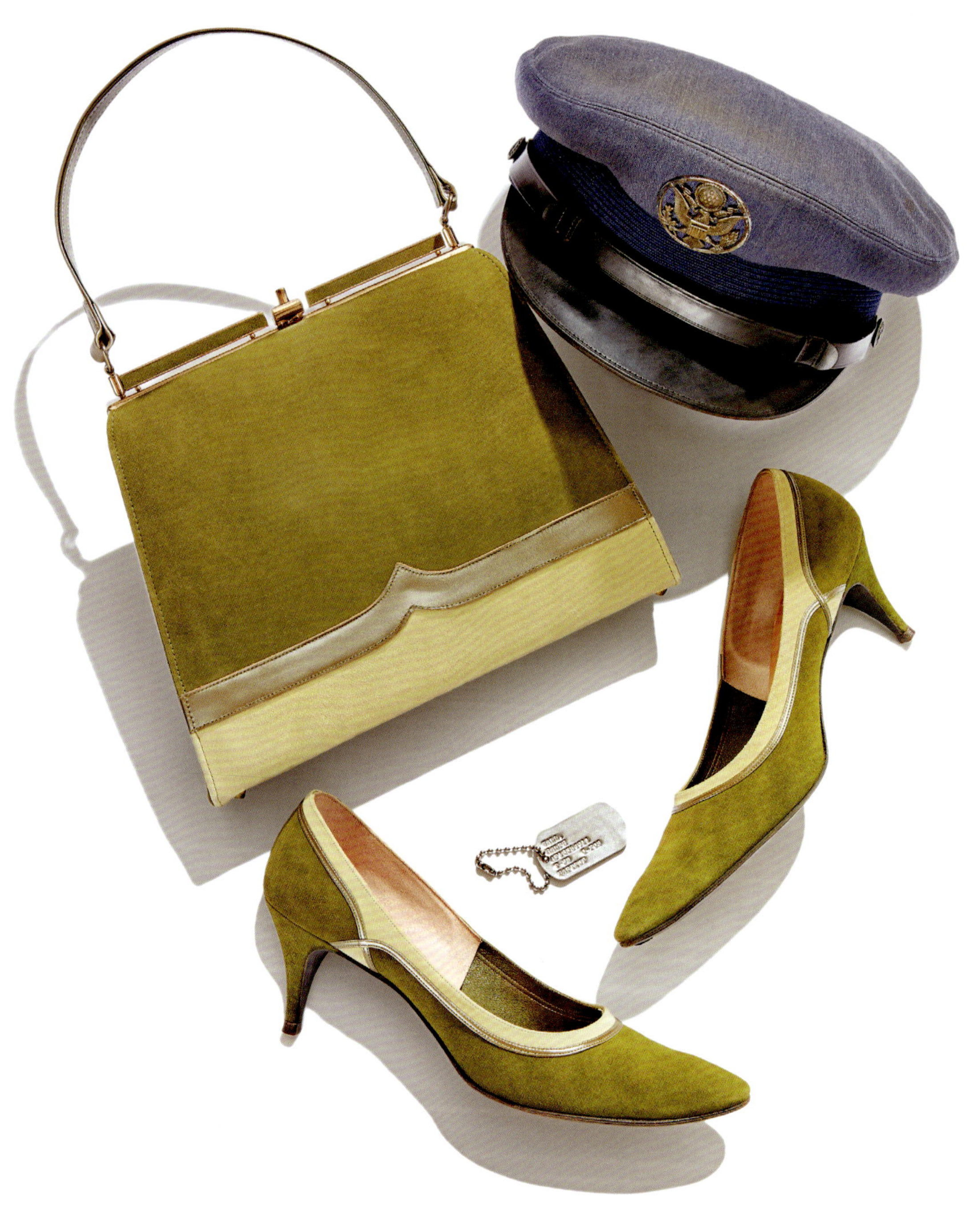

48. Betty Wall | PORT LAVACA, TEXAS

While her husband served in the air force during the Vietnam War, Betty Wall did not see or hear from him for an entire year. Raising their children, then aged nine and thirteen, was a full-time job, and she took on another—as a bookkeeper—to make ends meet. Three of her closest friends stepped in to help with the kids on days when Betty had to work. The sacrifice was great, but family and country were worth it.

There was one thing Betty splurged on while her husband was away—a new handbag and pair of heeled shoes, pictured. On the day in 1968 when her husband was finally to return to his base in San Antonio, Texas, she did a thing strong women know well—she put on a dress and those new heels and went to bring her husband home.

"I was nervous, but full of excitement to see my husband again," Betty says of going to greet his plane at the air force base. "The shoes cost $19.95, and the purse was really an extravagant purchase at $25, but after all, I was getting to see Ralph after 365 long days, and I wanted to look my very best!"

Ralph was welcomed home by a group of family and friends who threw him a party for every holiday he missed while he was away. He and Betty enjoyed nearly forty more years of love and marriage that included travel, double dates, and even starting a business together. (He had asked her to marry him on their third date—their love was meant to be from the start.) Ralph went on to serve in the air force for twenty years and retired as a senior master sergeant.

Ralph passed away in 2004, but Betty stayed in their home, living on her own, until just recently. While preparing for an upcoming move, she came across the heels and handbag she wore to the base to get Ralph.

"It was a reminder of what an outstanding man Ralph was and how much we loved one another," Betty says.

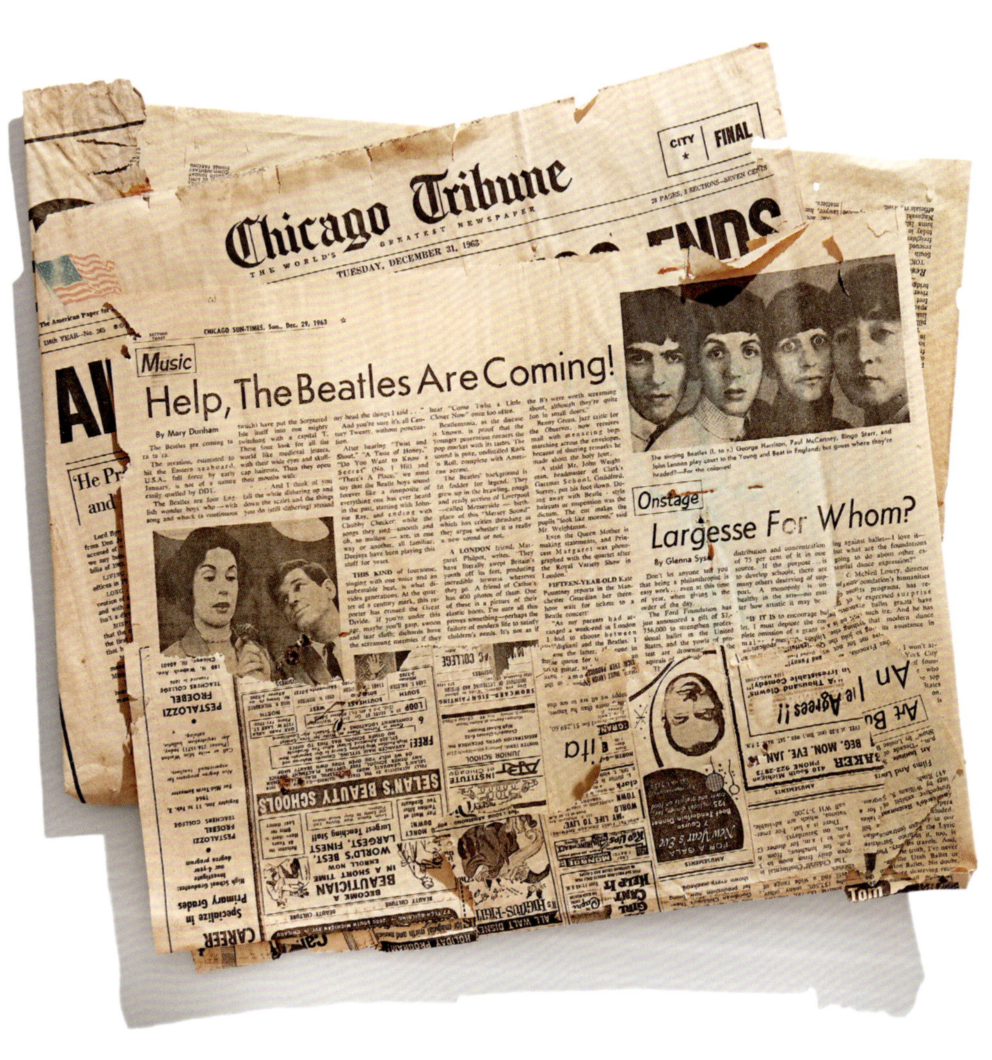

CITY ★ FINAL

Chicago Tribune

THE WORLD'S GREATEST NEWSPAPER

TUESDAY, DECEMBER 31, 1963

CHICAGO SUN-TIMES, Sun., Dec. 29, 1963

Music

Help, The Beatles Are Coming!

By Mary Dunham

The Beatles are coming ta ra ta ra.

The invasion, estimated to hit the Eastern seaboard, U.S.A., full force by early January, is not of a nature easily quelled by DDT.

The Beatles are four English wonder boys who—with song and whack (a continuous twitch) have put the Sceptered Isle itself into one mighty twitching with a capital T. These four look for all the world like medieval jesters, with their wide eyes and skull-cap haircuts. Then they open their mouths with:

". . . And I think of you (all the while dithering up and down the scale) and the things you do (still dithering) around my head the things I said . . ."

And you're sure it's all Century Twenty, without punctuation.

After hearing "Twist and Shout," "A Taste of Honey," "Do You Want to Know a Secret" (No. 1 Hit) and "There's A Place," we must say that the Beatle boys sound forever like a composite of everything one has ever heard in the past, starting with Johnnie Ray, and ending with Chubby Checker, while the songs they sing—smooth and oh, so mellow — are, in one way or another, all familiar. Deejays have been playing this stuff for years.

THIS KIND of foursome, singing with one voice and an unbeatable beat, is what divides generations. At the quarter of a century mark, this reporter has crossed the Great Divide. If you're under this age, maybe you'll gasp, swoon and tear cloth; diehards have the screaming meemies if they hear "Come Twist a Little Closer Now" once too often.

Beatlemania, as the disease is known, is proof that the younger generation corners the pop market with its tastes. The sound is pure, undistilled Rock 'n Roll, complete with American accent.

The Beatles' background is fit fodder for legend. They grew up in the brawling, rough and ready section of Liverpool —called Merseyside — birthplace of this "Mersey Sound" which has critics thrashing as they argue whether it is really a new sound or not.

A LONDON friend, Margaret Philpot, writes: "They have literally swept Britain's youth off its feet, producing incredible hysteria wherever they go. A friend of Cathie's has 400 photos of them. One of these is a picture of their elastic boots. I'm sure all this proves something—perhaps the failure of modern life to satisfy children's needs. It's not as if the B's were worth screaming about, although they're quite fun in small doses."

Benny Green, jazz critic for the Observer, now receives mail with menacing bugs marching across the envelopes, because of slurring remarks he made about the holy four.

A staid Mr. John Weightman, headmaster of Clark's Garmar School, Guildford, Surrey, put his foot down. Doing away with Beatle-style haircuts or suspension was the dictum. The cut makes the pupils "look like morons," said Mr. Weightman.

Even the Queen Mother is making statements, and Princess Margaret was photographed with the quartet after the Royal Variety Show in London.

FIFTEEN-YEAR-OLD Kate Pountney reports in the Manchester Guardian her three-hour wait for tickets to a Beatle concert:

"As my parents had arranged a week-end in London I had to choose between Modigliani and the Beatles. I chose the latter. . . .

The singing Beatles (l. to r.) George Harrison, Paul McCartney, Ringo Starr, and John Lennon play court to the Young and Beat in England; but guess where they're headed?—For the colonies!

Onstage

Largesse For Whom?

By Glenna Sys[illegible]

Don't let anyone tell you that being a philanthropist is easy work . . . even at this time of year, when giving is the order of the day.

The Ford Foundation has just announced a gift of $7,756,000 to strengthen professional ballet in the United States, and the yowls of protest are drowning . . . squeals of . . .

. . . distribution and concentration of 75 per cent of it in one source. If the purpose . . . is to develop schools, there are many others deserving of support. A monopoly is unhealthy in the arts—no matter how artistic it may be.

"IF IT IS to encourage ballet, I must deplore the complete omission of a grant . . .

. . . ing against ballet—I love it—but what are the foundations going to do about other essential dance expression?"

. . . McNeil Lowry, director of . . . Foundation's humanities . . . programs, has reportedly expressed surprise . . . ballet grants have . . . such ire. And he has . . . that modern dance . . . its assistance in . . .

SELAN'S BEAUTY SCHOOLS

BECOME A BEAUTICIAN IN A SHORT TIME

WORLD'S BEST, LARGEST, FINEST

CAREER

PESTALOZZI FROEBEL TEACHERS COLLEGE

Specialize in Primary Grades

"A Thousand Clowns"

An Irresistable Comedy!

Art Buchwald

FOR A GALA New Year's Eve

49. Jonathan Gordon | CHICAGO, ILLINOIS

Summer weekends in the 1980s, for Jonathan Gordon, meant being packed into a car with family and friends and heading for southwest Michigan's Harbor County, an idyllic string of small resort towns on Lake Michigan.

"Seventy-five miles from Chicago, but a world away," Jonathan says. Classic childhood memories were made there—rock skipping, apple picking, and countless hours spent freely in the great outdoors. But one memory really stuck: driving past the stately white gates that welcomed visitors to Grand Beach and the old Grand Beach Inn. Jonathan was always fascinated by the inn's storied past, which involved gangsters and gamblers in the 1930s.

Jonathan would grow up to become a Chicago real estate developer. But no matter how many new projects he took on, his appreciation for the past always tugged at him.

In 2018, Jonathan had a chance to meld the old and new in an adaptive reuse project. He gut-renovated a 130-year-old building originally built for Chicago's 1893 World's Columbian Exposition and turned it into a boutique hotel.

When he found out the Grand Beach Inn of his childhood had fallen into disrepair and was for sale, Jonathan's heart skipped a beat. "We knew it was our chance to put our stamp on the roadside hotel," he says. His team gutted the property right down to the studs and restored it to its former glory, the glory of Jonathan's rock-skipping years.

"We wanted to make a place where families could be together again in a thoughtfully designed setting, with a real sense of place and community. A place to make memories."

During the renovation, the inn served up some memories of its own. "Adaptive-reuse projects often turn up small treasures along the way," Jonathan says. This 1963 *Chicago Tribune* announcing "Help, The Beatles Are Coming!" was one of his favorites. It was pulled from the floorboards of what is now the inn's lobby.

"Our job was to understand the story of the property, its place in history, and continue as the caretaker of that story," Jonathan says. He intends to make the Grand Beach Inn a treasure for generations to come.

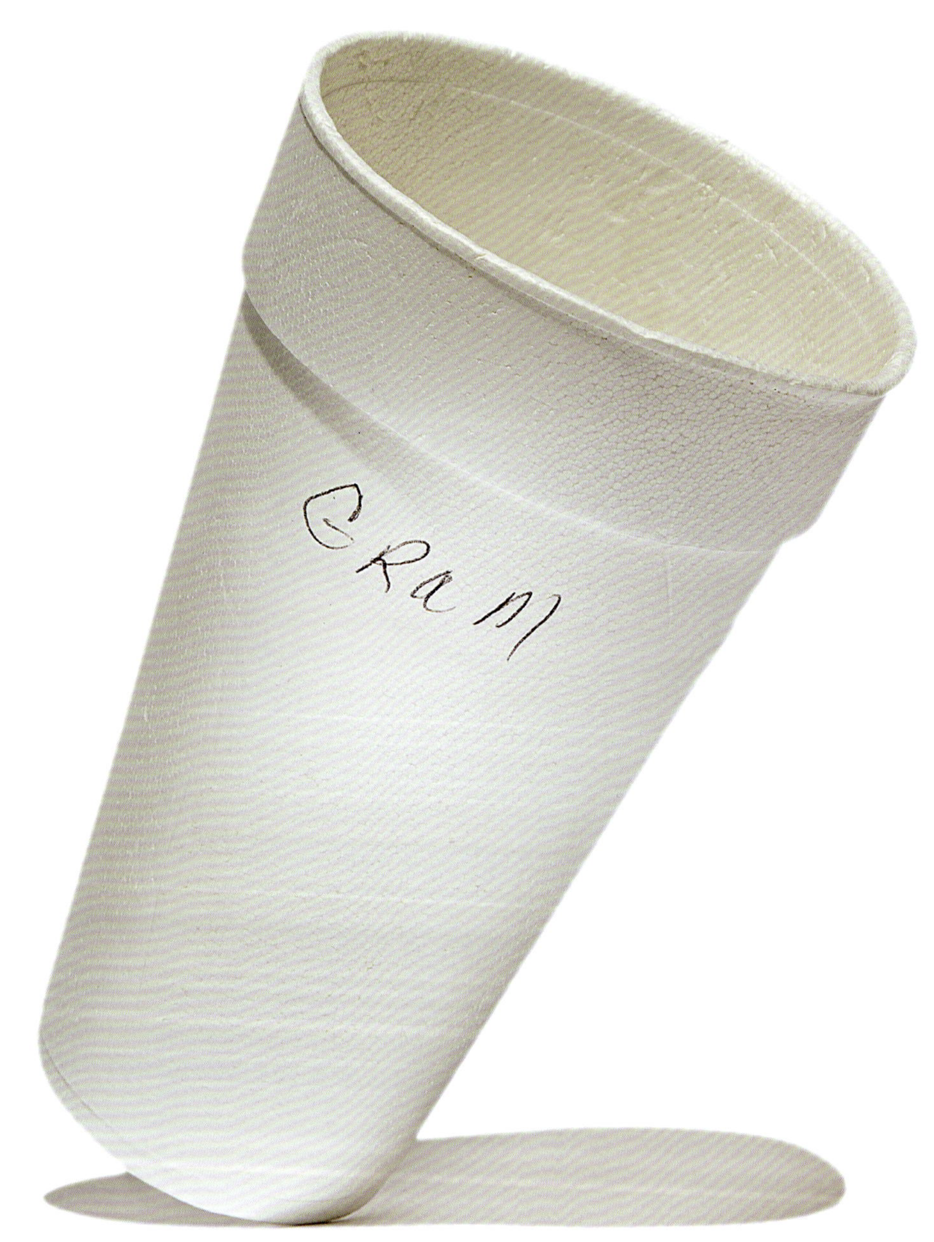
GRaM

50. Hannah Sellers Terry | NASHVILLE, TENNESSEE

Both of Hannah Sellers Terry's parents worked full time when she was a kid, so the grandmas in the family stepped in to help raise her. Gram, also known as Barbara Porter, was Hannah's maternal grandmother and was assigned the important task of school pickup duty. Gram would pull up to Hannah's elementary school each day with a homemade Oreo Blizzard in a Styrofoam cup, in a cooler, on ice to ensure perfect consistency when Hannah got in the car. That is how much she loved Hannah—and Styrofoam cups.

Styrofoam cups were practically Gram's calling card. With grandkids filtering in and out of her house constantly, she'd label her sweet tea so no one would drink it. When the family gathered at her house for holidays, everyone got a cup with their name on it. Even when Hannah would come home from college to visit, there were two cups, one labeled with her name, and one with Gram's.

"On the surface, it feels like she wanted people to make sure they knew which cup was theirs," Hannah says. "But I really think that she was the kind of person who wanted to make sure you felt cared for, safe, and loved. It was never about the cup. It was about the love and comfort that she wanted us to constantly feel."

Hannah says Gram was the quintessential matriarch—beautiful white hair, a friend to anyone she met, and with a laugh that would light up a room. She was always, always present.

"Ball game? Never missed one. Gymnastics meet? You bet she'd be there. School play? Front row," says Hannah. "She was incredibly special in our family, and we were all close with her."

Barbara passed away in 2021, and though it was devastating for the family to lose her, her grandson, Hunter, found something to hold on to. One last cup.

"The most constant piece of a memory that is still physically present," Hannah says.

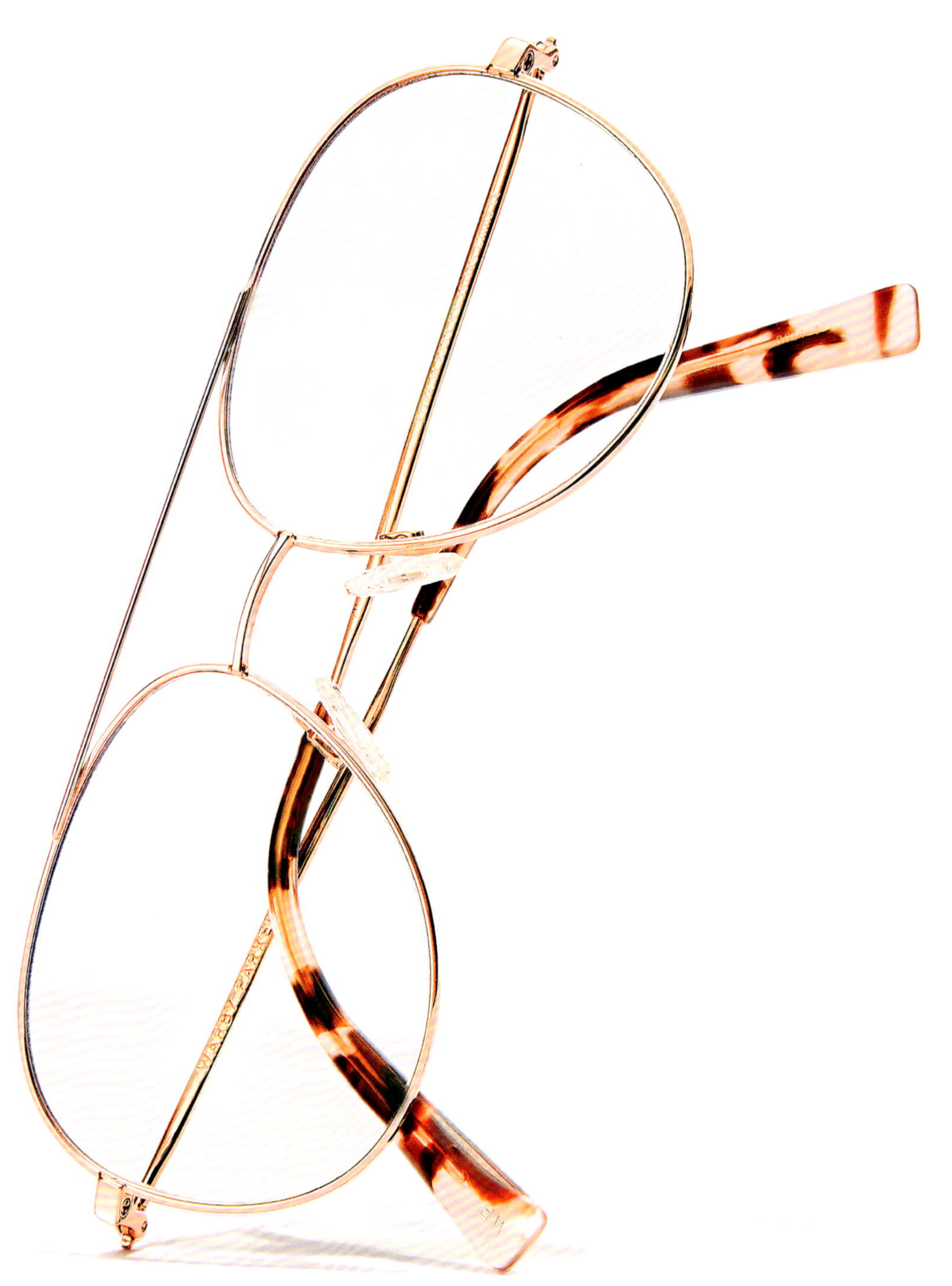

51. Susan Feldman | LOS ANGELES, CALIFORNIA

If "aging like fine wine" could be bottled and sold for all to enjoy, Susan Feldman would probably be the president of the company that does it. Or maybe she already is.

Susan built a career in fashion marketing and then, at the age of fifty-three, built another one as cofounder of One Kings Lane, the home-furnishings company that became a household name due in part to its fresh approach to individuality and craftsmanship at a time when other similar companies were hooked on big-box trends.

Susan sold the company in 2016. She could have called it a day and retired pool-side with a good book. But she wasn't done. "I knew I had another act in me," she says. She had identified another space in need of a redesign: the way the world perceived women and ageism.

"Women in their fifties and older are wealthier, healthier, and more engaged than any generation in history," Susan says. "They have great taste, hard-earned wisdom, and they're smart." Yet all around her, Susan was hearing the same thing. "These women led happy, full lives but, suddenly, they were starting to feel invisible." This got Susan thinking. *Where do women my age go to get inspired, to navigate the challenges of growing older . . . to feel like we're heard and seen?*

She did some research, but it didn't take long—there weren't many resources available. And so, much like in the entre-preneurial days of One Kings Lane, Susan moved into the space and spruced it up. And so began In The Groove, Susan's third—and arguably most important—career. She was a start-up founder at the age of sixty-three.

Susan designed In The Groove to be an online lifestyle resource with a stylish, empowering approach aimed directly at women fifty and older. "Party like it's 1979," the website proclaims. Wellness, beauty, and fashion are all hot topics. But the site doesn't shy away from serious topics like menopause.

While In The Groove is busy serving women of a certain age, they've got their eyes on the kids too. "It is up to our generation to rewrite the script for aging. We need to change the dialogue and show younger women the beauty in getting older," Susan says. "The time has come to reframe this conversation."

Fittingly, her brand's motto is #WeSeeYou. These eyeglasses are perfectly symbolic of her story—aging in style is her business.

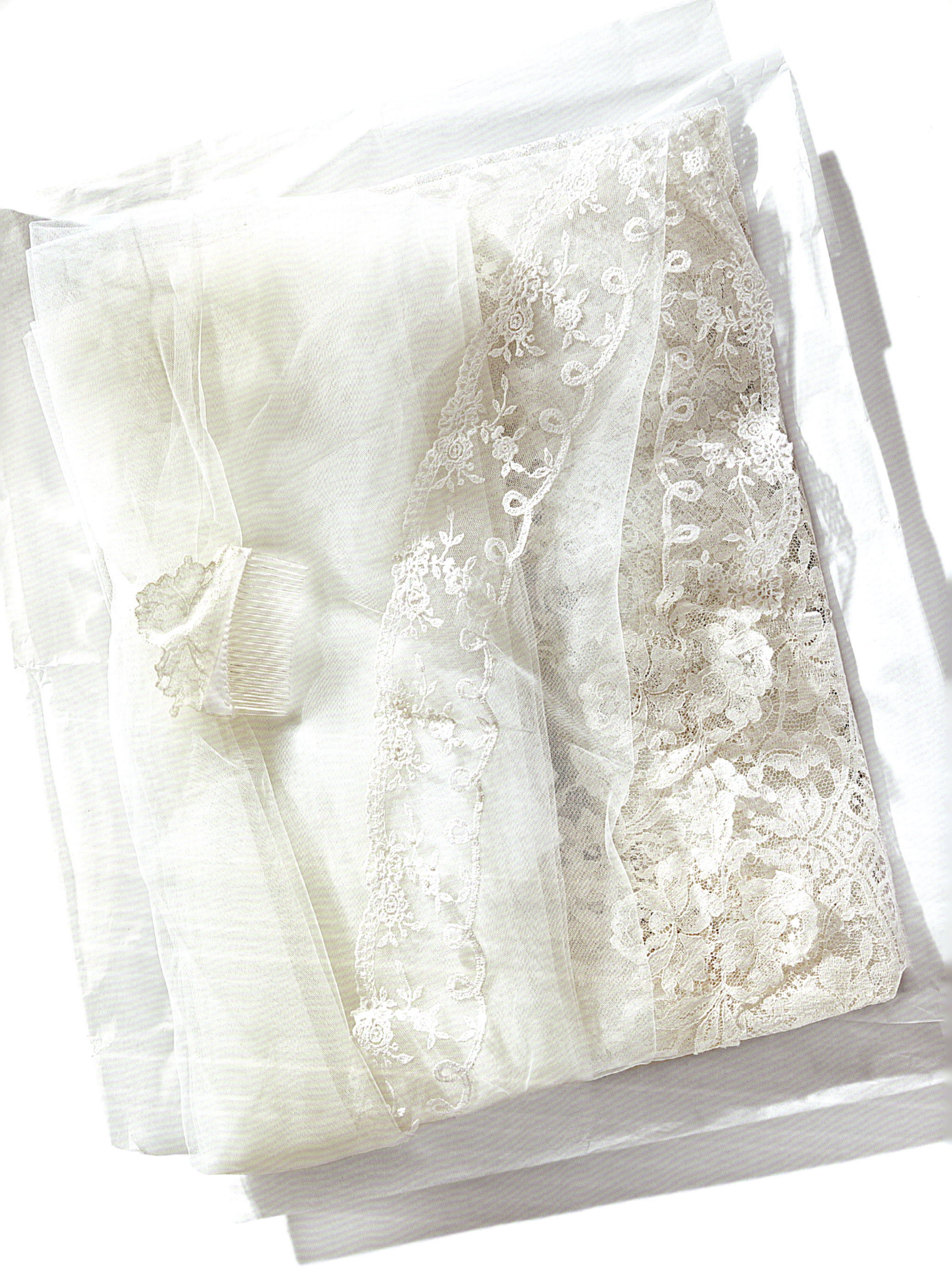

Mattie Kahn spent the hours before her wedding in a room with the most important women in her life. Just before the ceremony was slated to begin, music and merriment began and the groom appeared. He had come to symbolically lift Mattie's veil over her face—a tradition in Judaism called "the bedeken." The veil was an heirloom with a modern twist and a lasting connection to the one woman who couldn't be there—Mattie's grandmother, Ellen Kahn.

Ellen fled Germany in 1933, leaving most of her family belongings behind. This could be the reason, Mattie suspects, that her grandmother so loved to buy beautiful things not just for herself but for the whole family.

Ellen earned a reputation as an impeccable shopper with elegant taste. So much so that when her daughter, Felice, became engaged, Ellen signed up to shop for the dress and the veil, and even curated the reception. She bought a simple but elegant lace veil for her daughter.

In 1986, the veil would take part in another family wedding, that of Mattie's mother, Nessa. It was lent to anyone and everyone who could use it in the years that followed.

"It's been well worn and well loved over decades," Mattie says. When she and Jason Hellerstein became engaged in 2021, she knew she was next.

Mattie is a writer and so, by nature, did some investigating.

"After seeing it and thinking about how much my grandmother would have loved to be at our wedding, I really wanted to incorporate it," Mattie says. But she also wanted to give it her own touch. She found a designer to remake the veil, keeping intact the original lace her grandmother had picked out so many years ago.

"She would have been especially touched to have had a hand in creating this family heirloom, since she lost so many of her own family's most treasured pieces," Mattie says of her grandma. "The veil was a reminder of where I come from and in whose footsteps I walk. I hope I have a fraction of her grace, elegance, and absolute refusal to suffer fools."

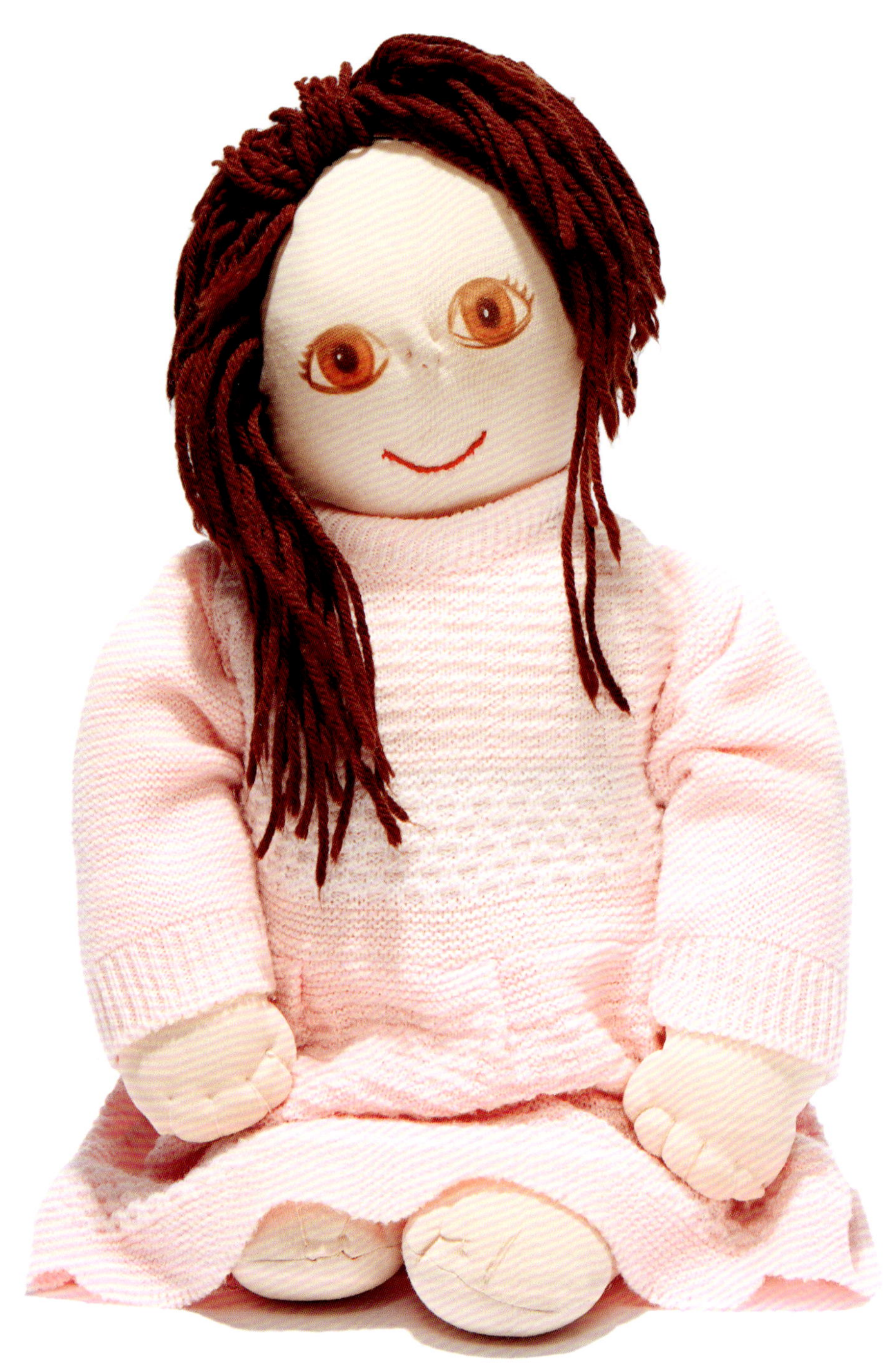

53. Tali Farhadian Weinstein | NEW YORK, NEW YORK

Tali Farhadian Weinstein's childhood Cabbage Patch Kid may not look like yours, but the story behind it will inspire you just the same.

Tali fled Iran with her parents in 1979. She was four years old, and the only toy she brought with her was a small stuffed animal. Her family settled in the New York City area and began to rebuild their lives in a world different from anything they had known.

A notably foreign phenomenon, especially for a young girl, was the Cabbage Patch craze of the mid-eighties.

"All the girls I knew had these dolls," Tali remembers. "Naturally, I really wanted one too. But we could not afford to spend that kind of money on a toy. So, we did what we knew how to do as immigrants: We figured out a way to do things a little differently. My mother was a talented seamstress—when we first immigrated, we had sewn our own clothes—and she decided that we were going to make the doll we could not buy."

Tali's mother sent away for a do-it-yourself Cabbage Patch Kid pattern. Though the doll was made with love, it was a challenge for the young girl to accept that it didn't look like the other kids' dolls.

Looking back on her childhood, Tali sees the doll as early evidence of an attitude that had been instilled in her all along—a true spirit of "DIY." It was this attitude that Tali would eventually integrate with her gratitude for the country that gave her family refuge and opportunity.

"Although I did not know what shape it would take, I always knew I wanted to be a public servant," Tali says. She attended Oxford as a Rhodes Scholar and graduated with a law degree from Yale. After graduation, she would clerk for Merrick Garland and Sandra Day O'Connor, and serve in the Obama administration's Department of Justice as counsel to Attorney General Eric Holder. She went on to be both a federal and a state prosecutor and has worked on everything from national security cases to fighting for women's equality. Her resume also includes professor, legal analyst, and the highly coveted position of mother.

"When I look at how much this country has given me—freedom, community, and so many opportunities—it's natural for me to want to give back and to use my freedom to figure out how best to do that."

Tali's homemade Cabbage Patch Kid remains the purest reminder of a long-held belief: A life is what you make of it.

Dayton Legal Blank Co. – 01003

Form No. 2-B Prescribed by Secretary of State (9-74)

DECLARATION OF CANDIDACY

PARTY PRIMARY ELECTION
FOR DISTRICT OFFICE

Representative to Congress (District), Judge of the Court of Appeals, State Senator or State Representative

To be filed with the Board of Elections of the most populous County or part County of the District not later than 4 P.M. of the 75th day before the day of the Primary Election.

Revised Code 3513.05, .07, .08, .09, .10, .191

NOTE – The Candidate must fill in and sign his statement of candidacy before Petitions are circulated.

I, GERRY TEBBEN (Name of candidate), *the undersigned, hereby declare under penalty of election falsification that my voting residence is in* I *Precinct of the* 4th Ward (Township) or (Ward and City or Village) *in the County of* Allen*, Ohio; that my postoffice address is* 1064 W. Market Street (Street and Number, if any, or Rural Route and Number) *of the* City (City, Village or Postoffice) *of* Lima*, Ohio; that I am a qualified elector in the precinct in which my voting residence is located. I am a member of the* Democrat *Party. I hereby declare that I desire to be a candidate for nomination as a candidate of the* Democrat *Party for election to the office of* UNITED STATES REPRESENTATIVE TO CONGRESS *for the* Full Term (Full term or unexpired term ending) *from the* 4th (Number of District) Congressional (Congressional, Appellate, House of Representatives or Senate) *District, at the Primary Election to be held on the* 3rd *day of June, 19*80*, and I hereby request that my name be printed upon the official primary election ballot of the said* Democrat *Party as a candidate for such nomination as provided by law.*

I further declare that if elected to said office, I will qualify therefor, and that I will support and abide by the principles enunciated by the Democrat *Party in its National and State Platforms, and that I have not voted as a member of a different political party at any primary election within the next preceding four calendar years.*

Dated this 4th *day of* March*, 19*80

Gerry Tebben
(Signature of Candidate)

Geraldine Tebben had raised eleven kids by the time she turned fifty-eight. It would be accurate to say she knew a thing or two about running an organization effectively and for the good of the people.

Politics had long been a family affair for the Tebbens, so when Geraldine grew frustrated with her local congressman, she decided to run against him.

"My grandma's home was the kind where politics were discussed at the dinner table, which was actually a picnic table in the kitchen to accommodate the size of the family," says Geraldine's granddaughter, Shannon. "I remember knowing she was special and different."

Both Geraldine and her mother, Muriel Shanahan, held office as the president of the Allen County Democratic Women, and Geraldine was a member of the executive board of the County's Women's Democratic Party. Her son Tom says that one of his earliest memories is helping his mom stuff flyers for the 1960 Kennedy presidential campaign.

By 1980, Geraldine had been paying close attention to her multiterm US congressman's voting record for years. And like any good mom and smart woman, she was fed up with what she saw as some poor choices. When his reelection came around and no one announced they would run in opposition, she stood up.

On March 4, 1980, Geraldine "Gerry" Tebben filed her Declaration of Candidacy, pictured, in the 4th Congressional District of Allen County, Ohio. Her husband, Joe, owned a rubber stamp and typesetting company, and got to work printing her campaign materials.

Geraldine ran on issues such as prudent spending, inflation, and unemployment. "We must send to Congress principled, conscientious people who will be responsive and responsible to ALL the citizens whom they represent," her candidacy flyer announced.

"She thought people deserved another choice," Shannon says of what motivated her grandmother. "The older I get, the more badass I realize that she was."

Geraldine lost the election. But her attention to politics at the local level, and her desire to make it better, had put her in perhaps an even more influential seat. She inspired her children, grandchildren, and a generation of girls who now know that if you're not happy with how things are going, you must get involved in order to change them.

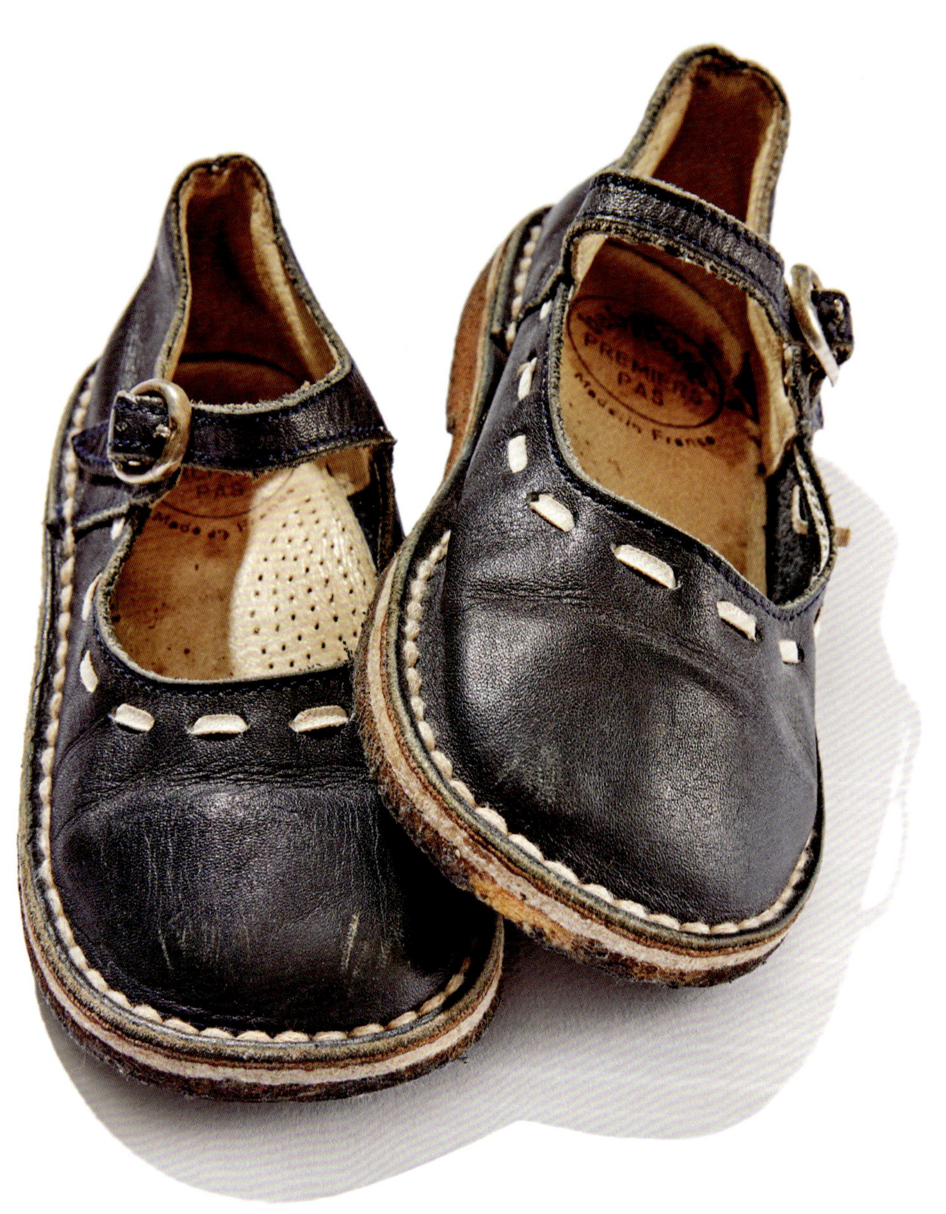
PREMIERS
PAS
Made in France

55. Rosanne Cash | NEW YORK, NEW YORK

Becoming a mother can fill your heart with joy. It might also break your heart and hand it back to you, rearranged. And if you let all of it happen, if you listen, and allow yourself to learn, you will become a much, much better person.

These are words of wisdom straight from the mind and soul of Grammy-winning musician and songwriter Rosanne Cash. You should listen to her. Not just because of the Grammys, but also because she is a mother of five.

Rosanne will freely admit that new little humans rocked her way of life. She was mostly tuned in to caring about herself and her career before her children arrived.

"I didn't know how to balance their needs with mine," she says of being a new mom. Humbly and humorously, she admits she learned on the job, the hard way—by having five kids, all with completely different needs. It was more than she could bear at times. And then, she noticed a shift.

"I changed. I listened more," she says. "They wanted to explain things to me and I adjusted my ears to hear."

She was getting the hang of it. Every challenge was a lesson.

"Boys and girls are so different," Rosanne says. "I didn't expect that, but I should have. The girls could be dramatic; their emotions were like big canvases of vivid color. My son is much more private. I learned very early to respect his need to work things out in himself—not with me—and his innate emotional reserve."

"None of them reflected myself back to me as I vaguely expected they would," Rosanne says. But it didn't matter. She had come to love them so much it hurt.

Pictured are a pair of baby shoes belonging to her youngest daughter, Carrie. To Rosanne, the time-stamped, well-worn shoes symbolize the toil and love required of raising all the kids. They represent momentous joy and shock waves of heartache. The little clothes, the growing up, the pushing away.

"I keep them because extraordinary people chose me as their mother before I deserved them," she says.

With the kids now grown, you'd think Rosanne would be free to resume caring mostly about tour dates and record deals. But Rosanne Cash, the mother, will tell you it's the opposite. The emotional tugs remain just as strong.

"They operate under their own imprimatur of their own destiny now. Most of the time I don't know what's best for them. They want to figure it out for themselves. They are doing it much more elegantly than I did," she says. "Hannah, Caitlin, Chelsea, Carrie, and Jakob—my relentless advocates to awaken."

They wanted to explain things to me and I adjusted my ears to hear.

—Rosanne Cash

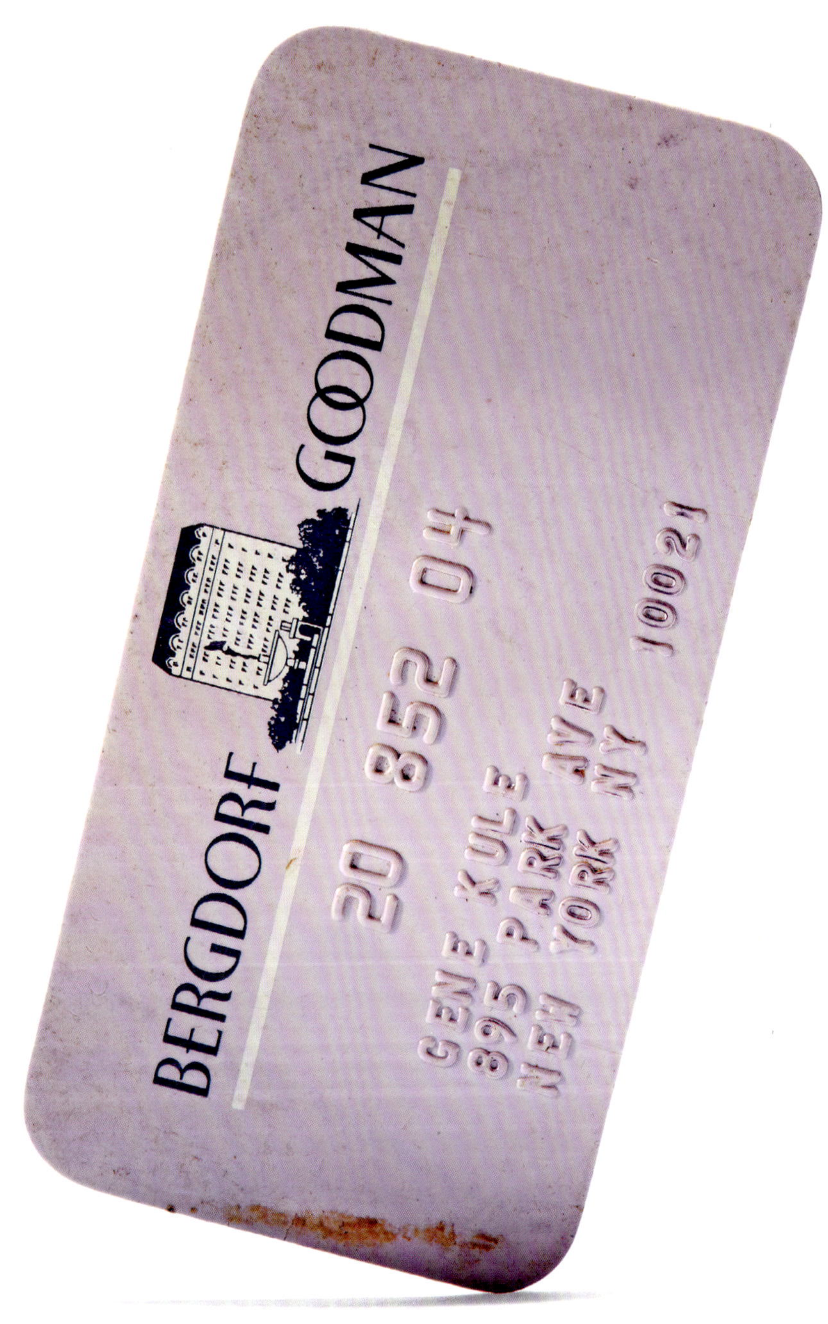
BERGDORF GOODMAN
20 852 04
GENE KULE
895 PARK AVE
NEW YORK NY 10021

Nikki Kule remembers every charm of legendary department store Bergdorf Goodman, right down to the dressing room chairs. It was there she would sit as a kid, watching her mother, Arlene, try on designer clothes. It was an early education in personal style and more.

"My mom liked to make a statement in a room," Nikki says. "Once, she was getting dressed up for an event, and she came into my room before she went out with my dad and was wearing a three-piece tuxedo with a matching satin head wrap. I thought, *How cool is my mom wearing the same outfit as my dad?*"

The Kule family knew a thing or two about pants. Nikki's father, Gene, was known in the fashion world as "The King of Pants" through his business, Happy Legs. He had a reputation for pioneering new trends and tailoring styles long before they were popular in mainstream retail and is even credited for bringing bell-bottoms to the American mass market from England.

Nikki's father also had another reputation—as a considerate and thoughtful business-man. "The way he grew his company . . . I grew up knowing I wanted to stay in the business through him."

Nikki attended design school and worked in the fashion industry for years, honing her innate love for fashion. These days, it would be fair to say that from "The King of Pants" Nikki learned to be the "Queen of Stripes." She is the founder and designer of her own fashion label, KULE—a collection of cult-classic striped tees, sweaters, and accessories, all designed with a nod to tradition with a playful twist. The goal, Nikki says, is to make dressing easy and fail-proof but fun.

In 2022, the KULE brand announced a collaboration with Bergdorf Goodman, the very department store Nikki used to frequent with her mom. "The Kule name alongside the Bergdorf Goodman name would have made my parents really proud," Nikki says. "Especially my mom, who always saw it as the pinnacle of retail."

While Arlene Kule undoubtedly used her credit card, pictured, to make many a glamorous entrance, it's important to note that the card is in Gene's name—evidence of the times. Until 1974, when New York congresswoman Bella Abzug had the Equal Credit Opportunity Act passed, women were not legally allowed to have credit cards in their name.

Women have credit cards with their names on them these days. And they put their names on their businesses too.

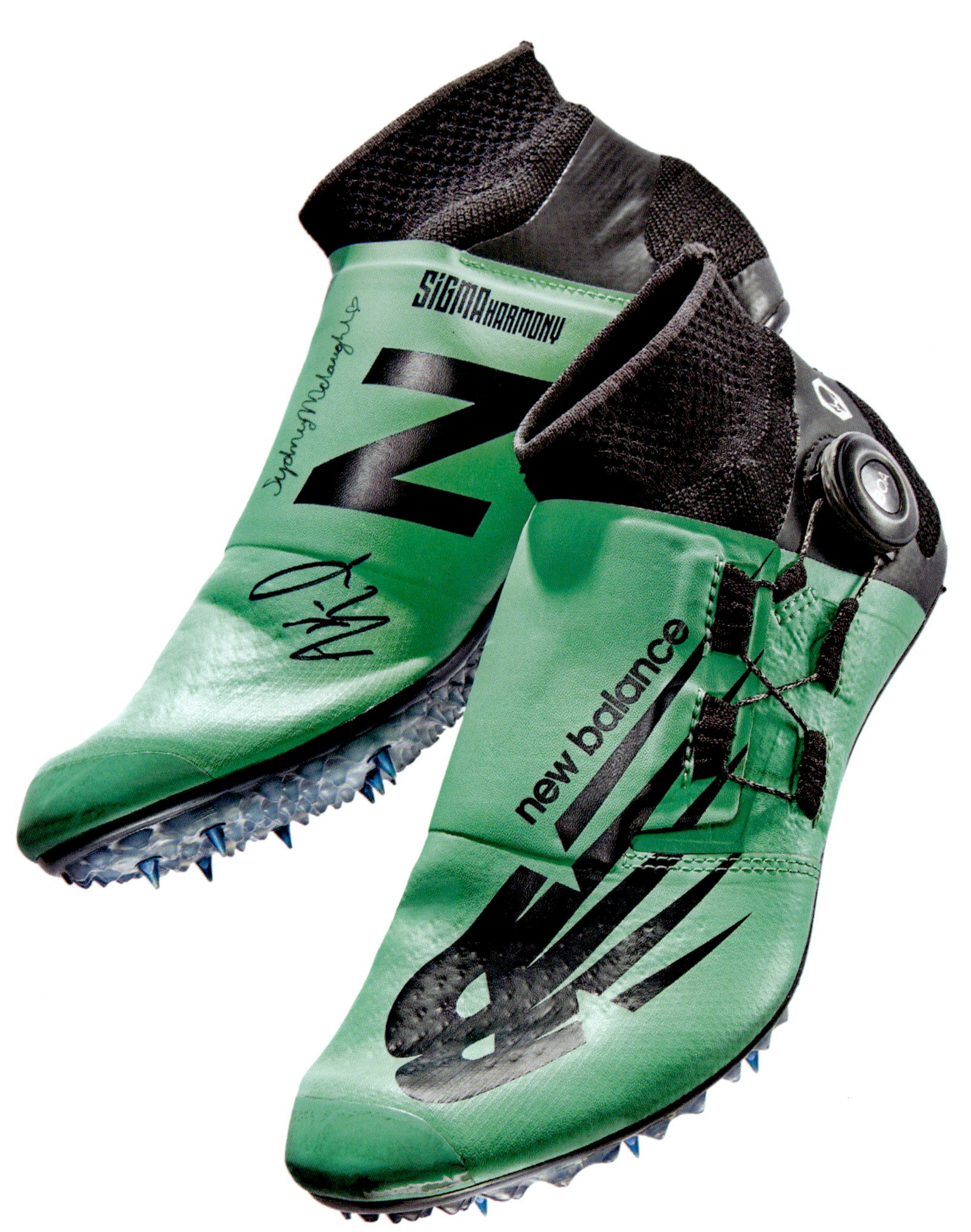
SIGMA HARMONY
new balance

Darrick Harris played basketball and soccer in college, but he graduated as a track star, setting records in the high jump and several sprints. Now Darrick, the visuals director of *Town and Country* magazine, and his wife, photographer Mei Tao, have their own track star on their hands—their daughter.

"It was evident she had some speed," Darrick fondly remembers of the early days of watching his daughter, Dashiel, compete at track events. Darrick and Mei lovingly—and fittingly—call their daughter Dash.

Dashiel ran indoor and outdoor sprints throughout high school. Darrick was always present, a proud dad in the stands. He was familiar with the challenges and rewards of running track. But he was, for the first time, also watching as a father.

"Having the opportunity to observe her as a competitor and a team member through triumphs and losses has been amazing," Darrick says. He could tell that her many accomplishments had given her confidence and humility, two important traits she would need as she grew into her own.

Dashiel's track shoes, pictured, just might say it all. Darrick and Mei originally bought them for her because of the laceless technology. But she personalized them one day at a high school track clinic by having Sydney McLaughlin and Ajee Wilson autograph them. Both women are record-holding champion runners.

Dashiel is now a member of the Emory University track team and things are clearly running smoothly. In her freshman year alone, she earned the honors of being named to the US Track & Field and Cross Country Coaches Association All-Academic Athlete list and US Track & Field and Cross Country Coaches Association South/Southeast All-Region Team. As a sophomore, she was named to the CSC Academic All-District team and her relay team earned, among other accomplishments, All-American honors in the NCAA Division 3 4×100 meter relay.

Given her track record, by the time this book is published, Dashiel will be a junior with plenty more honors to list—following in her father's footsteps, in her own way.

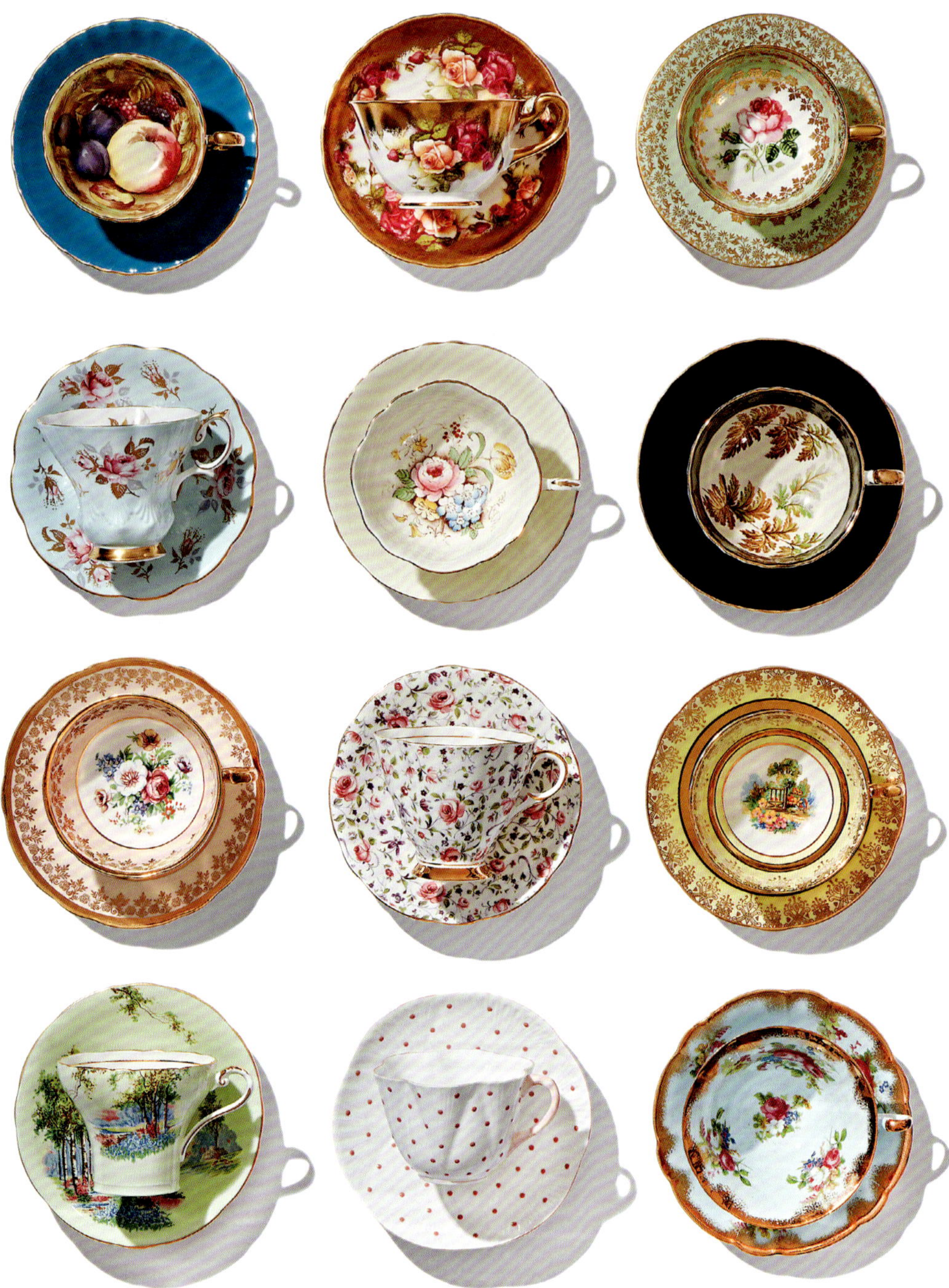

58. Jessica Geller | ESSEX FELLS, NEW JERSEY

Setting the table for Mom might seem like a chore to some kids, but when Jessica Geller was little, it was hands down delightful. Her mom entertained often, always using her best teacups. Jessica was drawn to the eclectic details of each cup, so setting them out for Mom meant exploring all the bright colors and patterns. She claimed the cup with the pink polka dots as her favorite.

What Jessica didn't know at the time was that her mother's teacups had a deeper story to tell. When Jessica's great-grandfather, Abe, left Russia in 1916, around the time of the Russian Revolution, he followed his seven sisters to Montreal, Canada, eventually leaving them to find work and start a family in the United States. Every time one of Abe's seven sisters would visit, she brought a teacup as a gift for his daughter, Mary. Pictured is only a fraction of the collection the sisters built for their niece, each piece evidence of an extensive and lasting family ritual. As a whole, the teacups are a symbolic gathering of good times, raised cups, and family connection.

Mary was Jessica's grandmother. Her teacup collection was eventually handed down to Jessica's mother. And that's how the little girl who loved the pink polka dots came to set the table with her family's brightly patterned treasures.

That Jessica took note of each artful detail or elegant feature may have been an early indication of where life would take her. Jessica is today one half of the interior design team Toledo Geller Interiors. She is now the third-generation keeper of the cups. It's a good thing there are enough to go around: In addition to a son, Jessica is mom to girls—twins—who she hopes will both want future ownership of the collection.

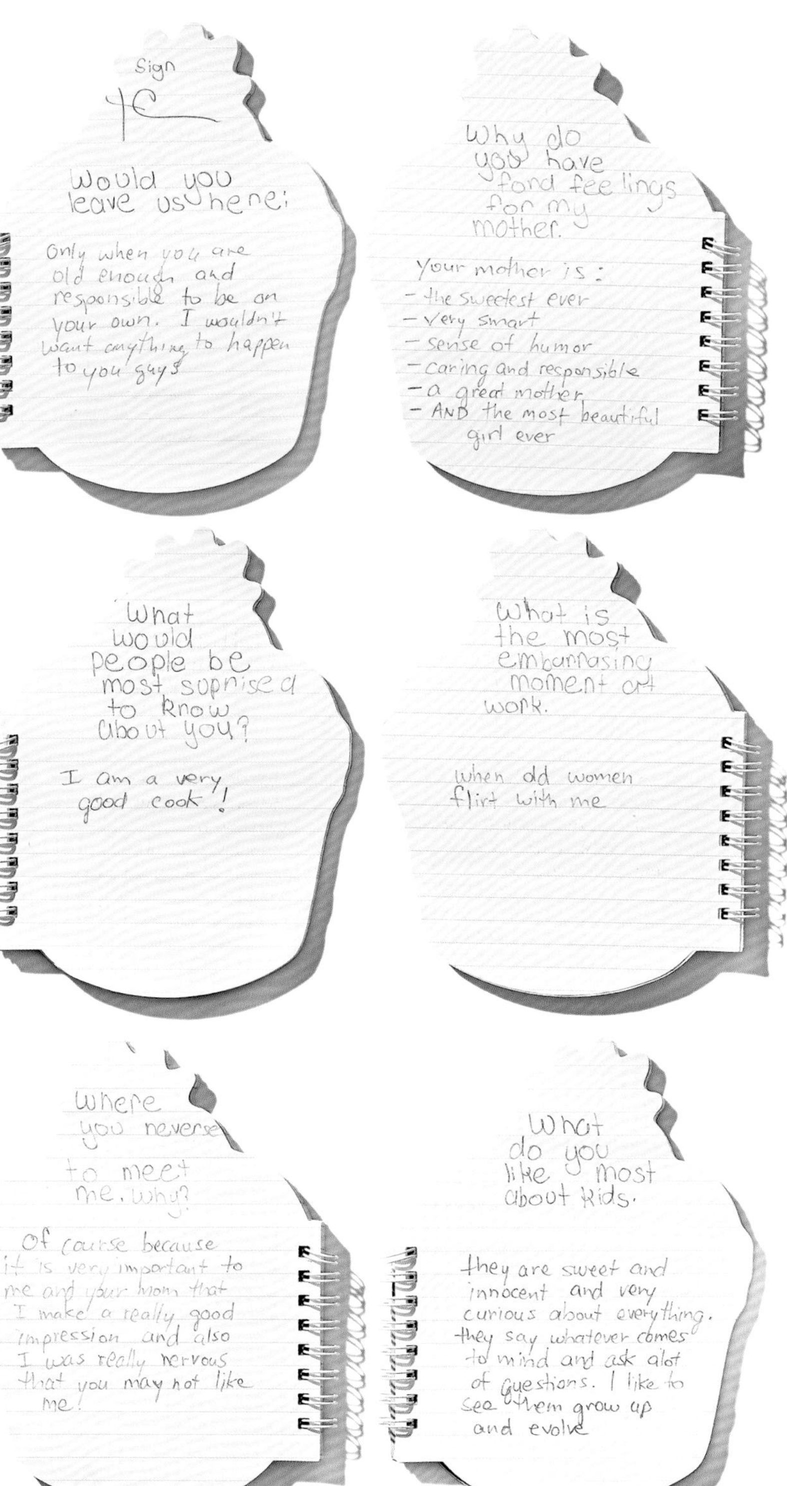
Sign
Would you leave us here;
Only when you are old enough and responsible to be on your own. I wouldn't want anything to happen to you guys
Why do you have fond feelings for my mother.
Your mother is:
- the sweetest ever
- very smart
- sense of humor
- caring and responsible
- a great mother
- AND the most beautiful girl ever
What would people be most suprised to know about you?
I am a very good cook!
What is the most embarrasing moment at work.
When old women flirt with me
Where you nerverse to meet me. Why?
Of course because it is very important to me and your mom that I make a really good impression and also I was really nervous that you may not like me!
What do you like most about kids.
they are sweet and innocent and very curious about everything. they say whatever comes to mind and ask alot of questions. I like to see them grow up and evolve

59. Beth Chappo | ZIONSVILLE, INDIANA

Beth Chappo was out for a casual night with her girlfriends when a guy named John crashed the party.

"I was in a very difficult season of life and certainly not in the dating mindset," she says of the night the universe introduced her to her future husband.

"You don't look like you're having a good time," he joked when he approached her. But they instantly connected. And then dated. His most difficult test was next: meeting Beth's kids.

"It was a mixed bag of nerves and excitement," Beth says of the day she introduced John to her two daughters for the first time. Her youngest, Campbell, jumped gleefully into his arms on sight. Her oldest, Chase, on the other hand, had a test for the new guy. She walked into the room dressed as a teacher. She had handily borrowed glasses, a belted skirt, and heels from Beth, who is a fashion and lifestyle digital creator. She had a notepad and pencil in hand.

Her notepad contained quizzical questions inspired by the curiosities of a nine-year-old mind: "Why do you have fond feelings for my mother? What do you like most about kids? Would you leave us?"

John was required to handwrite his answers and formalize them by signing on the dotted line, which Chase had penciled in. He passed the exam with charming, straightforward answers a child could understand.

"Not only did they immediately hit it off, but we all went to the movies later," Beth says. "It was a natural fit from the start. Never in my life would I have dreamt that moment would be the beginning of our beautiful life," she says. She married him.

Two years later, three days after Chase and Campbell's baby brother, Calvin, was born, John adopted Beth's daughters. Beth has kept the tiny notepad with Chase's exam all these years—a sweet reminder to take notes from the kids, and to love with openness, curiosity, and acceptance.

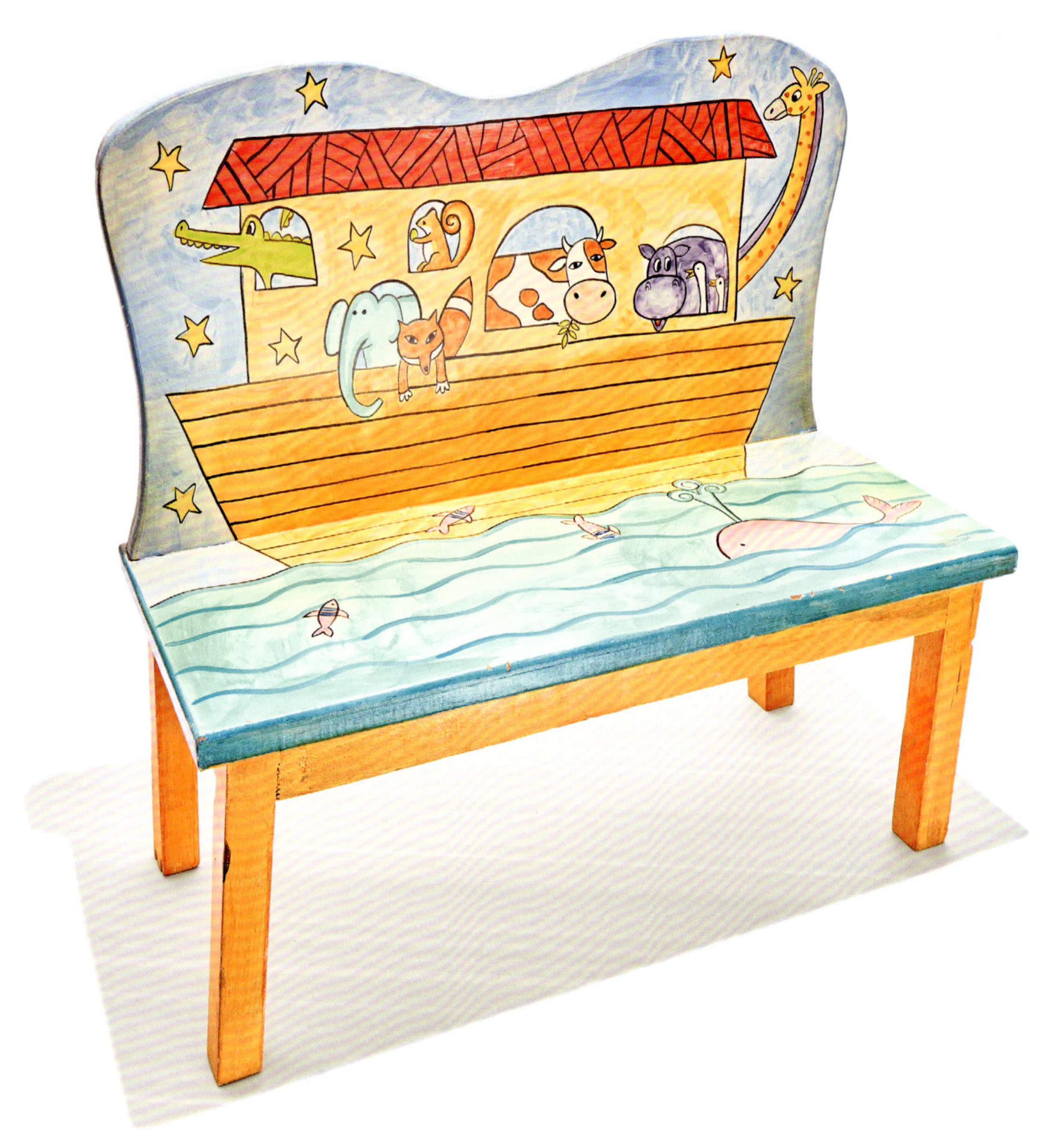

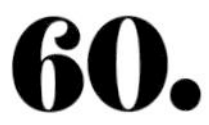

Tara Favors | SOUTH ORANGE, NEW JERSEY

Bringing tiny humans into the world involved a lot of consideration for Tara and Dale Favors, two newlyweds with busy, vibrant careers. Both worked in the financial industry and attended meetings at the World Trade Center every week. When it was attacked on 9/11, they had close connections to the building and knew of friends, colleagues, and neighbors who were lost. That day, they changed.

They knew it was time to start a family. "We wanted to bring some joy into the world," she says.

Early in her first pregnancy, Tara was out shopping when she found a little bench at a thrift store. It was sturdy and sweet and she could practically see her baby—and babies—sitting on it, reading, developing a love for learning.

Her vision would become reality. The bench would become the best seat in the house for her two young boys.

In time, the boys became young men, reading mostly on a computer. *Goodnight Moon* and *Whistle for Willie* would be replaced with assigned topics from teachers and professors. Tara's oldest, Dalton, is now a senior at Morehouse College, an economics and Chinese studies major. Her youngest, Davis, at the time of this writing, is a freshman studying acting at UCLA.

"Both boys have found their passions. It's amazing to watch what we so gently nurtured form its own roots. I couldn't be prouder of the foundation those early days provided."

A few years ago, with the boys grown and facing the age-old question of what to keep and what to toss, Tara decided she would pass the bench on to someone else. She listed it for sale on a Facebook page for local moms. Tara's girlfriends were not having it.

"Keep it for your grandkids, Tara. Don't let it go," one friend commented. "I was going to say the same thing," another wrote. Another girlfriend really got serious. "I'll keep it at my house if you just can't look at it anymore. In twenty years or so you'll be sorry you gave it up," she wrote.

Tara's girlfriends even started a hashtag campaign—#savebabybench. Tara changed the listing to "No longer for sale."

"They recognized it as an heirloom before I did," she says. "It represents family, learning, and vibrancy—which is who we are. I am glad I kept it and promise to protect it for the next generation to come."

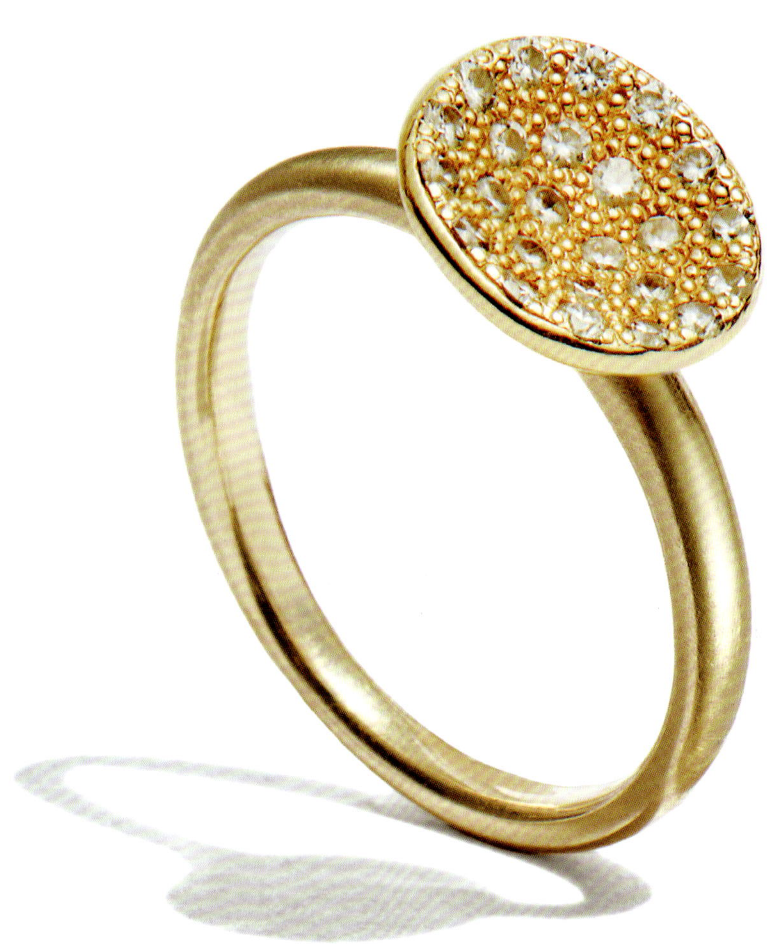

61. Amy Helm | WOODSTOCK, NEW YORK

Back in 2011, Amy Helm found herself at a jewelry shop with her father. He had come with a stack of bills and a loyal heart. She remembers the day exactly. The money, Amy says, was hard-earned and bookmarked for more practical things like electric bills and taxes. Yet, there they were at the jewelry shop.

"Some of the rings had diamonds, some were rubies set in gold," she says. "All six of them were paid [for] in cash. A big fat stack of cash, still covered in rubber bands."

Her father had gone to the shop that day, Amy says, "compelled to pay a debt of gratitude to some of the women who had saved him in one way or another over the years. Some had helped him through drug addiction or cancer treatments. All of them had seen him through the low tides of faith."

One of the rings was for her.

Together and individually, she and her father have supported and influenced each other and the musical community in all the best ways. Her father, Levon Helm, was a founding member of The Band. His contributions to music are deep and lasting—and very much alive in Amy's approach to her own music career. She played for a decade in his band, The Midnight Ramble Band, and in her own, Ollabelle. She counts several critically acclaimed solo albums to her name, and she produced an album for her dad. It won a Grammy.

Not long after her father bought the rings, Amy began to notice a change in him. His cancer had returned, but they wouldn't know it for a bit.

"One night, on a gig in Milwaukee, my dad uncharacteristically grabbed my hand in the middle of singing 'Gloryland,' an a cappella hymn that required as much voice and breath as all of us could manage. I wondered if he grabbed my hand for strength, but I felt his fingers fall on the ring and start to play with the little bowl-shaped center, touching it like a worry stone or lucky charm. A talisman to carry him through the song."

Four months later, her father was gone. His legacy, however, can still be heard.

In addition to being a touring musician, Amy now owns and runs Levon Helm Studios in Woodstock, New York. Once her father's home, stage, and recording studio, the space is now a music venue featuring bands and musicians from all walks of life, where bucket listers and music legends alike flock to be together, play music, and celebrate the power of community. Each show is a tribute to Levon's legacy and will continue for years to come if Amy has anything to say about it.

62. Jennifer Waterhouse | CHAPPAQUA, NEW YORK

In November of 2001, the *New York Times* ran a short story about Tom Brennan playing Grateful Dead CDs in the car at full volume, hoping his unborn son would hear the music. His young daughter, meanwhile, danced in her car seat in the backseat. The story appeared in a feature on 9/11 victims; Tom did not make it out of the South Tower of the World Trade Center. At the time, his daughter was seventeen months old and his wife, Jen, was pregnant.

Family, friends, and community surrounded Jen with support as she adjusted to raising the kids with only her memories of their father. There would be a lot to remember.

Jen always kept Tom in her casual conversations with the kids around the house, but sometimes, she says, she relied on others to share stories about him to give the kids a well-rounded idea of his personality. The resounding theme, no matter who you talked to, Jen says, was always Tom's love for the Grateful Dead.

"The kids and I planted scarlet begonias ("Scarlet Begonias" is the title of a Dead song) at his grave every Father's Day for many, many years. His love for music was a big part of him."

In 2003, Tom's friends and family established the Thomas M. Brennan Memorial Foundation. They held a golf tournament, raising funds for partial scholarships to Boston College. "The prize," Jen says, "much like the green jacket at Augusta, was a coveted and hideous homemade tie-dye jacket, an homage to Tom's love of the Grateful Dead."

And then, there was the briefcase. It contained a cassette collection of live Grateful Dead shows from all over the world, each with meticulous set lists in Tom's handwriting.

"It existed long before me," Jen says. She thinks he started the collection back in high school. It sat quietly in their home for years, but it undoubtedly held a lot of joy—and proof for the kids as they grew up of just how much love their dad was capable of.

These days, more than twenty years after Tom's passing, Jen says his love is very much alive in them.

"Thomas is the spitting image of his father," Jen says of her grown son. "His mannerisms and personality are much like Tom's. And Cat is constantly discovering and seeing lesser-known bands just like her dad loved to do."

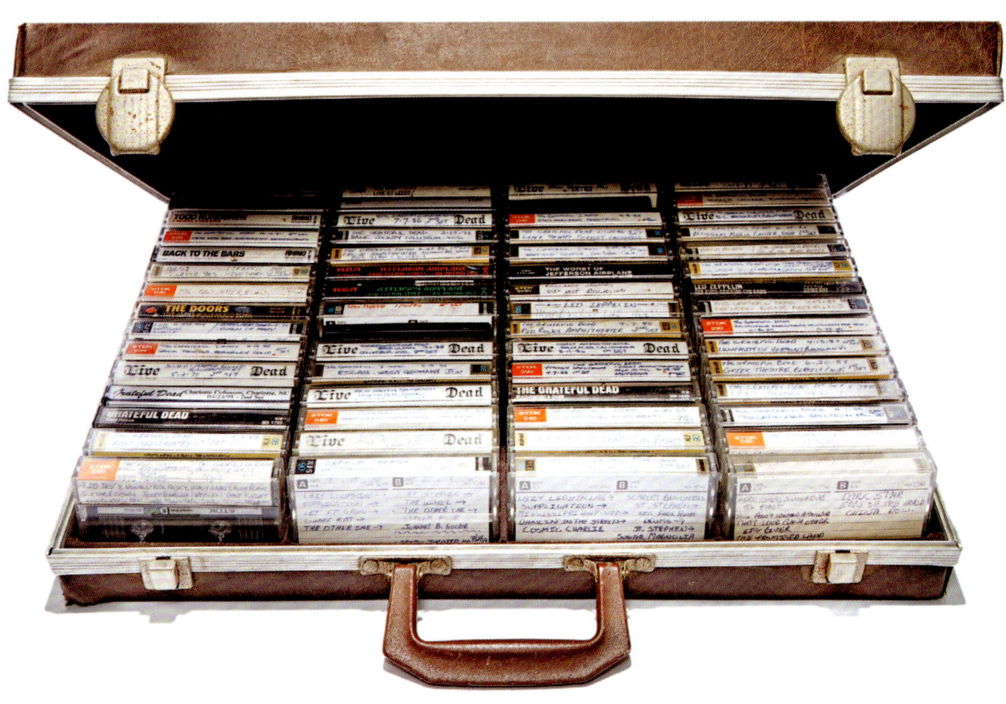
BACK TO THE BARS
THE DOORS
JEFFERSON AIRPLANE
THE WORST OF JEFFERSON AIRPLANE
LED ZEPPELIN
Live Dead
THE GRATEFUL DEAD
GRATEFUL DEAD

The twentieth anniversary of the terrorist attacks was a major and difficult milestone for the kids and Jen. "In a lot of ways, I think that is when they really came to terms with the tragedy," she says. She wanted to do something special for them to celebrate their dad, and what better way than through music.

Jen mobilized friends, family, and Tom's college buddies to make a modern-day mixtape—everyone contributed songs and memories that remind them of Tom—which Jen turned into a Spotify playlist for all to share. The playlist ended up being eight and a half hours long, a testament to just how much he was loved.

Jen's efforts to keep Tom present in the kids' lives came full circle recently at the Red Rocks Amphitheatre in Colorado. They went to see their first Dead show together.

"The set list was as if Tom made it himself," she says.

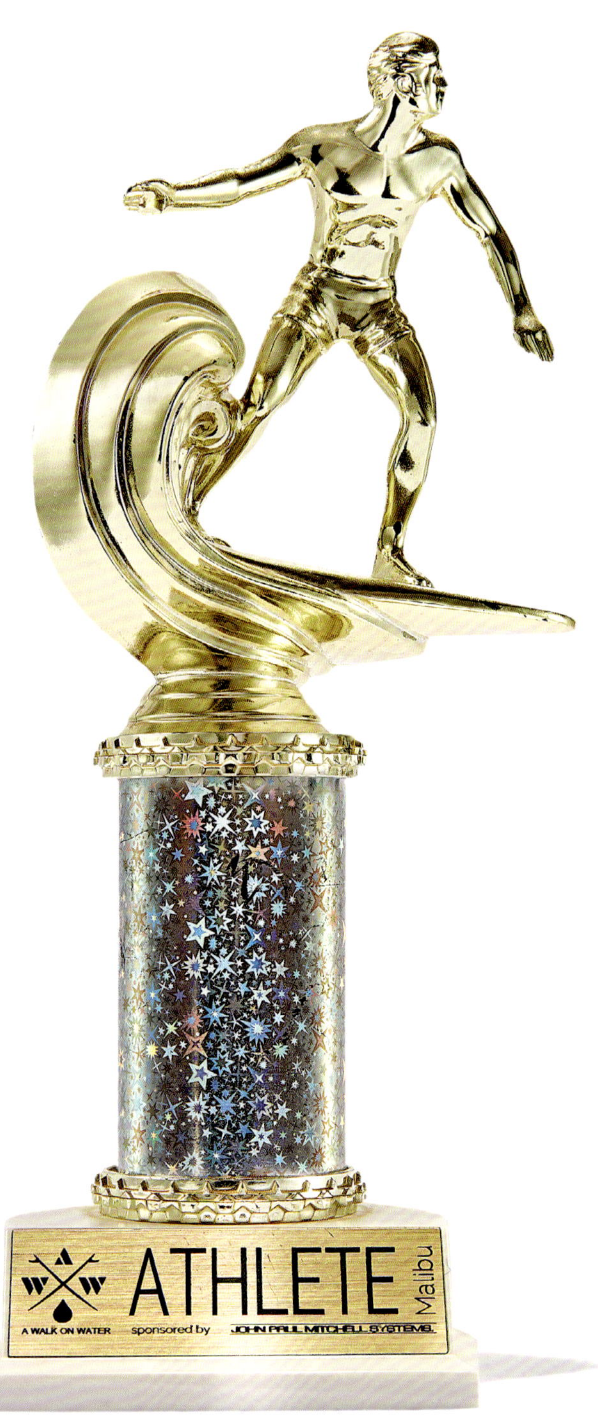
ATHLETE
Malibu
A WALK ON WATER
sponsored by
JOHN PAUL MITCHELL SYSTEMS.

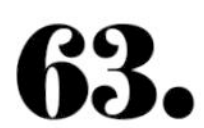 Walter and Clash Zamora | MONTAUK, NEW YORK

Walt Lindveld-Zamora has all the signs of a cool kid—vintage pickup truck, dark-rimmed glasses, a career as a creative director, and a son named Clash. But he's not too cool for a good, old-fashioned proud-dad cry.

"I cried like a baby," Walt candidly admits of the first time he watched his son catch a wave while surfing. A lifelong surfer himself, sharing his passion with his son got him right in the ticker. But it wasn't just catching the wave that filled him with joy. Walt and Clash had overcome a lot just to get to the beach.

"I dreamed of surfing and skating and hanging out together," Walt says of his thoughts when he found out he was going to be a dad. When Clash was diagnosed with Down syndrome, Walt's expectations were flipped upside down.

Walt has been raising Clash in the beachside town of Montauk, New York, where he is the creative director of the Montauk Beach House and a handful of other local businesses. The two surf and skateboard together in their free time, giving Walt glimpses of what he had always dreamt parenting would be—and more.

"What he's learning through surfing and skating is actually what he is teaching me," Walt says. "To not be afraid to take risks. I am learning to overcome my own fears and take chances so that I can open myself up to greater achievements."

Walt credits the surf-therapy organization A Walk On Water for being a huge part of getting Clash into the ocean and onto a board.

"Surfing pushes him past his comfort zone, which is critical for his growth," Walt says. "Just showing up to the ocean and facing the many different challenges is in itself a critical therapy toward the emotional processing and development he needs."

That day on the beach, when Clash first stood up to ride his board to shore, Walt realized all of his dreams had actually become reality.

"My boy and I would, in fact, share the bonds, the magic, and the healing power of the ocean and surfing. It was emotionally overwhelming, and one of the most beautiful things I have ever experienced as a parent."

This trophy represents Clash's first California wave, ridden under the close supervision of the good humans at A Walk On Water.

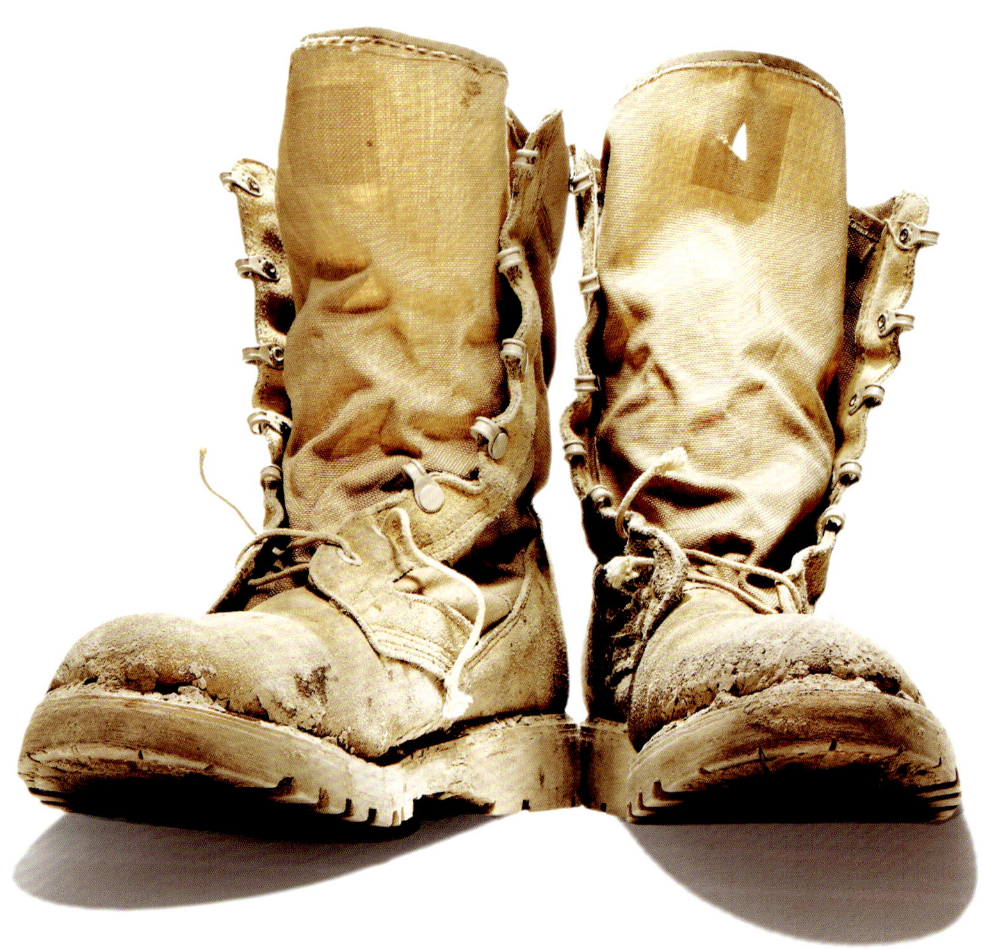

64. Lee and Bob Woodruff | RYE, NEW YORK

In 2006, Lee Woodruff received a plastic bag from an American military emergency room in Iraq containing her husband's wallet, watch, boots, and dented helmet. Her husband, ABC News correspondent Bob Woodruff, had been reporting on the Iraq War when a roadside bomb exploded, leaving him with a life-threatening traumatic brain injury. Lee put the bag in the garage. She couldn't touch it for nearly ten years.

Bob endured years of recovery and rehabilitation after the explosion. The toll taken on his wife and young children was immense. But Bob had survived. Their family had survived. And even though Bob was a journalist, military medical personnel had treated Bob like one of their own every step of the way, from the emergency room in Iraq to the Walter Reed National Medical Center in Maryland.

Lee was cleaning out the family's garage one day when she came across the plastic bag. She felt ready to open it. The boots were still caked in Iraqi dirt and dotted with blood. They were a terrible reminder of that devastating day. But facing the boots helped turn them into a symbol for a force of good.

During their time spent in military hospitals, the Woodruffs saw firsthand the extraordinary importance of support systems when veterans return home. The need extended beyond medical care to include veterans' families and caregivers. So, the Woodruffs founded the Bob Woodruff Foundation, a nonprofit dedicated to treating the heroes who stood up for their country with the same care the Woodruffs had received. The foundation's mission statement says it all:

"The Bob Woodruff Foundation ensures that our nation's impacted veterans, service members, and their families have access to the highest level of support and resources they have earned, for as long as they need it."

This image of Bob's combat boots, still standing after all these years, has become a symbol for the foundation's work.

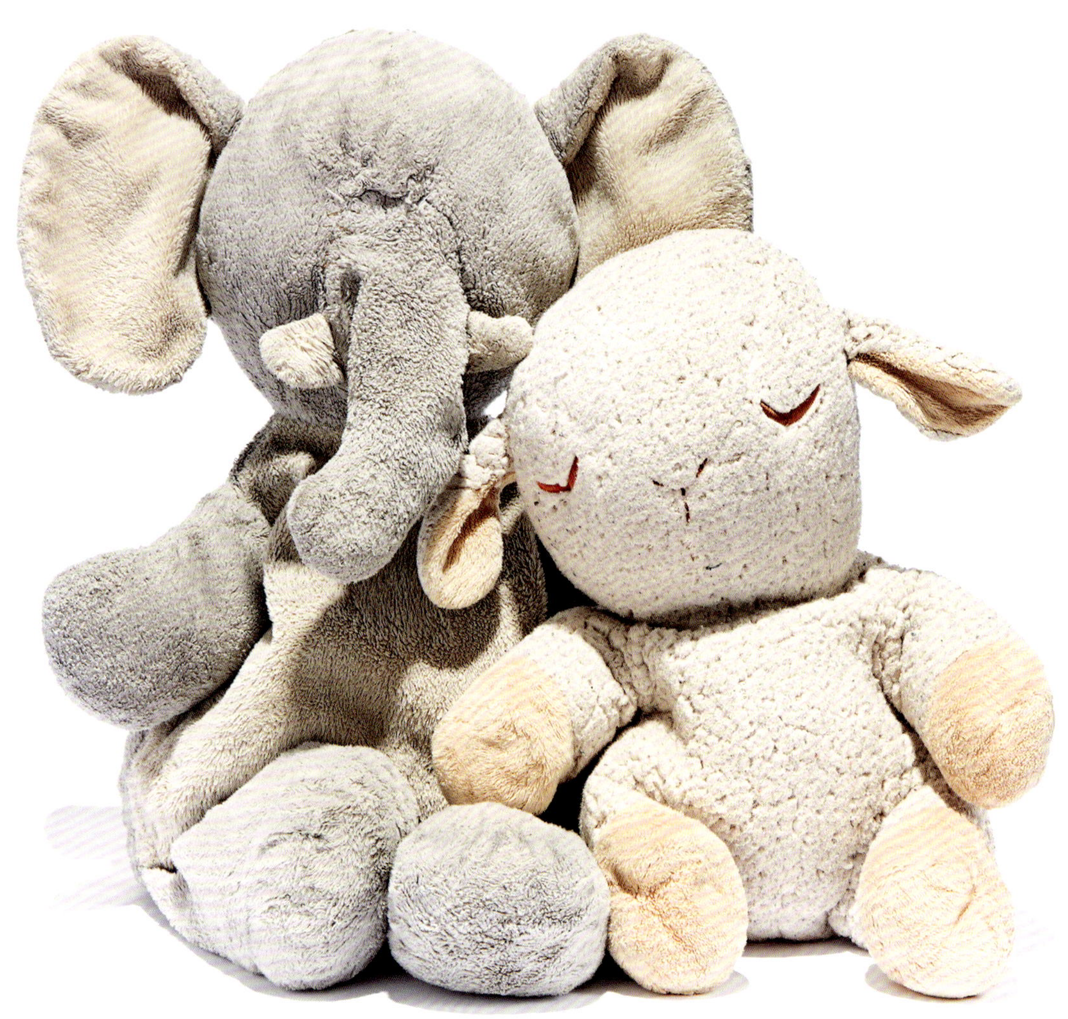

65. Tig Notaro | LOS ANGELES, CALIFORNIA

If the power lunch isn't your style, get yourself a reservation at Max and Finn's restaurant. Their lunch service is casual and filled with deep conversation. Plus, it will leave you stuffed. Regular patrons include luminaries such as Elephante and Lamby.

Elephante and Lamby are stuffed animals, but Max and Finn are real. The brothers, twins, have always done everything with their sidekicks—imaginary lunch dates included—practically from day one.

"Elephante and Lamby were the first expressions of love our children displayed that was from their own world," says their mom, Tig Notaro. "Seeing the care and love that Max and Finn put into Elephante and Lamby makes me feel like Stephanie and I have been doing an OK job so far."

The adventure of raising boys has been like nothing and everything Tig expected.

"I didn't expect them to be so exactly who I was waiting for all these years," she says. "There are no other two people who were supposed to be our children. I also never expected Pokémon to enter my life or vocabulary. But here we are."

Tig Notaro is a Grammy- and Emmy-nominated comedian, and though the kids inspire some pretty funny material on stage, she is as serious about her children as any other parent on the planet.

"Like most parents, I just want them to be happy, healthy, and safe—not just now, but long after I'm gone. I want them to know patience and compassion, that it's important to learn about other people's stories and lives, and to listen and consider differences," she says.

If the sweetly imaginative lunch dates with Elephante and Lamby are any indication, we see strong, sensitive gentlemen in this family's future.

"They make me excited about getting older," Tig says of the boys. "As much as I'm loving them at eight years old, I truly can't wait until two gigantic young adults are lounging around the house with us sharing whatever is going on in their hearts and minds."

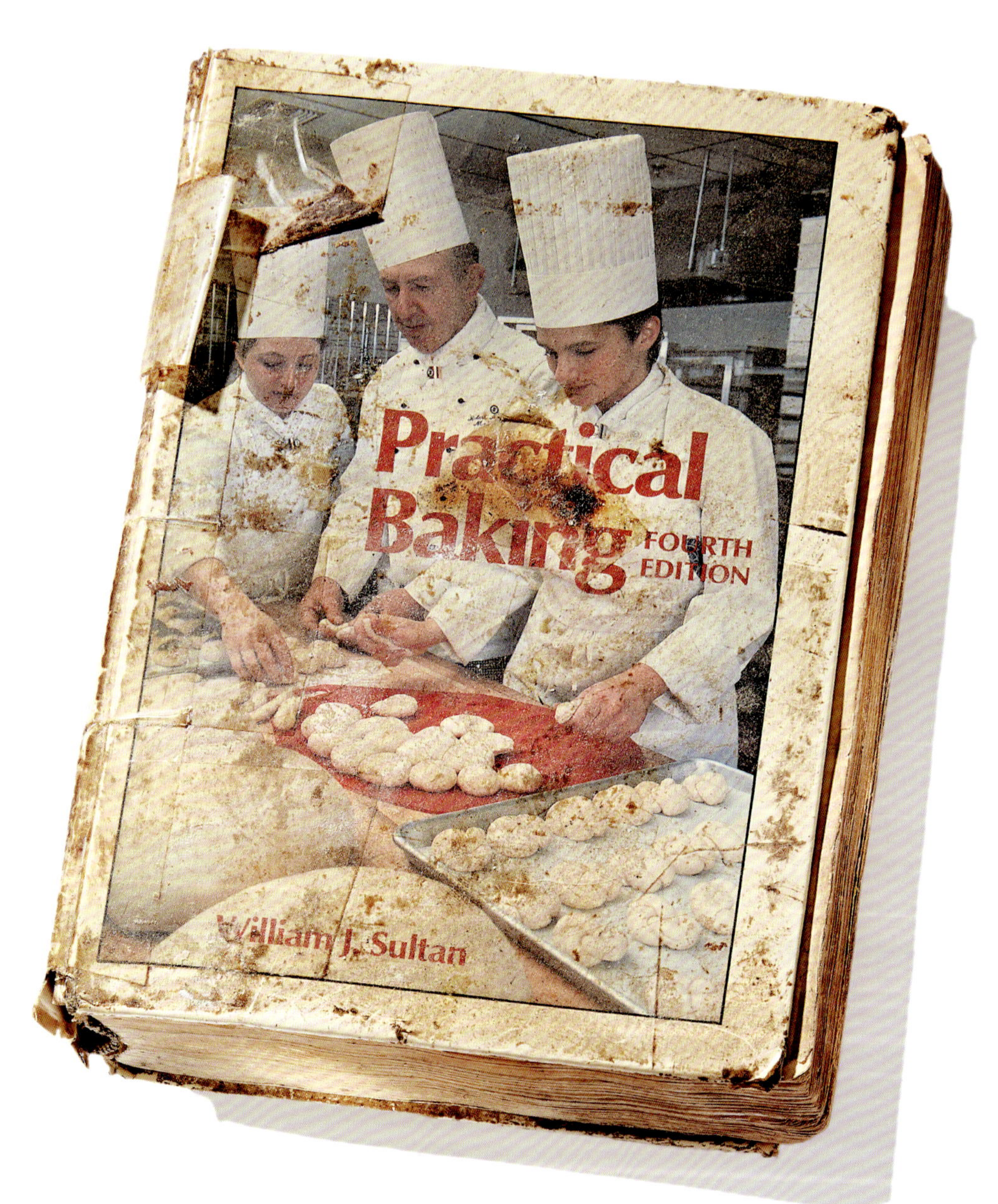
Practical Baking
FOURTH EDITION
William J. Sultan

66. Sue Brezack | OMAHA, NEBRASKA

In the early 1970s, Joel Brezack's job was to drive truckloads of cookies along a delivery route into New York City each day. The work was proving to be a not-so-sweet career choice—the pace was hectic and the commute was tiresome. So, he and his wife, Sue, thought about a move. Where could they find an easier pace and no traffic? They considered Sue's hometown, Omaha, Nebraska. There was no traffic there. There were no bagels, either, which would soon change.

"I think we're going to open a bagel factory," Sue remembers Joel saying one day. He and a childhood buddy came up with the crazy idea. Her reply was, "Are you kidding me?"

The couple made several research trips to Omaha, the Midwestern town better known for steakhouses, and found it was true: At the time, around 1976, there was no such thing as a bagel shop in Omaha. What did exist was an enthusiastic community ready and willing to support the type of establishment the Brezacks had in mind. After securing funding, they packed their mixing bowls and headed west.

The Bagel Bin, Omaha's first New York–style bagel shop, opened its doors in 1977. In addition to bagels, the Brezacks filled glass cases with kosher baked goods using recipes from Joel's Polish ancestors. Joel and Sue lived in her parents' basement until their bagels could pay the bills. It didn't take long.

Nearly fifty years later, their once-crazy idea is now a community staple. On any given morning, the shop is a hive of locals lined up out the door for a quick bite before heading to the office while retirees hold court at tables in the back, discussing world issues or reading newspapers over coffee. There is never not a child somewhere in the shop, strapped into a highchair, with cream cheese gloriously smeared across their happy cheeks. It's the kind of place that is part food establishment, part community clubhouse. The kind of place where everyone knows your name and your bagel order.

When Joel passed away in 2004, Sue made two of her sons, David and Scott, partners in the business and, together, they all took the reins. Support from the community and their customers poured in. "It was incentive to keep going in honor of Joel," Sue says.

In 2010, subzero temperatures froze the ventilation system for the shop's ovens, causing a devastating fire. The shop was destroyed but the Brezacks' spirit was not. Only two things survived the fire: an old picture of Joel and Sue's recipe book, pictured. Support once again poured in for the family business.

"Our customers are the only reason we rebuilt," Sue says. "And they remain the only reason I get up each day at 4 a.m. and put an apron on."

By two or three in the afternoon these days, she says, she is tired. But she is loyal to the customers who have been so loyal to her all these years. They often ask if they can convince her to keep the bagel shop open longer, into the evening for dinner.

"Put an apron on," she tells them.

Put an apron on.

—Sue Brezack

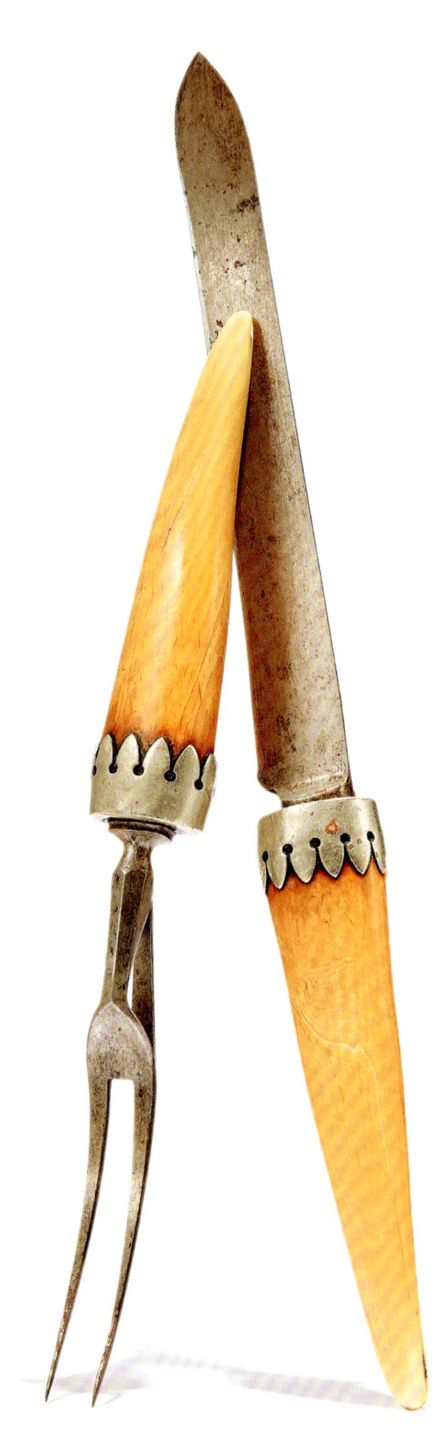

67. Andrew Zimmern | MINNEAPOLIS, MINNESOTA

Andrew Zimmern's ancestors left Germany in the mid-nineteenth century with very few belongings. This deer-antler-and-carbon-steel carving set made the cut.

The Zimmerns arrived in the Port of Charleston and settled in Atlanta. They were skilled butchers, but by the time the Civil War ended, they had lost everything. The carving set made yet another journey, this time north to New York City. The Zimmerns walked the entire way.

In New York, the next generation of their family became furniture makers, but their connection to food still flourished. Andrew remembers growing up in an environment filled with his parents' love for food, culture, and travel. By the time he was five years old, he knew he wanted to be in the food world.

"My parents were food geeks at a time when not a lot of people were," he says. "My dad liked to travel just to eat."

Andrew made good on his childhood dreams and became a chef. He got his start in the kitchens of some of the best restaurants in the business and has put his own stamp on food culture and many award-winning establishments. But the spirit for exploring and eating that his father instilled in him is perhaps most pronounced on television. As host of the Travel Channel's series *Bizarre Foods with Andrew Zimmern*, he earned James Beard Awards in 2010, 2012, 2013, and 2017 and won an Emmy, along with five nominations. To this day, Andrew can be found in the kitchen, on the radio, and on TV serving up his signature realism and passion for world food issues and culture.

When Andrew lost his father in 2015, he opened a box one day to find the family carving set. It was emotional, he admits. As a chef, he owns over two hundred knives. But none delivered the feeling of connection and tradition like the carving set.

"To use the same object for the same purpose that my great-great-grandparents did, it reminds me how special these pieces are. There is an electricity that goes back two hundred years. They are my heritage—sturdy and practical," he says.

Andrew is quick to point out that his family's carving tools are also a point of humility. It is not lost on him that the successful food career he built for himself stands on a foundation of ancestors who likely encountered lean years when there may not have been much meat to carve.

"I sit at the head of my family's table now," he says. "I take that responsibility with real reverence."

472-6488

SHIRLEY AKAWIE
ARTIST

LOS ANGELES, CA.

In March of 1957, a conflict broke out among the editors of the *Los Angeles Times Home Magazine*. A male editor seemed to be of the opinion that men work hard all day so their wives could have easy lives. Female editors strongly disagreed and subsequently dispatched a staff photographer to document the daily routine of a local housewife. They published the findings: a nonstop flurry of bed making, cooking, laundry, child care, and dishes.

"The housewife, we find, is doing her share," the newspaper subsequently stated.

That housewife was Claire Mazur's grandmother, Shirley Akawie. While her husband, Richard, worked as a scientist and engineer, Shirley's role within the family was to keep their home in order and raise their three daughters. That was just how things worked at the time. Once the girls were grown, however, the dish gloves came off.

In her newfound free time, Shirley took painting classes from a local high school art teacher. The hobby eventually became a full-time practice that would shape the next chapter of her life. Claire distinctly remembers her grandmother setting up her supplies whenever she came to visit, painting whatever was around the house. Florals were a favorite. Shirley's own home was filled with her watercolor works. Some works would be sold, others made on commission. As early as Claire can remember, she always understood her grandmother to be an artist.

When Claire was older and had a career of her own, she began to realize just how incredible her grandmother's "next chapter" had been. When Shirley passed away, her business cards surfaced among her belongings.

"In the place where a job title would go, it simply said 'Artist,'" Claire says. "I loved everything about what that symbolized. So many people struggle to call themselves artists because of fears or insecurities, but here she was, someone who hadn't started doing it until her late thirties, someone who wasn't represented by a gallery or legitimized in other typical ways. But she knew she was an artist. She was totally comfortable calling herself that and she was very proud of it," Claire says.

Harnessing creativity into purpose seems to be a trait Claire inherited from her grandmother. Claire made a career for herself doing just that—she is the cofounder of Of a Kind and A Thing or Two, both brands aimed at identifying "the next big thing" when it is still a small one, and giving emerging talent an audience. Along with her business partner, Erica Cerulo, she is also the author of *Work Wife*, a book about female friendships in the workplace.

Although Claire's career has taken center stage for a long time, and has always been focused on nurturing other people's creativity, she's making an effort to do something for herself that her grandmother would approve of: She paints as much as she can.

In the place where a job title would go, it simply said "Artist." I loved everything about what that symbolized.

—Claire Mazur

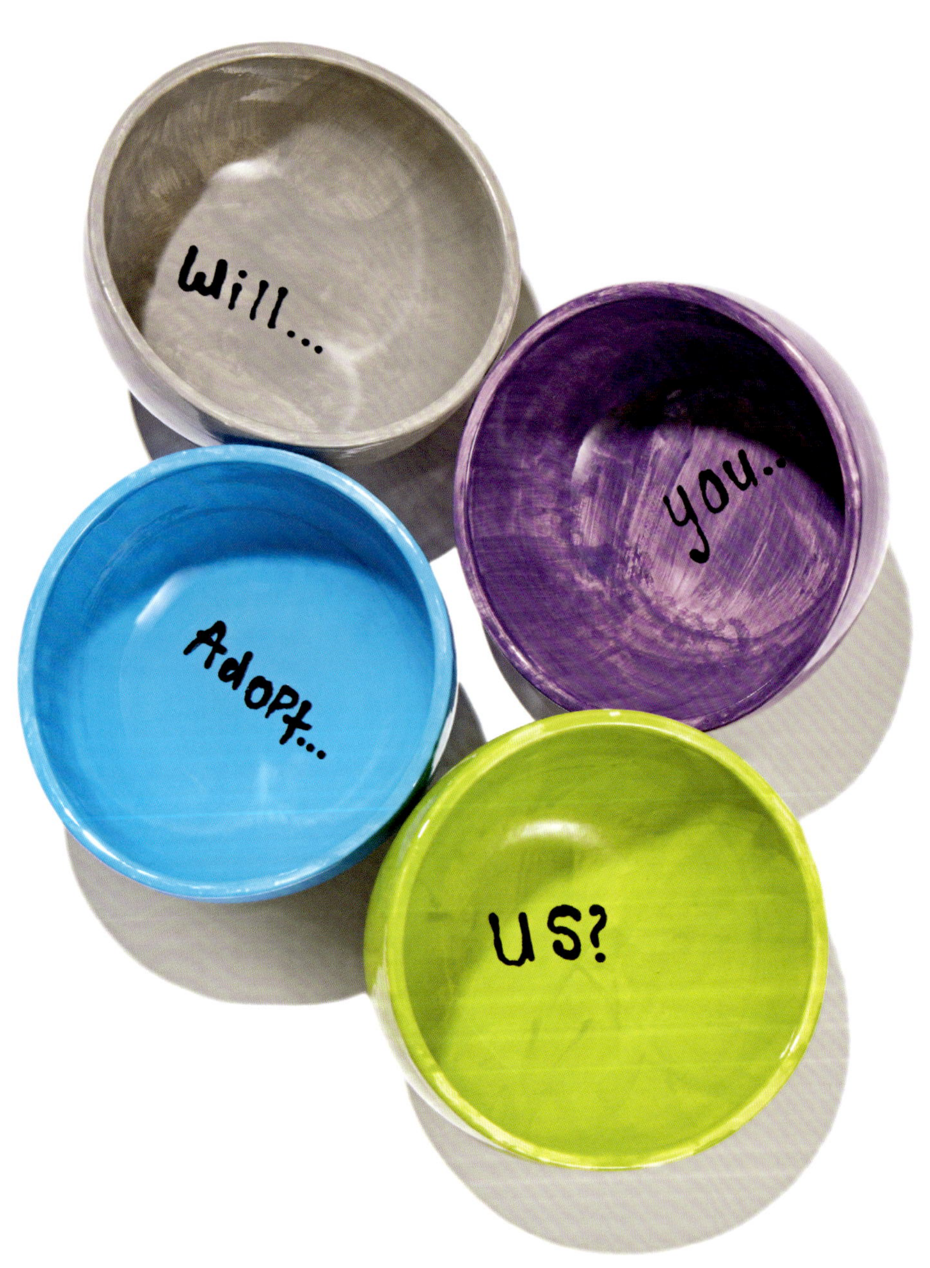
Will...
you...
Adopt...
US?

69. Christy George | KILGORE, TEXAS

As a newly single mom of two young kids, Christy George was taking her new normal one day at a time, just trying to make the best of it. That's when she crossed paths with a charming, handsome, younger man.

"Anything past a first date was out of the question," Christy jokes of Bradley. He was six years younger, not interested in marriage, and kids were nowhere on his radar.

"However, dates two, three, and four happened," she says.

Bradley eventually met Christy's daughter, Kennedy, who was six, and son, Trace, who was four. They became fast friends. Christy describes Bradley as a true kid at heart, so the bond was instant. Soon Bradley was going to soccer games, dance lessons, and getting invites to movie nights. When he told Christy he loved her, she had to remind him that she came as a package deal.

"I loved the kids before I loved you," he told her. She married him.

In the following years, Bradley would come to treat Kennedy and Trace as his own. "He never missed an event—ever," Christy says. "He is as special to the kids as they are to him." Bradley loved cereal, so the kids showed him how special he was to them by making him cereal bowls at the local pottery shop. He loved the bowls—they were deep and fit lots of cereal! Whenever he was up for a gift, he'd always ask for more bowls.

As the kids got older, they started to realize what Bradley meant to them. And so, one day, they decided to make him another set of bowls. Bradley unwrapped his gift, one bowl at a time, to reveal an important question.

"There were a lot of smiles, a ton of tears, and one big *yes*."

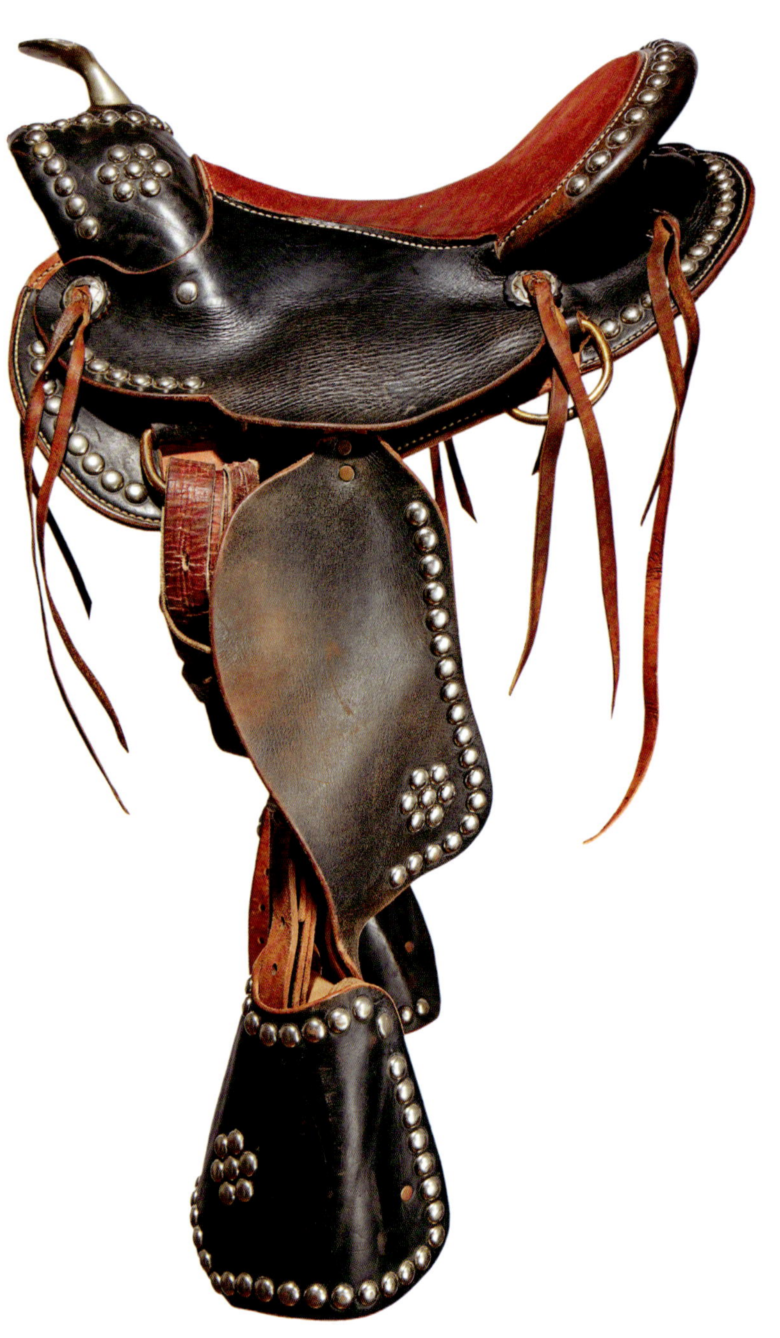

70. Kristin Thul | ALEDO, TEXAS

Harold Brooks didn't know it, but the day he went out to buy a horse, he would bring home much more.

Texas-born and married to his high school sweetheart, Harold was a POW during World War II. He made it home and spent his life surrounded by family—and horses.

One of those horses was Laura Lou. Harold brought her home one day, not knowing she was pregnant. Less than a year later, she gave birth to a black foal with a single white patch on her forehead. They named her Starbaby. Laura Lou died of an infection soon after giving birth, but Starbaby would carry on Harold's legacy for many years to come.

When Harold learned he would soon become a grandfather, he was ecstatic, according to the family, and went out and bought this kid-size saddle in anticipation of sharing his love for riding with his grandkids. He would pass away before getting that chance.

Kristin Thul is Harold's granddaughter. Before she was old enough to even sit upright, she says, her mom had her at the family ranch, sitting atop Starbaby in the very saddle her grandfather had been so excited to put her in. The family lovingly referred to Harold as Pop. His horse, Starbaby, would be Kristin's. Pop's legacy was alive and kicking.

"I developed a very special connection with Star at a young age," Kristin says. "She had a habit of being stubborn with many riders but would do anything I asked."

Kristin grew up with a passion for riding and knows she shares the same peace and tranquility in caring for and riding horses that Pop would have instilled in her. "Of all the heirlooms my family has," Kristin says, "the saddle is the most direct connection to the man I never knew but who started it all."

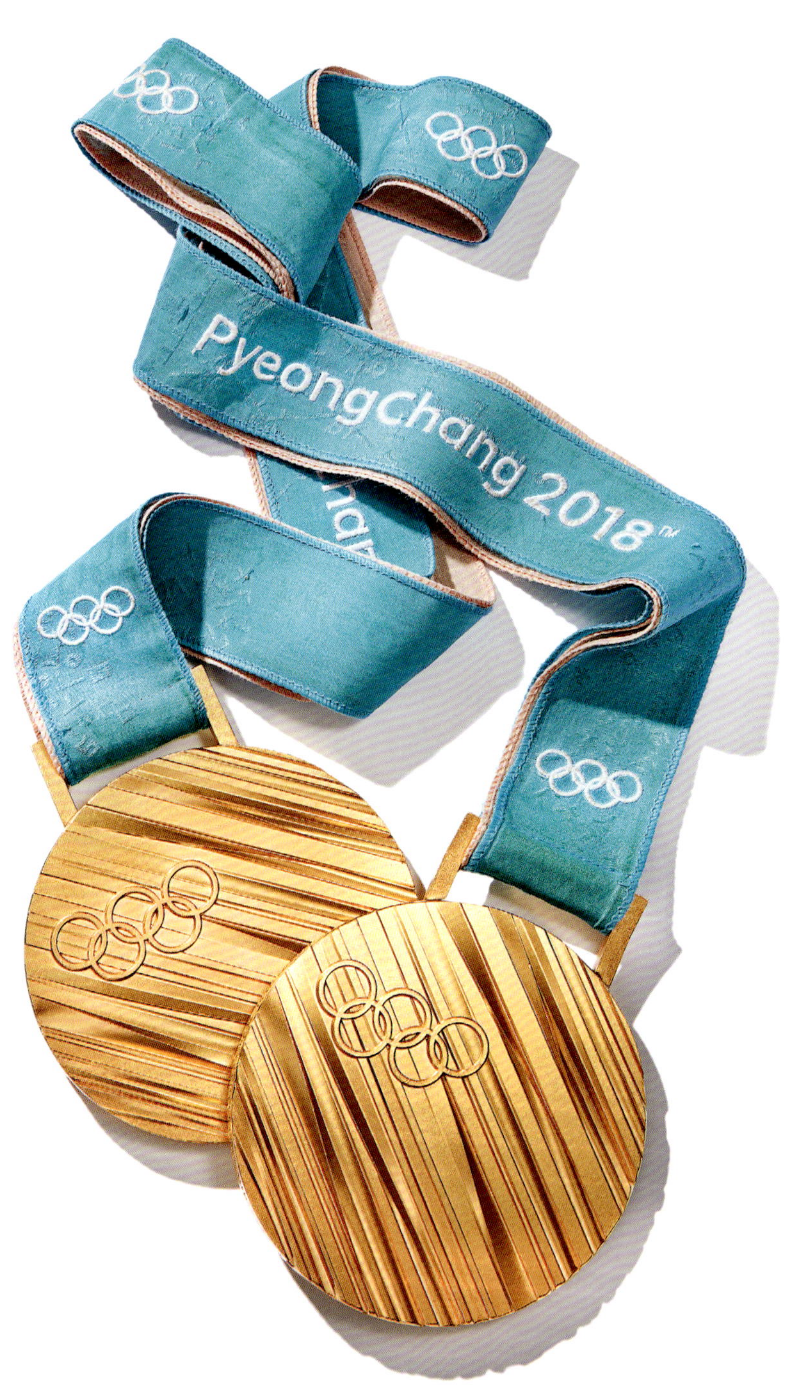
PyeongChang 2018™

At three years old, twins Jocelyne and Monique Lamoureux could be found laced into hockey skates chasing their big brothers around on the ice.

"We just did whatever they did," Jocelyne says. "The Twins," as they were referred to, grew up playing ice hockey with boys' teams because there were no teams for girls. This did not stop them from playing on the world's most prestigious ice.

Jocelyne and Monique played hockey throughout their high school and college years, where championships were won on a consistent basis. Their talent eventually landed them—together—on Team USA's Women's National Hockey Team for fifteen years, where they won six world championships and played in three Olympic Games. In 2018, in the gold medal game, Monique scored the game-tying goal. Jocelyne won the game in a dramatic sudden-death shoot-out. They returned from Pyeongchang, South Korea, with matching gold medals, pictured.

"Everything has always been 'we' and never 'me,'" Jocelyne says of her sister. "We have walked through life side by side. We have had the same goals and dreams since we can remember. So to accomplish a childhood dream together is what we always worked toward. We would not be where we are without each other."

In addition to the matching medals, the twins will be remembered for another hard-fought win. Along with their teammates, they have been advocating for years for gender equity in USA Hockey.

"Our fight for equity will always be what we are most proud of during our career," Jocelyne says. "It wasn't just us but our entire program that said, 'Enough is enough and we are going to stand up for change.'"

The twins recently retired from hockey to spend more time with family, but their impact is still being felt. In Grand Forks, their hometown, they created their true legacy, The Lamoureux Foundation, which funds extracurricular and educational activities for underprivileged kids.

"Our foundation gives back to youth in our home state of North Dakota. It's about meeting basic day-to-day needs for kids who may not get hot lunches during the school day, or even a young woman in need of feminine products," Jocelyne says. "Our hockey career has given us the platform to do this. There is so much more to our careers than just winning games and medals."

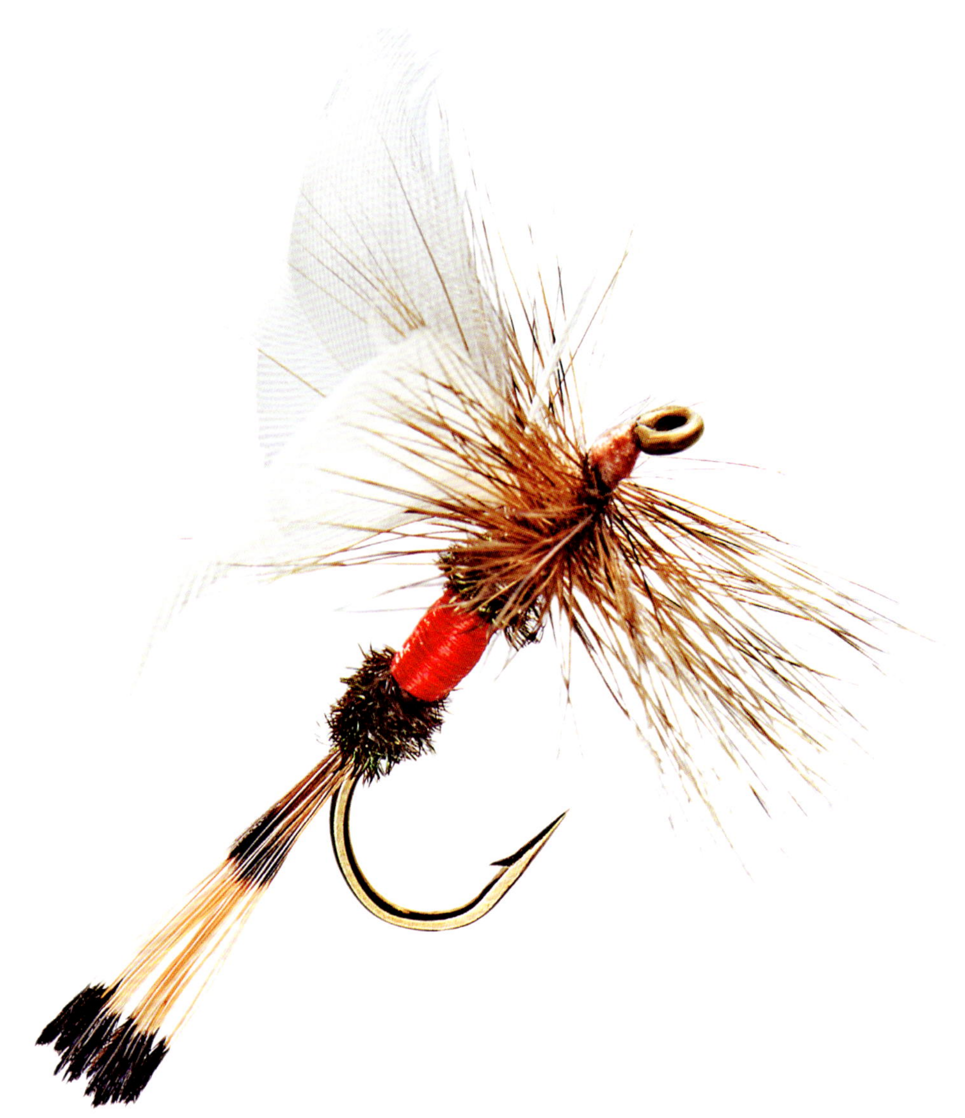

72. Melissa Chessher | DALLAS, TEXAS

I loved being a journalism school student, but it was clear from the start that I was never going to be a Pulitzer Prize–winning investigative reporter. But my writing professors, Bill Glavin and Melissa Chessher, didn't judge. This is the story of those two professors who profoundly impacted me and, as it turns out, each other.

Bill Glavin taught long-form nonfiction feature writing. He was a legend to thirty-eight years of students, as evidenced by the long line that formed in the hallway during his office hours. He taught methodically and wore sweater vests. He encouraged us to go deep for details and chase the nuances when crafting stories.

Professor Melissa Chessher had a different approach. She turned her students into a magazine staff on the first day of class and told us to publish an issue over the course of the semester. Everyone was assigned a position—writer, editor, designer. Then, she just kind of turned us loose. She had a very specific agenda, mind you, but under her watchful eye, we got to run amok in all the best ways, chasing leads, meeting deadlines, and making something together. This gave us the space to identify our strengths and to figure out what we really wanted to bring to the table. I appointed myself a staff photographer, which explains a lot now.

These very different professors laid a foundation for my work that I am ever grateful for. I still hear Melissa in my head to this day when I type, and consider her a mentor. When I asked if she would be willing to submit an heirloom for this book, she left me speechless when she suggested she might contribute the story of a keepsake from her mentor: Professor Bill Glavin.

As head of the Magazine Department, Bill hired Melissa to the S.I. Newhouse School of Communications at Syracuse University the very year I became their student. The two became lifelong family-level friends over the twelve years they taught together.

"I was definitely a student of his ability to teach well and with care," Melissa says. Bill Glavin always cared deeply, she says, both about people and their story. This affected Melissa greatly, both as a professor and as a human.

Melissa was a single parent with a young daughter when she started teaching in his department. But Bill always supported her, making sure she knew the best farm for the freshest, fullest Christmas trees, the best theater in which to see the latest Harry Potter movie on opening day, and he even advised on the safest paths through their hilly neighborhood in snowy Syracuse. "I benefited greatly from his kindness over the years," she says.

"Even students who [had] long left his class would call him to talk about how to soothe a colicky baby, deal with a difficult boss, or know if they'd found 'the one' to marry," Melissa says. His students and colleagues were his family, and his kindness extended beyond campus.

Professor Glavin was diagnosed with cancer in 2010.

"When he became sick, I received the gift of being able to return all the grace and support he had shown my daughter and me," Melissa says. She went to his doctor appointments with him, brought him dinner, and on Friday nights, watched Harry Potter movies with him. When the time came, Melissa took Bill to hospice.

"On the last night of his life, he struggled to sit up and then, after settling into a comfortable position, announced that he needed to return to his classroom," she says.

When Bill's will was shared, in addition to his relatives, he had included Melissa. He'd left her, among other things, his beloved L.L. Bean Subaru, some books, and two fishing reels. Bill loved fly-fishing—he loved reading about it, making his own ties, and visiting Montana to fish. And that is the reason this tiny lure, the first fly tie he ever made, holds such a huge meaning for Melissa.

"It reminds me of the expansive entirety of this special, magical, kind man and of all his gifts. Its smallness exists as the exact opposite of the impact he had on me, my daughter, and the thousands of students who shared a classroom with him."

As a kid, Karen Hofmann loved soccer, but there were no soccer leagues for girls in her town. So, she played with the boys. There on the field, at the age of eight, she says she learned a special brand of fearlessness and confidence—two tools needed to score major goals later in life. But they weren't the only tools she would need.

Off the field, Karen grew up around architects and aerospace engineers—people who were curious and skilled at affecting the human experience through design. Karen inherited this curiosity and earned a degree in psychology. Not satisfied with one, she earned another—in product design, from ArtCenter College of Design in Pasadena, California.

At design school, she remembers sitting in class next to brilliant minds and forward thinkers who would go on to work for brands such as Toyota and Nike, and for the *Star Wars* franchise.

"I was constantly inspired by incredibly talented people and surrounded by support," she says. "When you see yourself as not the best, that makes you strive to be better," she notes. Her determination and work ethic would drive her straight to Michigan, where she landed a job after graduation in vehicle interior design with Johnson Controls Automotive Systems Group. (The nearly 140-year-old company is behind many of the modern technologies in cars.) There, Karen found herself at the intersection of technology and traditional design.

"I caught the wave of 3-D software. But I'm also very analog—you have to learn by hand before you go digital," she says. Sketching, conceptualizing, and visual thinking with pen and paper have remained important processes throughout her career. Pictured are her most important tools—the pens, pencils, and markers she has used over the years to conceptualize and manifest some of her best ideas and design work.

Karen holds patents from her days in automotive design—third-row seating systems, cargo systems for truck-bed storage, and a tailgate video display. She even got to teach a few classes on behalf of her company to students at her alma mater. The opportunity shifted Karen into a different gear.

She took a position as a professor of product design at the very institution that had educated her. She was now designing lessons and coursework, and it was thrilling in a way she never expected. Within eight years, she was chair of the Product Design Department and then, in 2018, provost of the entire school. She had gone from

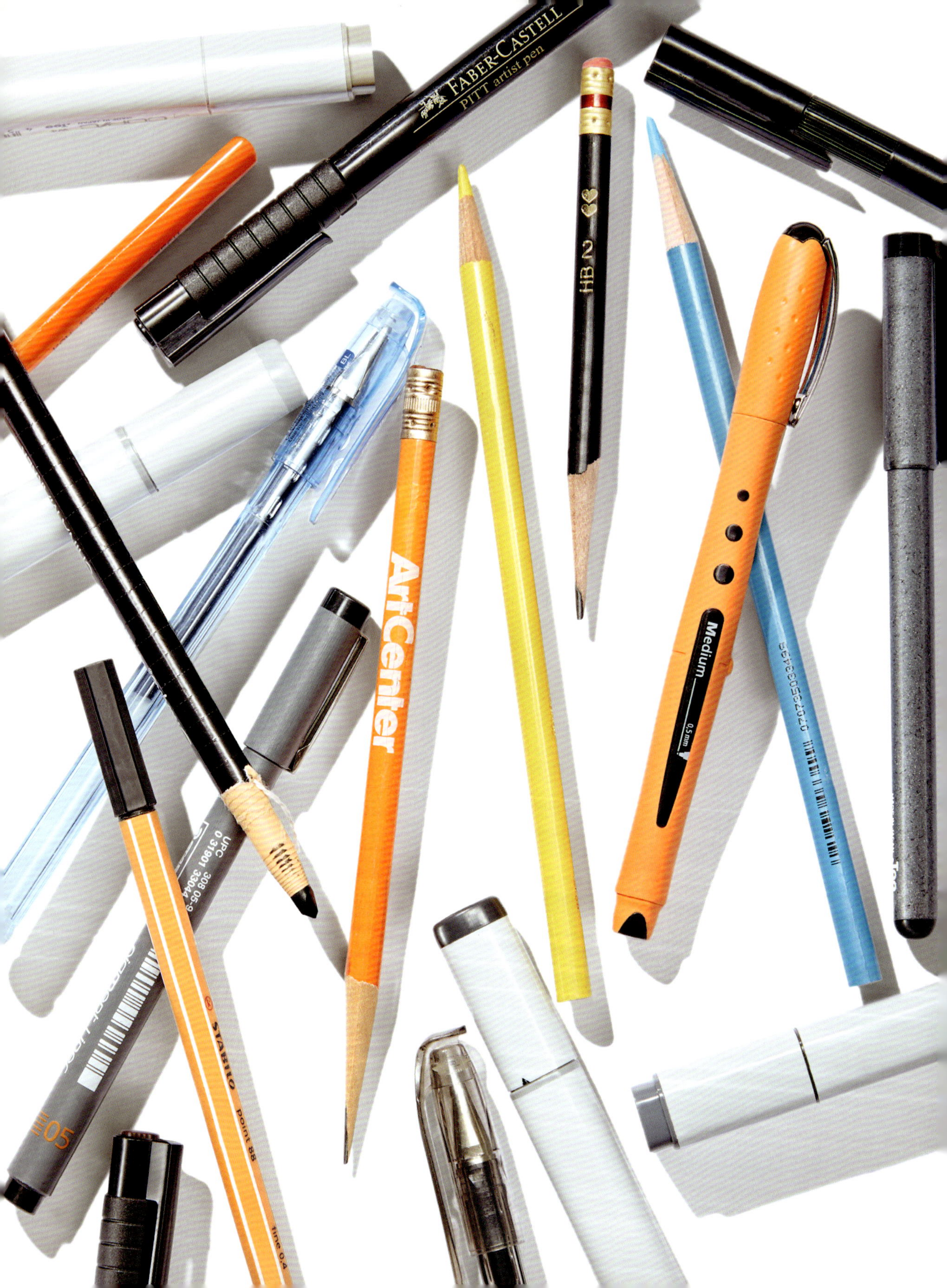
FABER-CASTELL
PITT artist pen
HB 2
ArtCenter
Medium
0,5 mm
STABILO
point 88
fine 0.4
UPC
0 31901 33044
308 05-9
05

designing tangible objects to designing goals, teams, and futures.

"I was designing their whole learning experience and it was incredibly rewarding," she says. That's when she decided to throw her hat in the ring for something bigger.

In 2021, the Board of Trustees of Art-Center College of Design was looking both nationally and internationally for a new leader. Karen wanted the job. The process of getting it was rigorous. She would have to show them she could design the ultimate product—the future of their school. All of her confidence and fearlessness and extensive experience turning ideas into reality would culminate in a boardroom in Pasadena.

In 2022, Karen Hofmann was named the school's first woman president and also the first alumnus to serve as president.

She says her favorite part of the job is seeing talented students from all over the world come to Pasadena to learn the creative skills needed to turn their big dreams into reality. "I still believe students should think, sketch, and learn with their hands before they sit down at a computer," she says. And she is a practice-what-you-teach kind of leader—she keeps her own pens and pencils handy at all times.

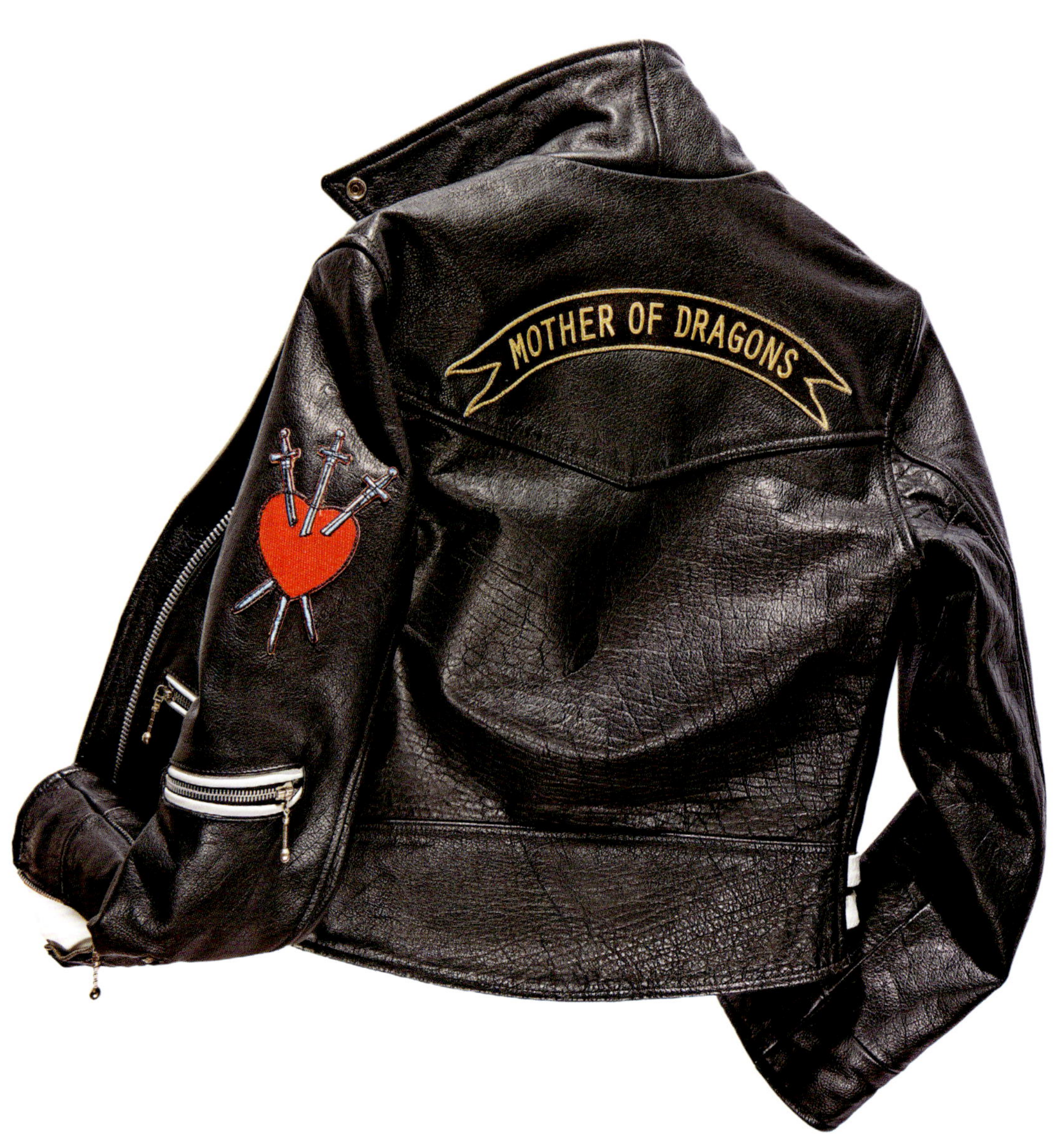
MOTHER OF DRAGONS

74. Jill Kargman | NEW YORK, NEW YORK

Jill Kargman's affinity for the dark side can be traced all the way back to *Sesame Street.* As a toddler, her favorite character on the show wasn't the lovable big yellow bird. It was the count in a black cape. Ask her about her favorite childhood *Muppet Show* guest host. Was it Julie Andrews? No, it was Alice Cooper, the heavy-metal rocker. But the kid with a love for black capes and dark eyeliner would grow up to be very much a point of light.

"My parents, brother, and I are all pretty morbid," Jill only half jokes. "But my family's awareness of death actually makes us happy, because morbid people live in the moment," Jill says. This life approach has served Jill well. Her ability to find light among the hard truths, mixed with a searing sense of humor, formed the distinctive voice she is known for in pop culture. And possibly one of the reasons she's alive.

In 2017, Jill had a stage 0 lump in her breast and learned she carried the CHEK2 gene mutation, making her a terribly good candidate for developing breast cancer. She chose to have a preventive double mastectomy—a humbling and difficult decision, and also an act of defiance.

This trademark boldness earned her spots on the *New York Times* bestseller list as the author of twelve books, one of which she aptly named *Sprinkle Glitter on My Grave.* Another book, *Momzillas*, was adapted into the television series *Odd Mom Out*, which she created, wrote, and produced for the Bravo Network.

So what does the queen of dark humor watch on her own TV? The HBO series *Game of Thrones*, of course. Jill says she hit superfan status immediately. "I hate fantasy and zombies, but I do love medieval style and righteous violence," Jill says. "The triumph of good over evil spoke to me."

Her favorite character was the damaged visionary, Bran Stark. The other was Khaleesi, a mother of two kids just fighting to survive. (Her kids just happened to be fire-breathing dragons.)

Jill was a new mom of three kids under the age of five when she found this MOTHER OF DRAGONS patch on a trip to Nashville. It resonated, to say the least. She had the patch sewn onto her prized leather jacket, pictured. It was the perfect badge of honor for where Jill was at the time—which was completely underwater.

"I was kind of drowning in my life with three kids under five," Jill says. "Kids are a blessing, but having three little ones was super tiring, and I basically didn't sleep for eleven years."

The patch emboldened Jill to own her role as a mom and reminded her to embrace precious life moments. "I suddenly felt like I had my own armor. Like I could take on the world," she says. "Wine and good friends helped too," she jokes.

These days, the Mother of Dragons reigns supreme. She is healthy, happy, and as fiercely goth-glam as ever. The kids, Sadie, Ivy, and Fletch, are teenagers. She and her husband, Harry, have worked endlessly to instill in them a sense of hard work, humor, and strength. "It's easy to complain about teenagers, but I actually love hanging out with mine," she says. "My dragons are all grown up, but I'll always love my memories of wearing this jacket when they were newly hatched."

75. Jenny Faw | EASTHAM, MASSACHUSETTS

On paper, Jenny Faw is my second cousin, but in life, she assumed the role of big sister—showing me the ropes and putting me in my place when I needed it. I often needed it.

When I was younger, Jenny was the modern-day pioneer of our family—pushing her way forward "back East" to New York City from our family roots out on the Great Plains. She grew up in Manhattan, Kansas, and ended up in Manhattan, New York. When I was growing up, in my somewhat conservative family, Jenny was the cool kid who came around for the holidays. Her jackets were black leather, she had an angel tattoo, and her hair was always impeccably cut because she was a Vidal Sassoon model. She was also an artist.

Jenny ran a design business from a bright tin-ceilinged loft in the Flatiron District of New York City. She was a painter, but she didn't just sit around and paint—she was a boss. The loft was always abuzz with coworkers, clients, fax machines, and ringing phones. There was a long wooden table in the middle of the open loft that served as her board room. Deals were made there. And man, she was getting paid.

The first time I went to New York to visit her, I was ruined—I would never be able to live anywhere else, and I knew it right then. The creativity she surrounded herself with was intoxicating, and I was drunk with it. She is the first person who introduced me to the idea that creativity could be a career, but only if I took it seriously.

Pictured is a matchbook from the restaurant where I had my first meal ever in New York City, The Coffee Shop in Union Square, a casual but glamorous gathering spot for a generation of New Yorkers. There, tucked into a leather banquette next to my cool cousin in the big bustling city, I was home.

I wanted to be like Jenny so badly that I moved to New York City probably thirty seconds after graduating from college. She has been my North Star ever since. She taught me to be firm and kind in business, to worship my friends like family, and to drink lots and lots of margaritas. Everyone who knows her know her heart only loves, it does not judge. She sees the best in everyone, automatically. We are all so lucky to be loved by this bright force of a human.

So, when I saw her at the hospital, hooked up to a chemo needle, my world was rearranged. The North Star had cancer. I know I saw fear in her eyes that day, and also a fire in her heart.

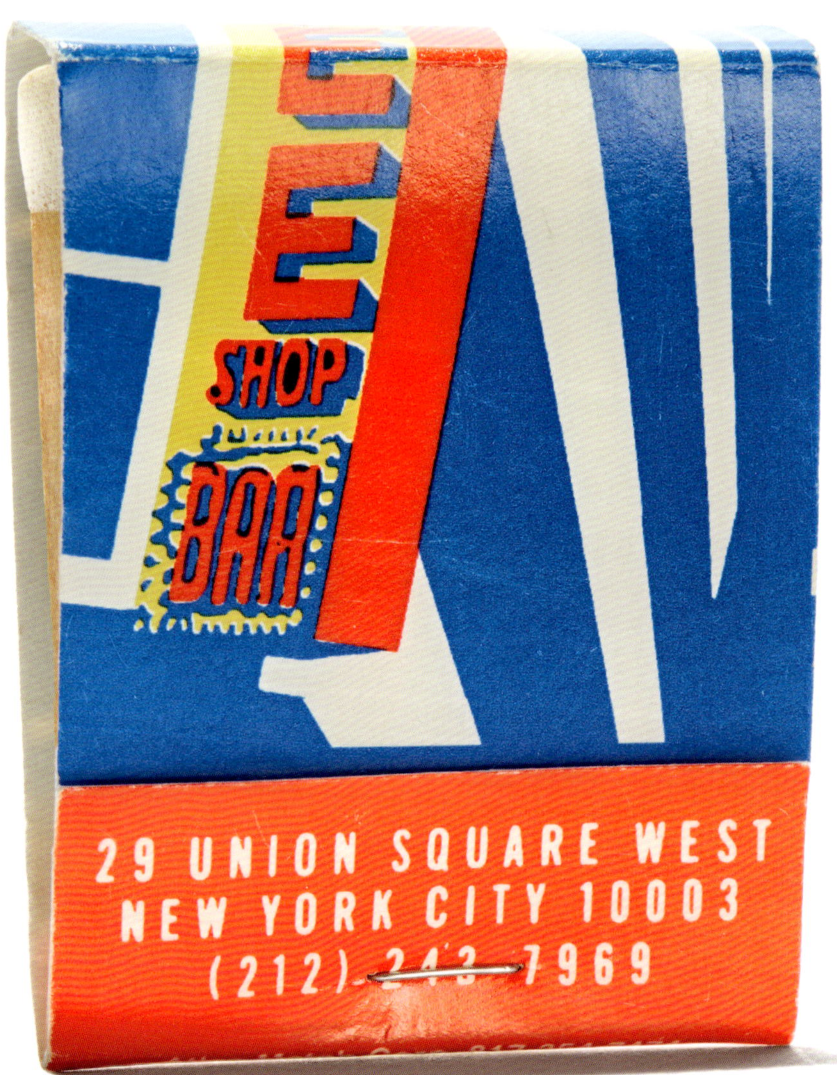
SHOP
BAR
29 UNION SQUARE WEST
NEW YORK CITY 10003
(212) 243-7969

Jenny would go through her cancer treatments with her trademark attitude—fierce, bright, and powerful. Seeing this changed me. It was one thing to look up to someone as a kid. It was a different thing entirely to watch them overcome something truly frightening with grace.

She showed cancer the door. No one was surprised.

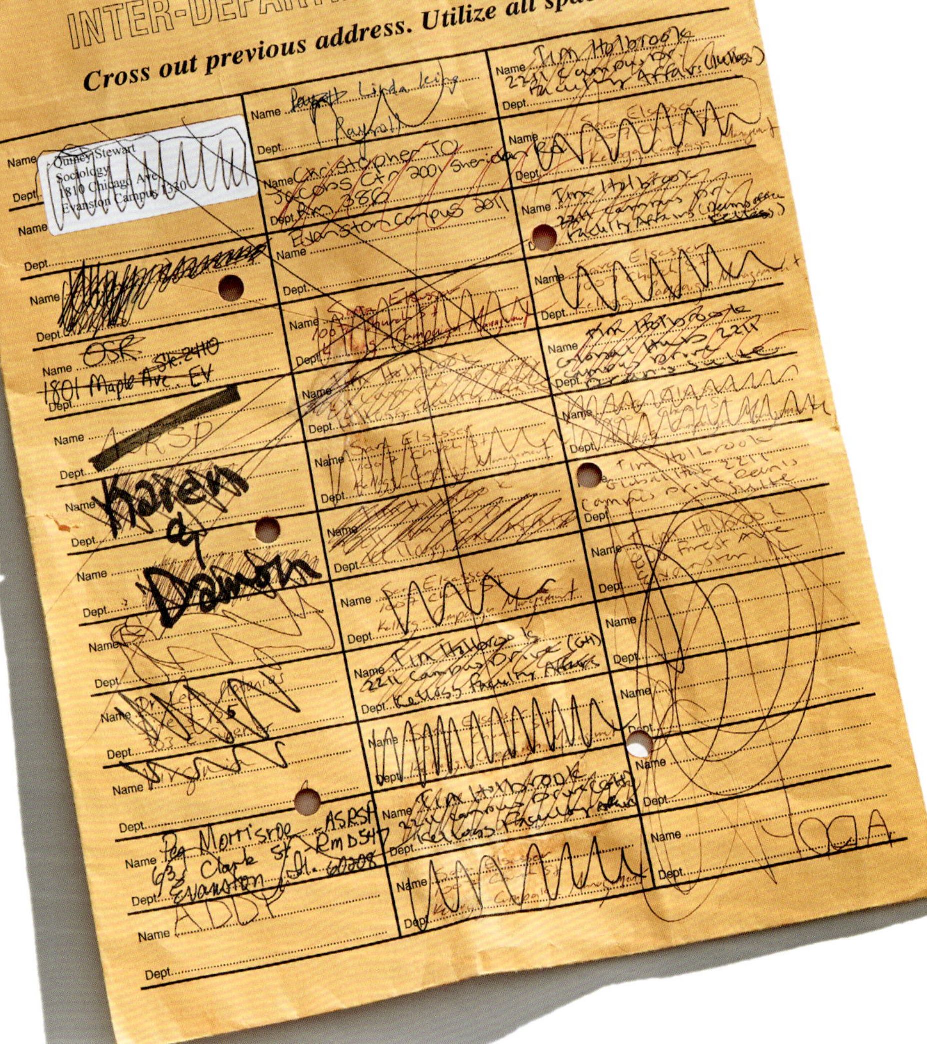
INTER-DEPARTMENT DELIVERY
Cross out previous address. Utilize all spaces.

76. Sara Elsasser | GLENCOE, ILLINOIS

Imagine, in this age of all things digital, sitting at your office desk one day when a bright yellow envelope shows up. Despite not expecting anything from anyone, it has your name on it.

This happened to Sara Elsasser. When she opened the envelope, she found a note from a coworker named Tim. Through the office grapevine, he heard she hated an inbox full of emails, but he wanted to introduce himself. So, he got creative and sent her a good, old-fashioned handwritten note via interoffice mail.

To Tim's surprise, the yellow envelope landed on his own desk the next day with a note from Sara.

It was official. "We were office pen pals," Sara jokes. The two exchanged notes for a time. That's when Sara's pen pal asked her out on a date. Using interoffice mail, of course.

The date was first-class. But even after, Sara and Tim continued their correspondence using the yellow envelope.

"The notes we wrote and sent in the envelope allowed us to share details about ourselves in an old-fashioned sort of way," Sara says. "Communication was slowed down because it was via snail mail and writing things pen to paper forced us to be thoughtful about what we shared."

And it worked. Tim eventually asked Sara to marry him, via the interoffice envelope.

The couple is now married and has four kids. This is the envelope that started it all, signed, sealed, and delivered.

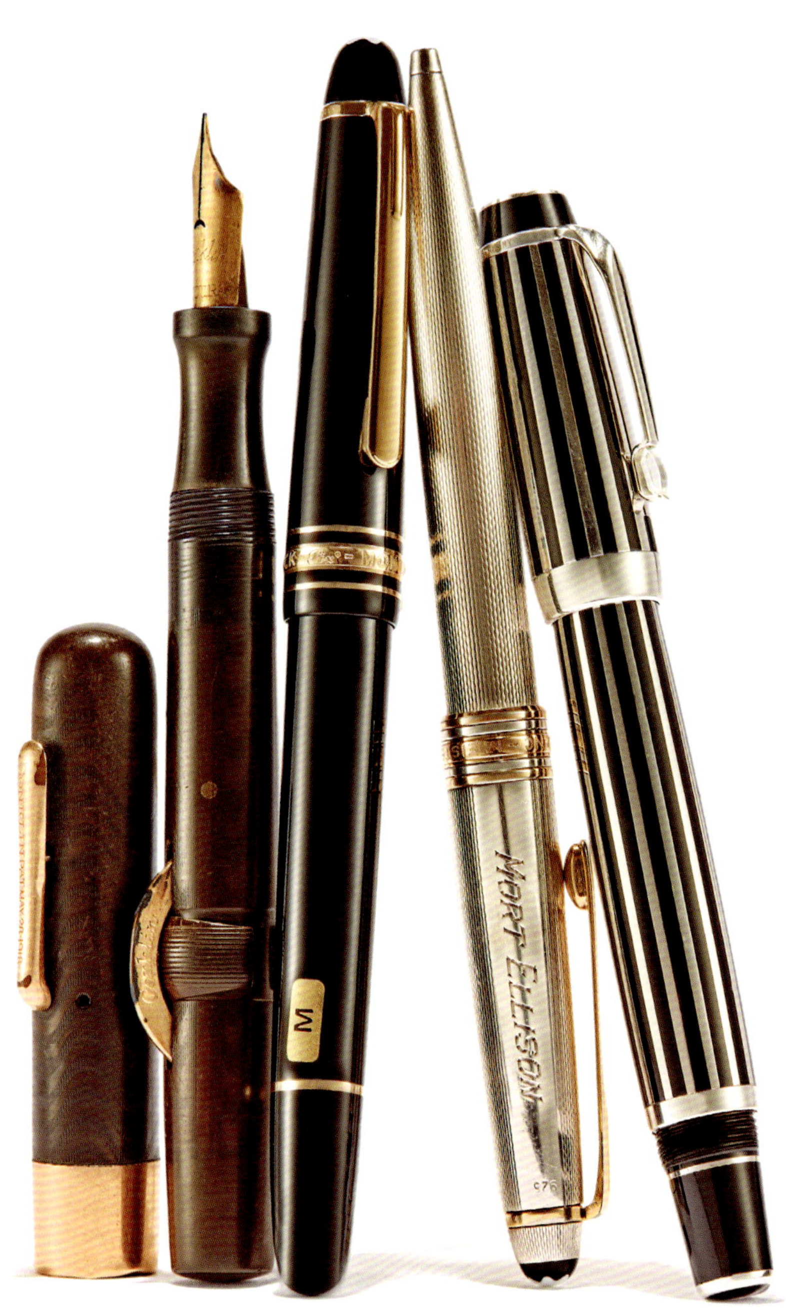
M
MORT ELLISON

77. Lauren Fox | CHARLESTON, SOUTH CAROLINA

Lauren Fox's father, Morton Ellison, was such a devoted pen collector that each morning as he dressed, he chose one to wear for the day and then matched his tie accordingly.

"He dressed to impress and that always included at least one pen. On some days, two," Lauren says. Pens were treasures to him. She thinks she knows where this came from.

The brown pen on the left belonged to Morton's father and was the only tangible thing he ever really had that connected them. When Morton was seventeen months old, his father died, leaving his mom to run the family shoe business, Ellison's Shoes, in Charleston, South Carolina. Morton would grow up to earn a degree from the Citadel and was headed for medical school, but he was forever loyal to his single mother—he took a year off to help her with the family shoe business and never left. He ran Ellison's until his retirement.

"These pens signed thousands of sales orders and contracts and kept a family business going for ninety-one years," Lauren says. Her father always kept the brown pen in his desk at the store.

Lauren was allowed to play, albeit cautiously, with some of the pens when she was little, but she grew up to take them very seriously. After college, she was recruited to work for luxury pen maker Montblanc, making her father ecstatically proud.

"His pen collection grew exponentially while I worked there," she jokes.

Over the years, these pens were undoubtedly used for many of Lauren's life's moments: notes to Lauren at summer camp, tuition checks for her education, and lots of generous giving to worthy causes.

"He was the kind of man who volunteered as the chair of our synagogue's cemetery committee for over forty years, because he wanted to do a kindness for someone who could never thank him," Lauren says. "He taught me to give without an agenda."

When Lauren's father passed away, she became the keeper of his many pens. These days, she signs contracts and legal documents with them in her job as an attorney. But she recently got a promotion: She was named a Charleston County magistrate judge. You can bet the desk in her chambers will hold a few pens.

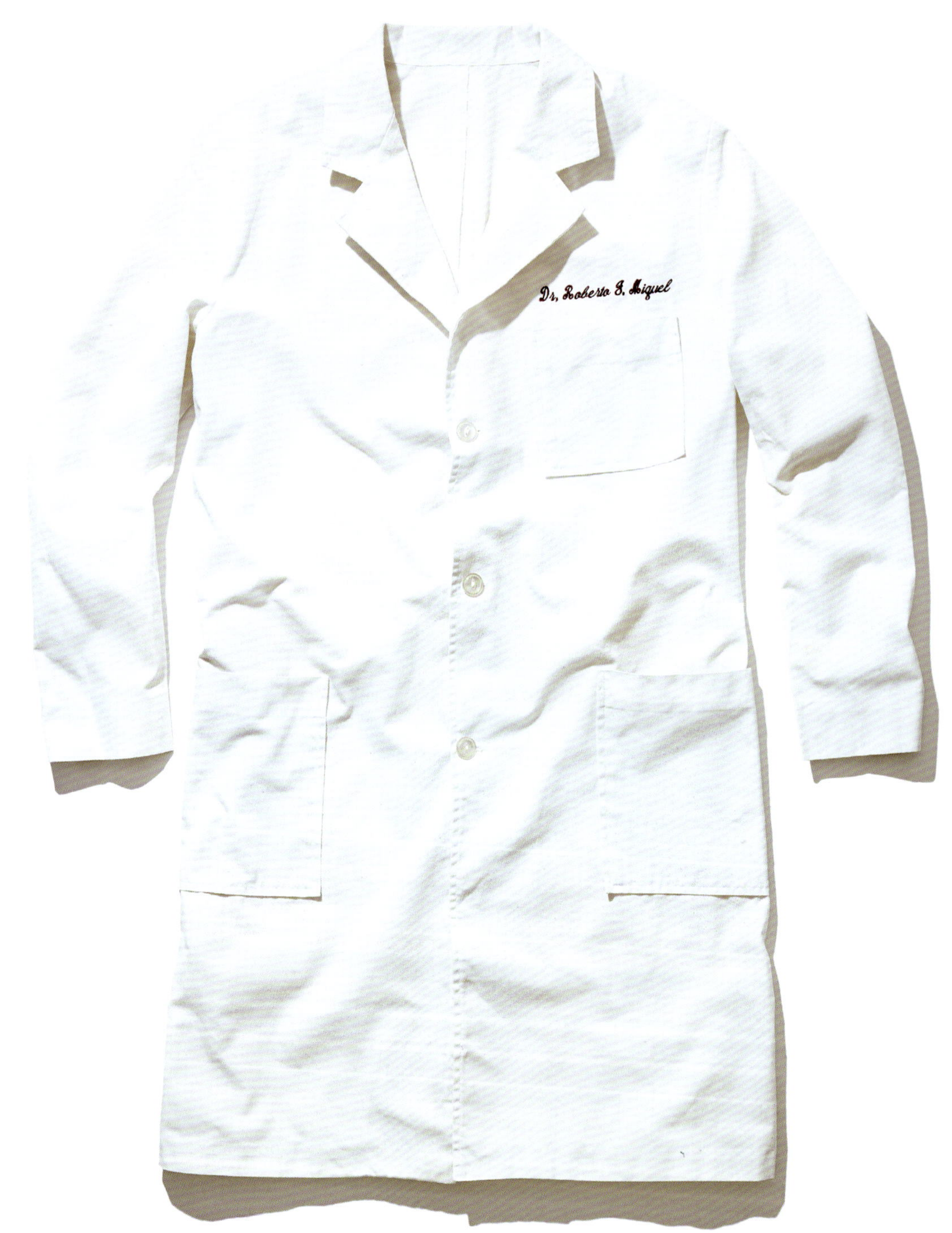
Dr, Roberto S. Miguel

78. Alex Miquel | WEST PALM BEACH, FLORIDA

Fourteen thousand Cuban children were evacuated to the United States in the years following the Cuban Revolution. Fearing what the future might hold in Cuba's growing militaristic political landscape, many parents sent their children, alone, to the United States under a program called Operation Peter Pan. At the time, it was the largest movement of minor refugees in the Western Hemisphere. Alex Miquel's father, Roberto, was one of them.

Roberto was just a teenager when he and his siblings left Cuba without their parents. They arrived in the United States speaking no English and had only hope that their family would reunite. For many, this never happened. The Miquels were some of the lucky ones.

When Roberto's family arrived, his father took a job cleaning office buildings in Miami, even though he had been a surgeon in Havana. Determined to follow in his father's footsteps, Roberto went to medical school, put down roots in West Palm Beach, set up a medical practice, and started a family.

Roberto raised his sons in an environment of hard work and compassion. His son Alex remembers frequently visiting his dad's office at a young age, and also joining him for rounds at the hospital or nursing homes on the weekends.

"I fell in love with his passion for helping others and the mutual respect he showed for his patients, and they showed back to him," Alex says. He knew he wanted a future in medicine.

In high school, Alex admits, his education suffered because he loved sports and having fun more than academics. He enrolled in a local community college after graduation, unsure of his path. One night, after returning home from being out with his college buddies, Alex came home, hugged his parents good night, and went downstairs. Five minutes later, he heard a commotion upstairs. His father had suffered a massive heart attack. He passed away that night.

Less than four months later, Alex enrolled in medical school.

"After my father passed, I remember thinking, 'I couldn't help the one person I would want to help, so I will make it a point to help as many people as I can, however I can, whenever I can,'" Alex says. He ended up graduating magna cum laude. He now practices family medicine in his hometown of West Palm Beach.

Throughout Alex's medical education, training, and career, he has always kept this white lab coat hanging in the closet or on a hook in his office. His father's name, "Dr. Roberto J. Miquel," is embroidered over the chest pocket. The coat has always been a reminder of why he does what he does—and that he has a lot to be proud of.

I will make it a point to help as many people as I can, however I can, whenever I can.

—Alex Miquel

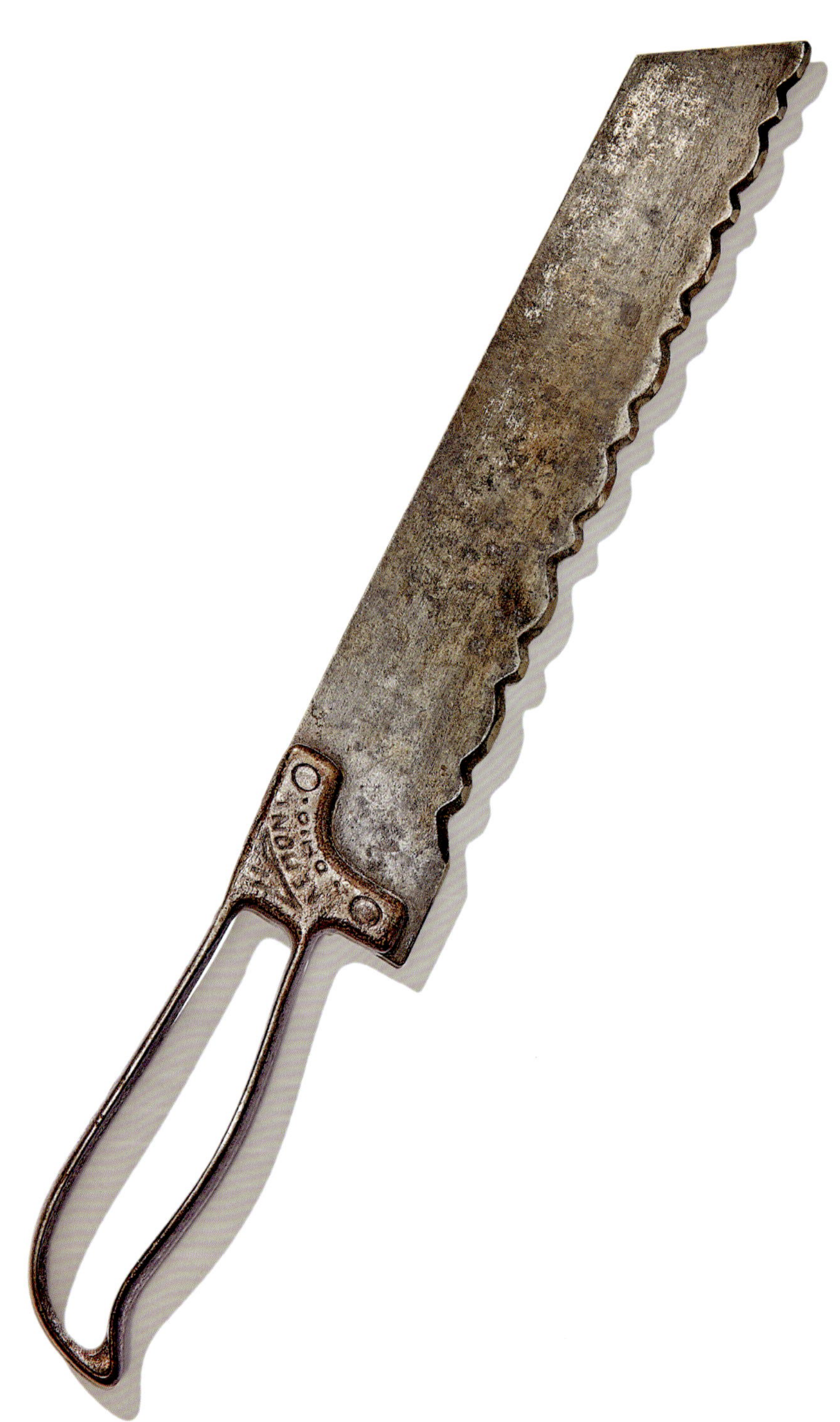

79. Amanda Hesser | NEW YORK, NEW YORK

Heirlooms passed down through the generations of Amanda Hesser's family include Civil War–era forks and a circa 1877 carbon-steel bread knife from Ohio. Also passed down: a deep appreciation for working with simple kitchen tools that function exceptionally well.

It's no wonder then that Amanda, a *New York Times* bestselling food author, went on to cofound Food52, a kitchen and lifestyle brand based on this example of simplicity and functionality in the kitchen.

But before she was the boss of her own company, she learned the ropes in the family kitchen. The kitchen was the nucleus of the household, especially at her grandparents' house on the Chesapeake Bay. Her grandfather, a carpenter, built the kitchen, and her grandmother operated it. There was always action there, Amanda says. "It was the place to be."

Summers meant countertops lined with Ball jars awaiting jam or vegetables for pickling. Colder months meant hearty meals prepared with meat from the chest freezer in the garage. Amanda got to help in the kitchen if she was lucky, but mostly, her grandmother and mother ran a tight operation.

"There was a hierarchy," she says. "The kids were the support crew." But Amanda observed and absorbed a love for the art of food preparation and togetherness. One very specific early memory is of her grandmother with this late-nineteenth-century bread knife—graceful with its scalloped-edge blade, and utilitarian with its boxy industrial handle.

"She'd hold the bread with her left hand and cut with her right," Amanda says of her grandmother. "Her fingers were so knobby and crooked; I was always sure she'd slice one off, but the knife's unusual shape belied its sharpness and the knife would just slide through the bread effortlessly. The knife was always ready to cut any loaf into thin, gauzy slices or beefy slabs."

Amanda asked to be the next keeper of the bread knife when her grandmother passed away at the age of 102.

"It reminds me of our family values and the tradition of being in the kitchen together," Amanda says. Hierarchy and all.

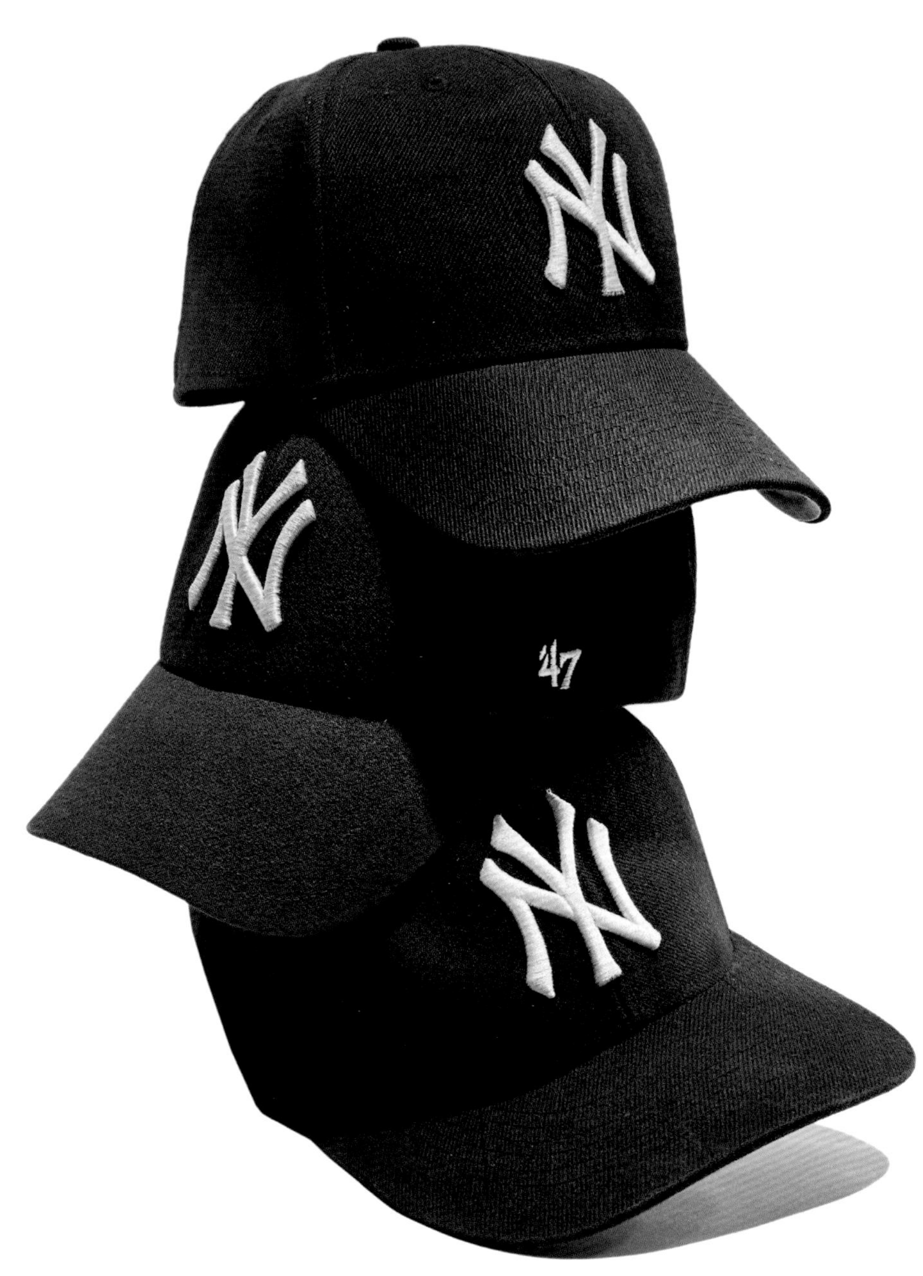
'47

80. Jodi Peckman | NEW YORK, NEW YORK

Jodi Peckman first met Barack Obama in 2008, just as he was about to receive the Democratic nomination for president. She was the photography director of *Rolling Stone* magazine at the time and had come to Raleigh, North Carolina, with a crew to photograph Obama for what would be the first of his many *Rolling Stone* covers. They got their shot. He told her he liked her hat, a classic navy-blue wool New York Yankees baseball cap.

The second time Jodi was sent to oversee the photography of President Obama, he walked onto the photoshoot set and, upon seeing her, exclaimed, "How about those Yankees!" She was wearing the hat again.

In fact, you'd be hard-pressed to find Jodi without her trademark cap. She has more than a few, all for various occasions and loved for different reasons. As an author and visual creative, she adores the graceful elegance of the font and logo, designed by Louis Tiffany (yes, that Tiffany) in 1877. She loves baseball, primarily for the hometown pride the Yanks represent. But most of all, she says, the hat is just a cool version of a basic necessity.

"It keeps the sun off my face and is an easy uniform when I'm traveling," she says. "On photoshoots, if any one was looking for the person in charge, they knew to look for the Yankees cap."

The third time Jodi and her team photographed President Obama, he asked her if she was in a bad mood. He was joking with her—the Yankees had just lost in the playoffs.

"He remembered the hat every time," she says, amazed to realize just how memorable she was while wearing it. (Jodi served for thirty years as the photography and creative director of *Rolling Stone* magazine, so the list of movie stars and rock gods who remember her—and not just for the hat—could likely fill a stadium.)

One of Jodi's most memorable trips to photograph the president was at his place of employment.

"You're not really going to wear that?" her boss asked as she headed into the White House in her Yankees cap. Respectfully, Jodi removed it when she stepped into the Oval Office for the photoshoot. But when President Obama walked in, he still asked her about the Yankees.

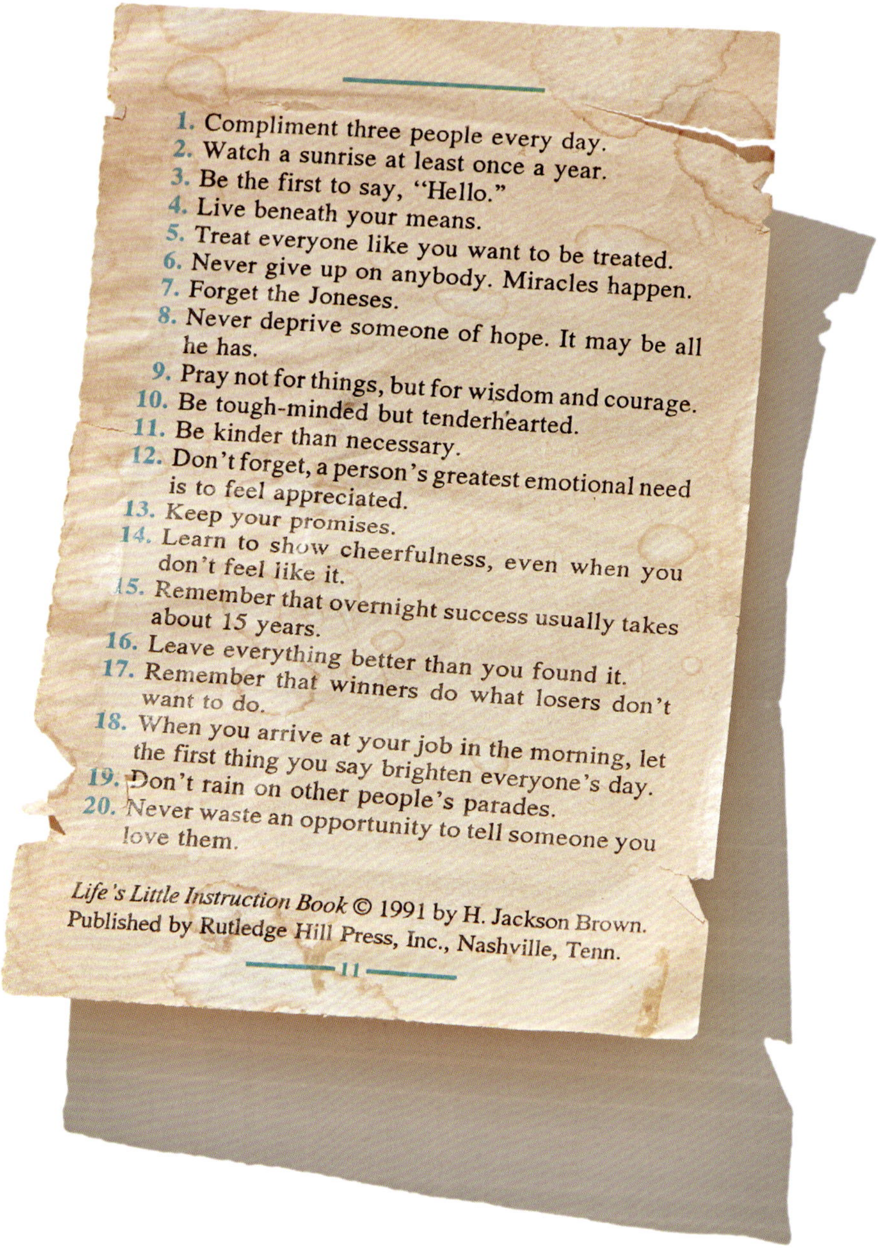

1. Compliment three people every day.
2. Watch a sunrise at least once a year.
3. Be the first to say, "Hello."
4. Live beneath your means.
5. Treat everyone like you want to be treated.
6. Never give up on anybody. Miracles happen.
7. Forget the Joneses.
8. Never deprive someone of hope. It may be all he has.
9. Pray not for things, but for wisdom and courage.
10. Be tough-minded but tenderhearted.
11. Be kinder than necessary.
12. Don't forget, a person's greatest emotional need is to feel appreciated.
13. Keep your promises.
14. Learn to show cheerfulness, even when you don't feel like it.
15. Remember that overnight success usually takes about 15 years.
16. Leave everything better than you found it.
17. Remember that winners do what losers don't want to do.
18. When you arrive at your job in the morning, let the first thing you say brighten everyone's day.
19. Don't rain on other people's parades.
20. Never waste an opportunity to tell someone you love them.

Life's Little Instruction Book © 1991 by H. Jackson Brown.
Published by Rutledge Hill Press, Inc., Nashville, Tenn.

81. Kaylea Nixon | MCKINNEY, TEXAS

If the well-worn edges and abundant coffee stains are any indication, this tiny piece of paper holds big purpose.

Kaylea Nixon's father, Glenn Race, clipped the "Twenty Rules to Live By," an excerpt from *Life's Little Instruction Booklet*, from a newspaper long ago. She can still see her dad reading it each morning, coffee in hand. "Like brushing his teeth or saying 'I love you' before leaving for work," Kaylea says, "reading the list was part of his morning ritual."

"He used the list to set the intention for his day," she says.

Glenn passed away suddenly in 2014. It was at his celebration of life that she realized he had truly been living his list every single day.

"I was stunned by how many stories were shared by the hundreds of people who attended. It felt like they were reading off this clipping, line by line," she says, even though none of them knew the clipping existed.

Several of her father's coworkers remembered him as the first person to welcome them into the office in the morning (see no. 3).

One told her he always kept his word (see no. 13).

More than a few people her father had mentored over the years told Kaylea that he had never given up on them (see no. 6).

"This list was the ethos he chose to live by," she says. "He left everything better than he found it." (See no. 16.)

Even though celebrating his life and love brought joy to Kaylea when her father passed, she will tell you honestly that she still struggles.

"So many things were left unsaid, and I didn't get to say good-bye." Having this well-loved piece of paper is a comfort for her. "It's almost as if my dad is whispering with a warm hug," she says. "Hey, Pumpkin, when was the last time you watched a sunrise? You should do that soon, it's good for the soul." (See no. 2.)

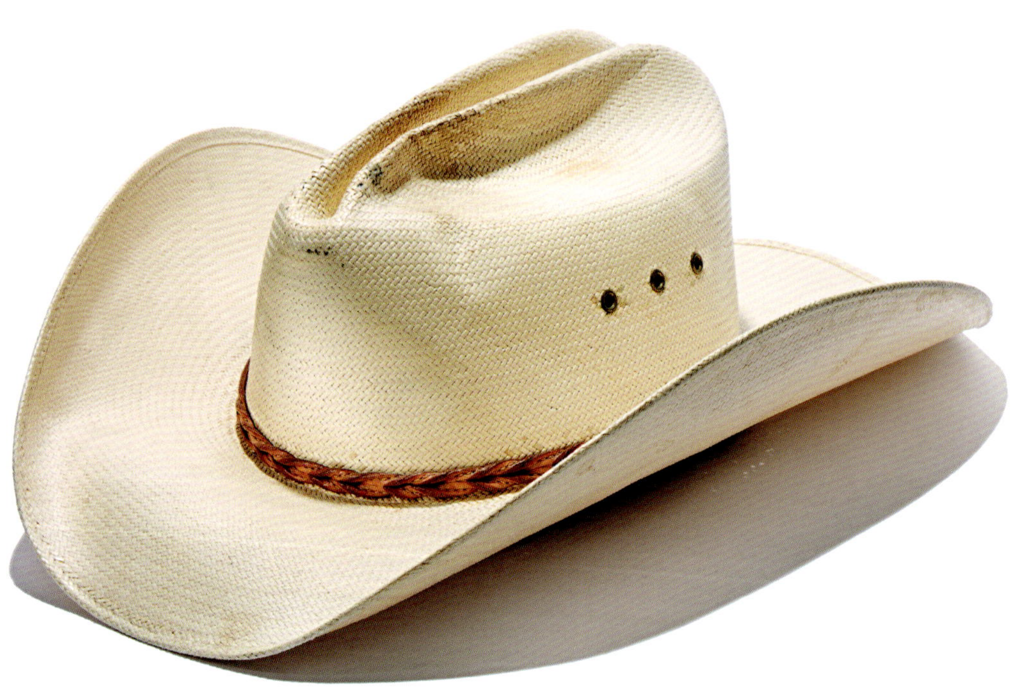

82. Jerry Novak | OMAHA, NEBRASKA

Once my brother and I were grown and well on our way to adulthood, my father, Jerry Novak, went out and bought himself two things: a bright-red sports car and a horse. The car didn't last—it sat too low to the ground. The horse offered a better view. To this day, my father still has framed pictures of his horse hanging in his house, right next to photos of my brother Andrew and me. Gold Rush was his name.

For ten years, Gold Rush loyally put up with my father, who was less cowboy and more of a shiny penny loafers and pressed shirts type of guy. Whenever we'd meet my dad for dinner, we couldn't go anywhere nice. He was always with Gold Rush, so he was always decorated with bits of hay, and he always, always smelled like a barn.

Dad is older now, and I'm sure he'd love to ride again but, he'll jokingly admit, that horse has left the barn. So, he recently gave me his cowboy hat from the Gold Rush years—a thin, airy summer-weight roping hat. It's beat up and stained, but it represents something I would like to remember about my dad—that he is a man who always had a certain motivation for fun and adventure. Human, yes, but our father just the same. One that fell in love with an incredible living thing rather than a sports car. This will be his legacy and the hat will tell his story.

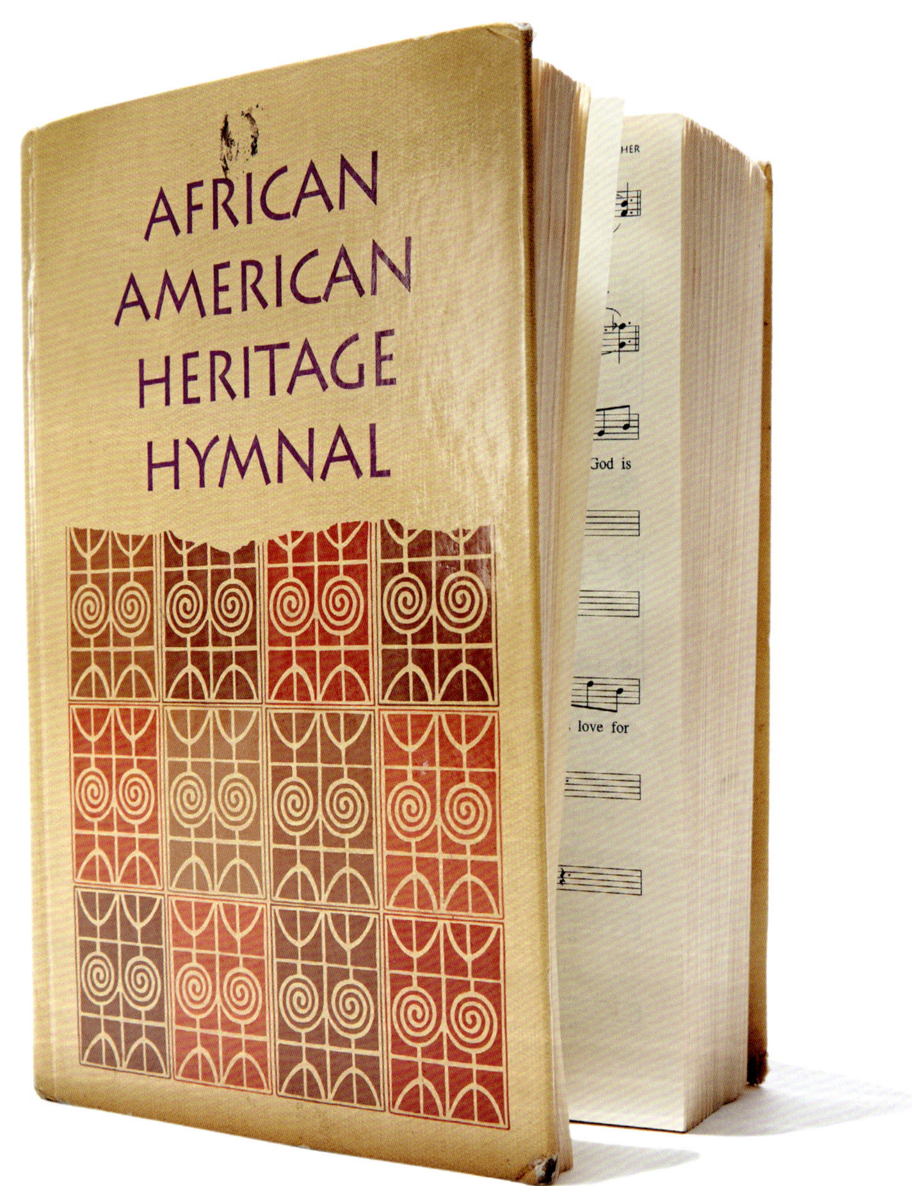
AFRICAN
AMERICAN
HERITAGE
HYMNAL
God is
love for

83. Essence Carson | LOS ANGELES, CALIFORNIA

Essence Carson credits a wooden record player in her grandparents' home for first introducing her ears to the wondrous sounds of music.

"I had an instant connection," she says.

Her grandparents saw the connection and enrolled her in her elementary school's band. The joy stuck—she played a part in her middle and high school bands, too. But she always had a connection to another beat—the basketball. And like playing music, she was really good at it.

"I was born and raised in the inner city of Paterson, New Jersey. There were few outlets for kids, so sports was the best way to stay out of trouble, make new friends, and learn what it takes to work together," she says. And shooting a ball into a makeshift hoop nailed to a tree brought just as much satisfaction as honing her skills on the court.

Essence's love for basketball and music was a natural life lesson in balance, responsibility, and time management. These life skills would lay the groundwork for a successful college education—and career.

Essence earned a basketball scholarship to Rutgers University, and from the minute she arrived, she was putting points on the board. Recognitions include Big East Academic All-Star and Big East Defensive Player of the Year, which she earned three times. Only one other female college player holds this record.

The New York Liberty drafted Essence straight out of college. In 2011, she was voted a WNBA All-Star. Her professional career spanned the next thirteen years, including a WNBA Championship with the Los Angeles Sparks.

Off the WNBA court, Essence was still playing that graceful balance to make room for music. Even while playing for the Sparks, she worked for Universal Music Group, serving on several of their labels. She is now the director of label operations and distribution at Guin Records, a boutique label tuned in to the development of emerging artists.

Although most of her career was spent making a name for herself on the court, her hymnal, pictured, a gift from her church choir, has always been her most valuable playbook.

"The hymnal symbolizes the role music has played in my life from a young age. It stands for family, faith, and unity. It represents the past, present, and the guiding light to my next stop on my musical journey."

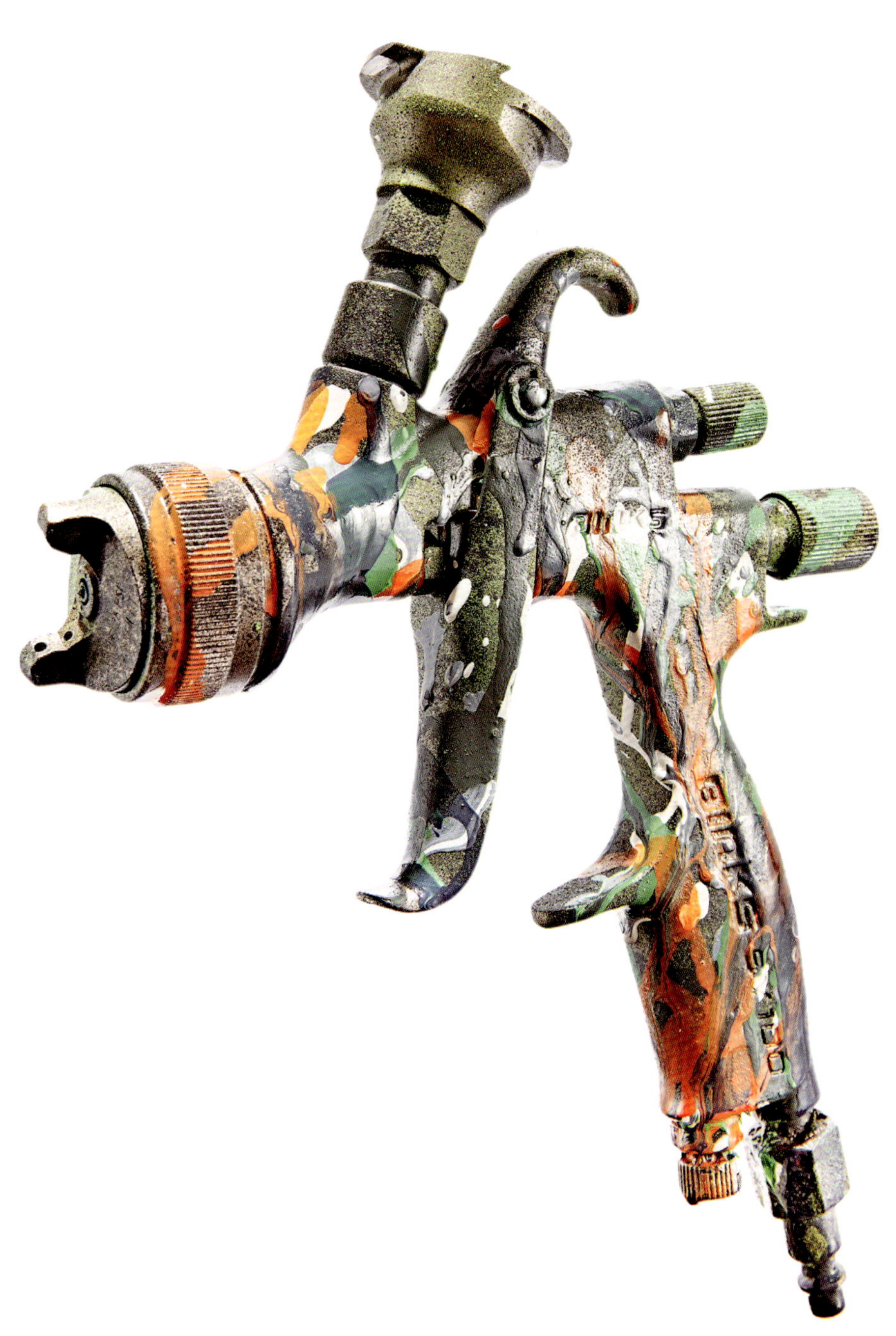

84. Meg Piercy | CHICAGO, ILLINOIS

Expecting your first child is a time full of unknowns. But once the baby is born, one thing is certain: You're gonna need a place to change all those diapers.

Meg Piercy and her husband, Joe, one day found themselves very pregnant but not so financially ready for all the demands a new baby makes on one's bank account. That's when they found a dresser in the alley behind their home. To some, it looked like the neighbor's trash. To Meg and Joe, it looked like their nursery's new changing table.

They took the dresser home and gave it a thorough cleaning. Next, Meg taught herself to sand and paint by watching videos on YouTube, and she gave the dresser a coat of bright-white paint to match the nursery. By the time their son was born, so was their future business.

The new parents started restoring other pieces together—often after they had put the baby to bed. Their work sold quickly on Craigslist and Facebook. Improving what already existed, it seemed, was proving to be a popular concept. The business quickly outgrew what the family home could handle. They moved the operation to a local storefront, showroom, and warehouse space, and began hiring a team to scale up the business.

Today, the company, which Joe affectionately named MegMade, has grown into something of a modern heirloom empire. Their team actively searches flea markets and garage sales for quality antique furniture in need of a makeover. Then, the pieces are restored at the company warehouse and customized according to client preference. No piece is off-limits—hutches, accent tables, and desks are only the start. No paint color is too wild. The concept earned MegMade an HGTV series called *Renovation Goldmine* in 2021.

The company recently expanded to lighting, upholstery, and paint. Meg now offers interior design services while Joe oversees aspects of production, marketing, and financials.

"As a small business, we wear many hats," Meg says. Today, a community of artisans, interior designers, and consumers look to MegMade for furniture with vintage vibes and modern attitude. The inventory is always changing, but the one thing you will always find is a Chicago mom of three armed with a dream and a paint sprayer.

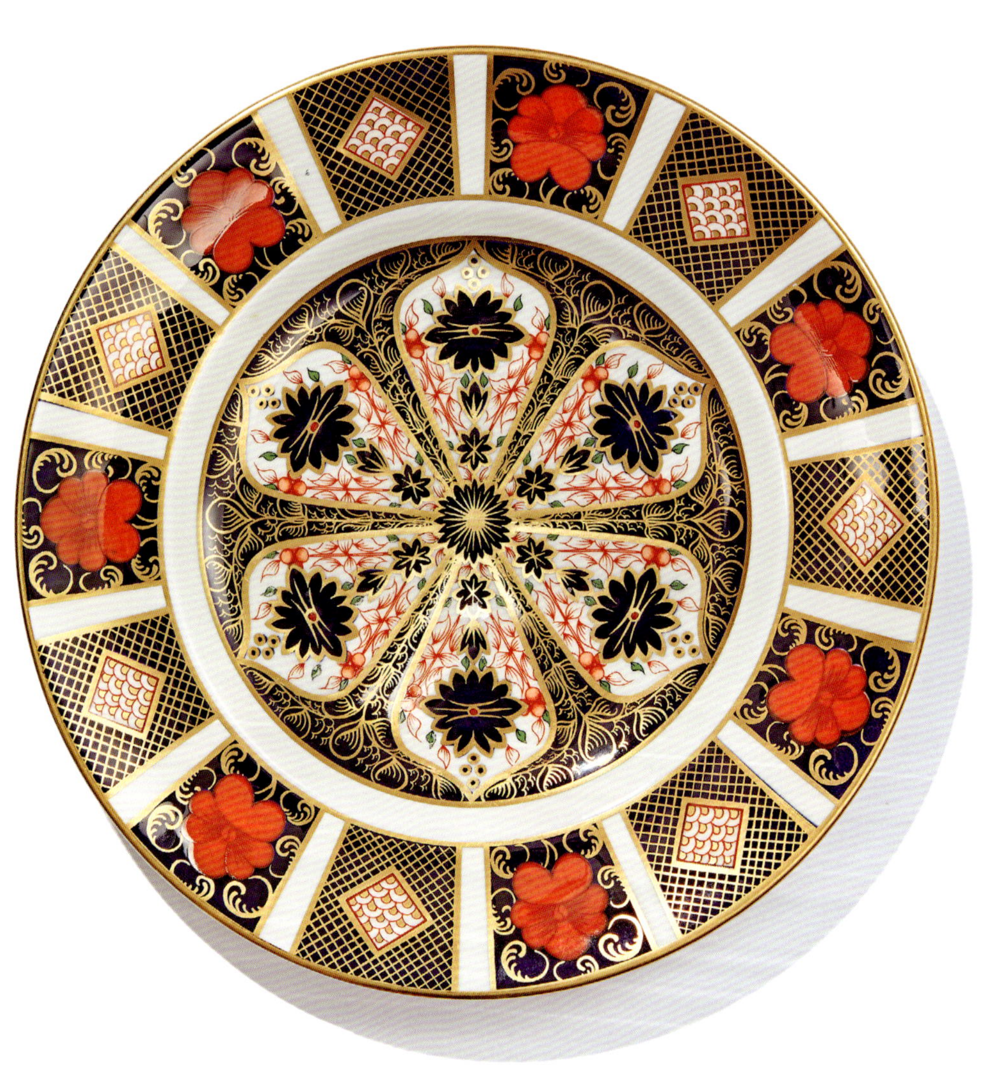

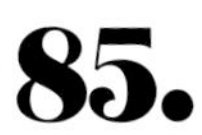 Josh Greene | NEW YORK, NEW YORK

The Royal Crown Derby china company first offered their Old Imari pattern in 1901, but by the 1970s, it was the contemporary and stylish thing to put on your dinner table (and on your wedding registry).

Josh Greene's mother, Wendy, was one of the young brides-to-be that chose Old Imari for her home. She put the entire set on her wedding registry and wedding guests got the dinner party started, so to speak, but the registry did not yield the complete set. So, several years after her wedding, Wendy went to Neiman Marcus and bought the rest of it herself.

"Twelve settings," her son, Josh, says. "Dinner plates, salad plates, cups, saucers, and servers." He grew up with an appreciation of the bold pattern and rich colors.

In the 1980s, when the Greene family moved, an entire box of Wendy's Royal Crown Derby china went missing. When she unpacked the moving boxes, somehow only six salad plates of the collection had arrived. Her set was once again incomplete.

As Josh grew older, his mom did a thing many moms do—she started to think about passing her treasures on to her kids. Wendy had crystal and sterling, and Josh adored it. But all he really wanted, he remembers, was the Royal Crown Derby china. It didn't matter that only six salad plates remained. "It was the one thing I really felt the beauty in," he says. And he's a professional at finding beauty—both literally and figuratively. Josh is the principal of his own interior-design firm, Josh Greene Design, and was named to the *Architectural Digest* 100 list in 2021.

Recently, Josh bought a new home, and his mother gave him the plates as a gift. They have a healthy serving of symbolism for him, and he plans to build back the set, piece by piece, so that he can have their beauty—and the story—at his own dinner table.

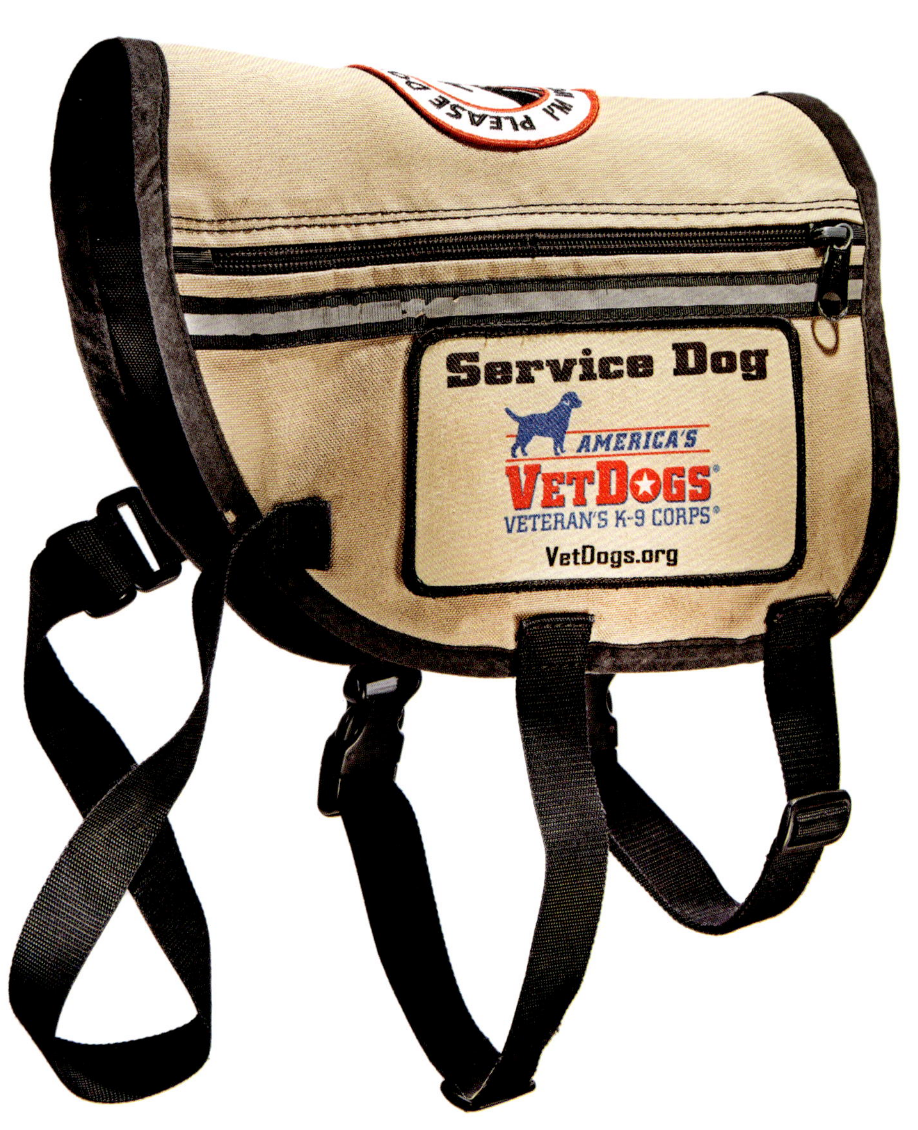

Service Dog
AMERICA'S
VETDOGS®
VETERAN'S K-9 CORPS®
VetDogs.org

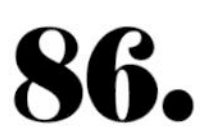

Gretchen Evans | BRUNSWICK, MAINE

Gretchen Evans is one of the most decorated female veterans in the United States. She enlisted at the age of nineteen and served the army in so many capacities in the following twenty-seven years, her career could fill this book several times.

In 2005, as command sergeant major in Afghanistan, a rocket blast left her deaf and with a traumatic brain injury. Her injuries forced her into a new kind of battle—retirement.

"I had lost my identity as a soldier and a leader," she says. "I was uncomfortable in a culture I had not been a part of for twenty-seven years. And I was deaf. My days were spent trying to convince myself I still had a purpose outside of the military."

She didn't know it yet, but what seemed like the end of life as she knew it was actually the beginning of her next tour of duty. At the time, physical activity was one of the few things that felt good and familiar to Gretchen and helped with her PTSD. But while out for a run one day, she was hit by a cyclist, thrown into traffic, and broke her clavicle.

"Another kick to the curb," she says. The cyclist didn't know, of course, that she was unable to hear his shout of "passing you on your left."

At the hospital, doctors chastised Gretchen for being out on the road alone. Their message was loud and clear—with her deafness, she was different now. She couldn't do things she used to do. Gretchen was running dangerously low on hope.

"But then I got angry," she says. "And I thought, 'No. I want my life back. I want to live.'" At the hospital, her audiologist suggested the possibility of a service dog. Gretchen felt a flicker of hope in her chest.

Once home and recovering from her injuries, she discovered an organization called America's VetDogs. They provide veterans and first responders with service dogs at no cost. Their mission statement resonated with Gretchen: "Our mission is to help those who have served our country honorably live with dignity and independence."

Gretchen recalls typing a one-sentence message to them: Can you help me? She clicked send and prayed. They responded in fifteen minutes with a one-word message of their own: Yes.

"For the first time since my injuries, I had hope," she says.

America's VetDogs had never trained a dog for a deaf person, but they were not deterred. They trained a Labrador/golden retriever named Aura to hear for Gretchen. Aura could alert her to sounds such as the doorbell, traffic, text alerts on her phone, people behind her, and just about anything that made a sound. Gretchen too trained before meeting Aura.

On the day VetDogs handed Gretchen the leash, she knew her life had changed. "I felt the love flow from Aura's leash attached to her collar through my hand into my heart like a strike of lightning. I had ears that could hear, I had a partner that went everywhere with me, I had unconditional love, I had a battle buddy. I had *hope*."

With her heart and hope revived, Gretchen wasted no time stepping back into a life that felt right for her—one of service and leadership. In 2019, she founded Team Unbroken, an organization of mostly veterans who survived life-changing injuries and who compete, together, in athletic events. Their rally cry is fitting: "What's within you is stronger than what's in your way."

The team navigates jungles, cliffs, and extreme conditions in all kinds of athletic competitions with Gretchen as their leader. "To prove to the world we are not broken," she says.

For her vast and continued contributions through Team Unbroken, Gretchen received the Pat Tillman Award for Service in 2022. As Gretchen took the stage to accept her award, Aura, now retired, watched comfortably from the audience with Gretchen's husband. Their second service dog, Rusty, accompanied Gretchen to the stage. She thanked Rusty for his service. They wore matching tuxedo shirts.

What's within you is stronger than what's in your way.

—Team Unbroken motto

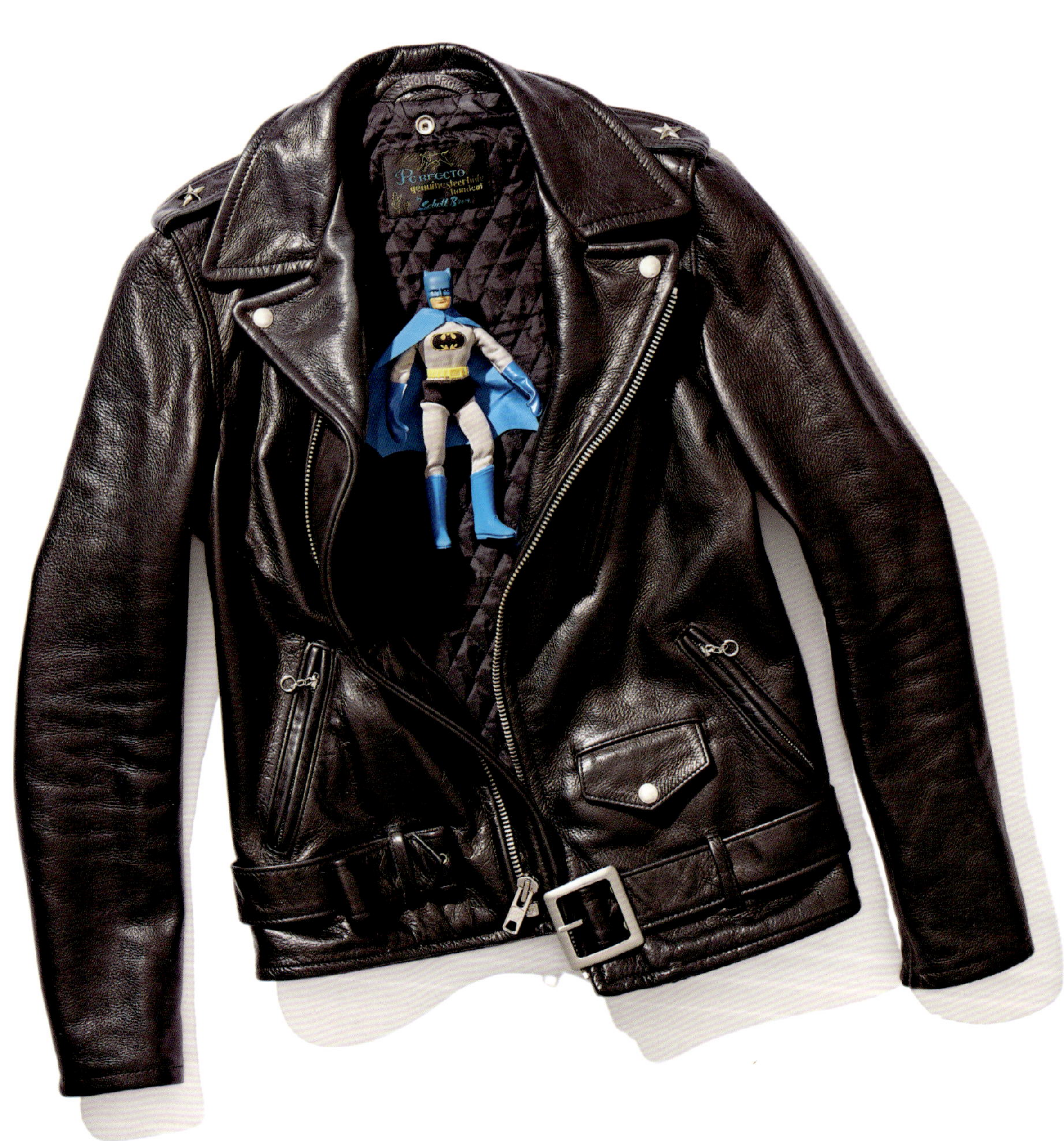
PERFECTO

Vlad Duthiers holds a master's degree from Columbia School of Journalism, won an Emmy for his work with CNN in Haiti after the 2010 earthquake, and is a Peabody-winning reporter for his work in Nigeria when Boko Haram kidnapped nearly three hundred teenage girls. He is a CBS News national correspondent. He speaks Haitian Creole, and French, and is learning Mandarin. Ask him about all of this and he will not hesitate to set the record straight.

"I'm just forever a nerdy, geeky kid," he says.

Vlad spent a lot of his childhood on his own, surrounding himself with books and music. He had only a few friends, and most of them were superhero figurines.

"I was a child of immigrants who grew up speaking French, a bookworm with a difficult-to-pronounce name, which often made me the target of bullies," he says. "I was the opposite of cool."

Yet Vlad was enamored by kings of cool like Marlon Brando and Elvis. When he first saw Henry Winkler as the Fonz swagger across the television screen wearing his trademark black leather jacket, he had to have one. He saved enough money from babysitting his little brother to buy a leather jacket—the "Perfecto" from legendary motorcycle jacket designer Irving Schott.

Strutting down the halls of his high school, he may have looked cool, but he was still the same inside. "It didn't matter what I wore," he says. "I was, in fact, a huge nerd. My life revolved around *Star Wars*, *Star Trek*, Dungeons and Dragons, and comic books." He loved Batman the most. "He doesn't have superpowers. He's just smart," notes Vlad.

These days, the Perfecto Vlad purchased as an adult, pictured with Batman, is his uniform when he is not on TV in a suit and tie. He has a loving wife, a daughter, a vibrant career, and a wonderful community of friends and colleagues.

Dare we say Vlad has officially achieved coolness? Again, he'll set the record straight.

"Anytime I start to feel cool—because of all the amazing things I get to do in my job—I just think about my childhood geekdom that gave me so much joy during periods in my life that often felt very bleak. And I realize, it doesn't really matter what people think. It only matters how I feel. And in my Schott Perfecto, I feel like me. Hero. Geek. Bibliophile. Dreamer."

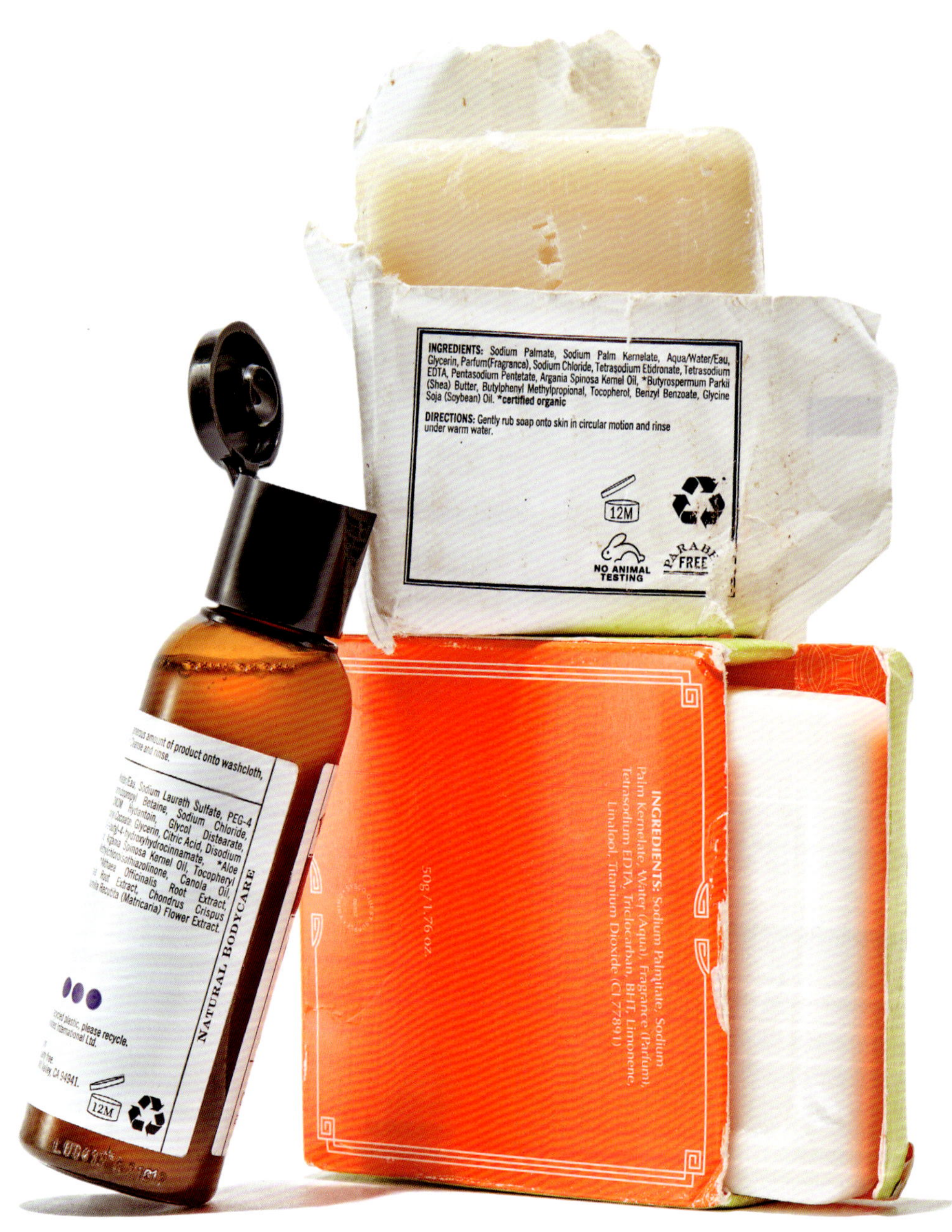
INGREDIENTS: Sodium Palmate, Sodium Palm Kernelate, Aqua/Water/Eau, Glycerin, Parfum(Fragrance), Sodium Chloride, Tetrasodium Etidronate, Tetrasodium EDTA, Pentasodium Pentetate, Argania Spinosa Kernel Oil, *Butyrospermum Parkii (Shea) Butter, Butylphenyl Methylpropional, Tocopherol, Benzyl Benzoate, Glycine Soja (Soybean) Oil. *certified organic
DIRECTIONS: Gently rub soap onto skin in circular motion and rinse under warm water.
12M
NO ANIMAL TESTING
NATURAL BODYCARE
INGREDIENTS: Sodium Palmitate, Sodium Palm Kernelate, Water (Aqua), Fragrance (Parfum), Tetrasodium EDTA, Triclocarban, BHT, Limonene, Linalool, Titanium Dioxide (CI 77891)
50g / 1.76 oz

88. Derreck Kayongo | ATLANTA, GEORGIA

If you've checked into a hotel room recently and noticed that the collections of complimentary soap bars and shampoos have been replaced by large pump bottles attached to the wall, it's due in part to Derreck Kayongo.

"Soap is like air," he says. "You never miss it until you don't have any." He knows this firsthand. Derreck and his family fled Uganda for a refugee camp in Kenya when war broke out. There, he noticed so much sickness. And one of the reasons was simple: There was no soap, a basic tool in combating bacteria and disease. This was a hard thing for Derrick to accept. His father had been a soap maker for much of his life. He knew the value of soap all too well.

Derreck eventually came to America for college, landing first at a hotel in Philadelphia before starting school. One of the first things he noticed was the many different soaps in the hotel bathroom.

"Soap for face, soap for hair, soap for body," he says. It seemed excessive. And it was. When he learned American hotels threw out eight million bars of soap a year, he decided to do something about it.

And so began The Global Soap Project—a program designed to collect and sanitize used bars of soap from hotels and distribute them to communities in need. The endeavor was one part environmental—soap chemicals slow down earth's decomposition process and pollute water supplies. The other half was humanitarian—there were communities in Africa in dire need of soap.

If the idea of repurposing soap sounds strange, Derreck explains that it's just science. "Germs need to breathe to procreate," Derreck says. "So you suffocate them." The sanitization process involves peeling back the surface of a bar of soap, which removes 90 percent of the bacteria. From there, the bars are crushed and put into a vacuum where all the air is removed.

With the help of the Centers for Disease Control and Prevention and some African-based nonprofits, The Global Soap Project delivered one hundred thousand tons of soap to organizations and communities in need. The project also caught the attention of the hotel group Hilton Worldwide, which donated 1.3 million dollars to help with distribution.

Derreck says The Global Soap Project inspired further collaboration with Hilton and other large hotel chains to address the need for further waste reduction in the industry. "Over time, it gave us all a clue that soap could be distributed in liquid form, and conditioners and shampoos in large containers, which would, in turn, cut down on waste. That idea populated the industry and it's now the norm rather than the exception," Derreck says.

Derreck says one of the biggest luxuries of having lived in America is being given the opportunity to solve a problem. Getting hotels to cut down on waste is an accomplishment of gigantic proportions, but Derreck is ever humble.

"America is a society of hardworking people who want to solve problems, and they're good at it," he says. "I'm very proud of how the hotels responded—they responded with innovation."

Next time you pump a dollop of soap or shampoo into your hands in a hotel room, it's not just for looks. It's for the greater good of the planet.

Soap is like air. You never miss it until you don't have any.

—Derreck Kayongo

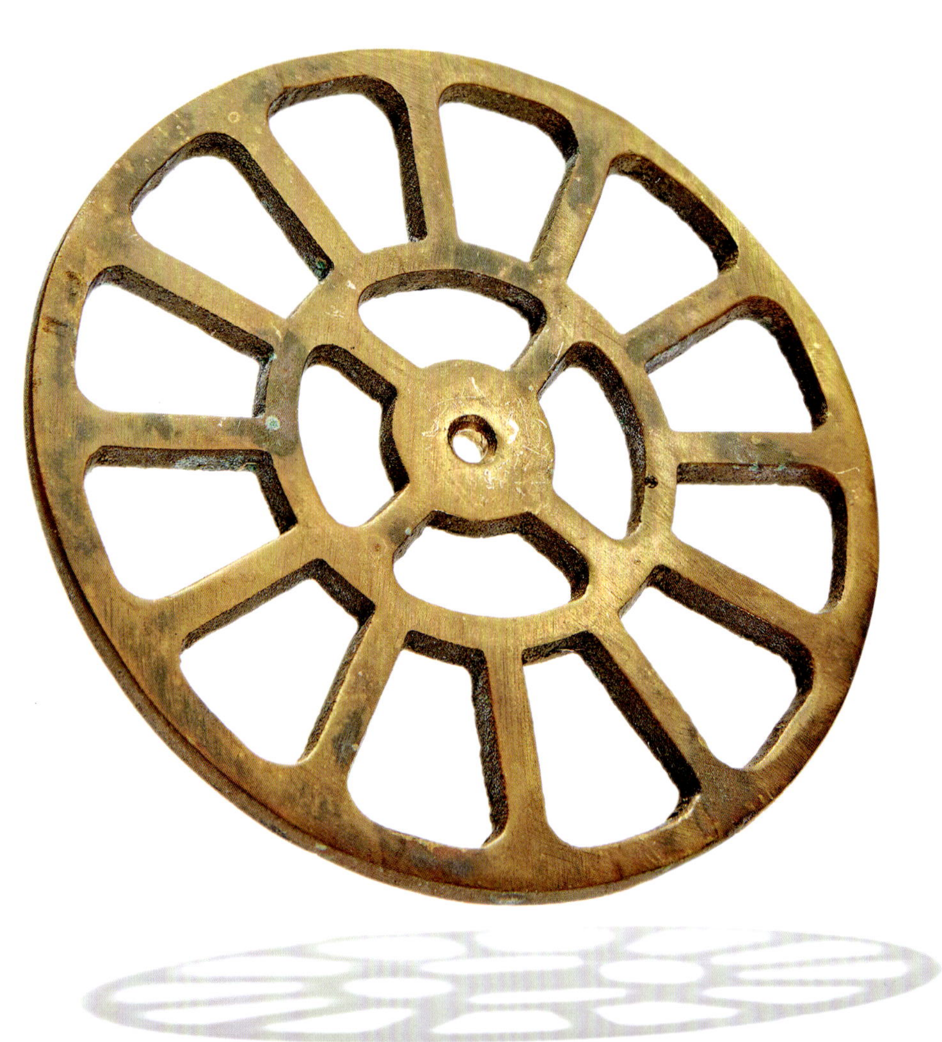

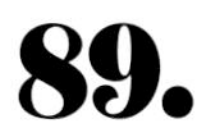 Kelly Cutrone | NEW YORK, NEW YORK

Fun fact: Kelly Cutrone's first job was as a kids' baseball umpire at her hometown ball field. Not so fun fact: The kids' parents weren't having it.

"Are you really putting a girl on the field? Get her out of there," they would scream as their kids took the field. She was thirteen. Many of the boos came from moms. This was Kelly's first brush with the societal construct that women were not equal to men. She was young but wise enough to know this was a total foul.

By her twenties, Kelly was beautiful, married to an artist, and making regular appearances in the social scene pages of *Vogue* magazine.

"I had done all the things society had told me to do to be successful," she reflects. "But it wasn't enough."

She soon found herself separated from her husband and the company she founded, living in a Los Angeles hotel, selling her books to pay the bills. That's when she had a chance encounter with a man at a bookstore. They had crossed paths at the distinct moment when Kelly needed to find something she had lost long ago—the power to be her true self. He would guide her to the teachings of the Divine Mother, a spiritual being and belief that true femininity is rooted in fierce compassion and intelligence, not looks or status. It was a startling contrast to the place society had relegated her to.

Today, she is a *New York Times* bestselling author, reality television personality, mother, and the force behind People's Revolution, a public-relations agency specializing in fashion and lifestyle brands. Her assertive and self-assured style of doing business is rooted in her spiritual connection and keeps her grounded in a world that once sidelined her. Her mission, both personally and professionally, is to keep the conversation about female equality front and center. And to make sure women know it's on them to support one another, not turn on each other, like those moms at the baseball field.

Pictured is the Mother's symbol, which hangs at the entrance to Kelly's home. It's her most tangible connection to the bigger power that keeps her in her own.

"It's not enough to sit and meditate," she says. "You have to connect with the divine and bring it down to where you are." And it's working.

No one is telling Kelly to get off the field now; she wouldn't if they did.

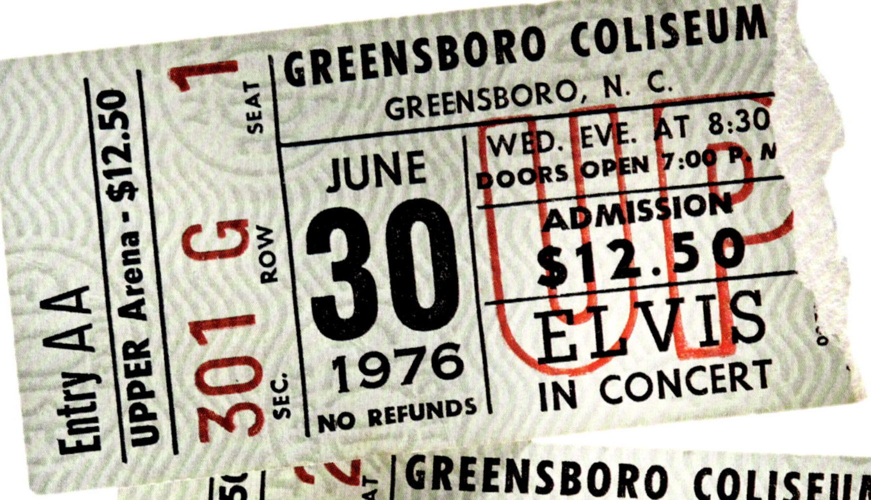
GREENSBORO COLISEUM
GREENSBORO, N. C.
Entry AA
UPPER Arena - $12.50
301 G 1
SEC. ROW SEAT
JUNE
30
1976
NO REFUNDS
WED. EVE. AT 8:30
DOORS OPEN 7:00 P. M
ADMISSION
$12.50
ELVIS
IN CONCERT
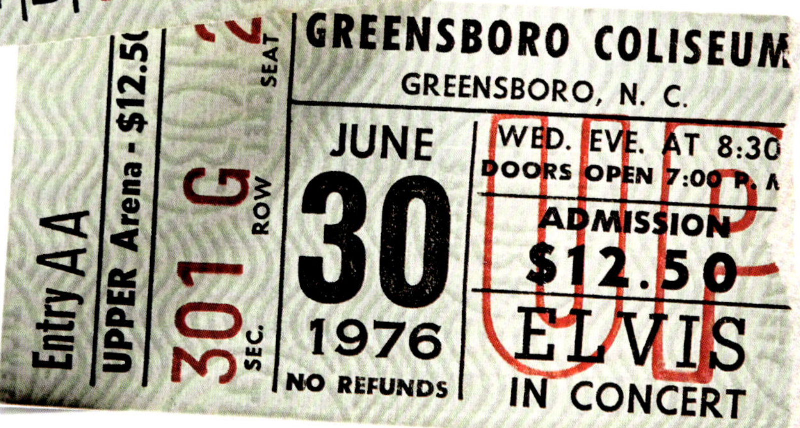
GREENSBORO COLISEUM
GREENSBORO, N. C.
Entry AA
UPPER Arena - $12.50
301 G
SEC. ROW SEAT
JUNE
30
1976
NO REFUNDS
WED. EVE. AT 8:30
ADMISSION
$12.50
ELVIS
IN CONCERT

90. Adam Lucas | CHAPEL HILL, NORTH CAROLINA

Adam Lucas knows his wife, Jenn, well, and when it comes to gift giving, she prefers experiences over things.

"We've been on trips, we've had unique dinners, we've gone to concerts," he says. "But one of her favorite experiences will always be missing." Jenn was born just months before Elvis Presley's death, but she grew up to be a superfan. She's been to Graceland and has more than a few Elvis T-shirts in her closet. When the 2022 biopic *Elvis* was released, she made sure they had tickets for opening day.

The one thing she will never get to do, however, is see Elvis live in concert. So, Adam did the next best thing—he bought her tickets to one. (It was a symbolic gesture—the tickets were collector's items from eBay.)

"What could be a more unique experience," Adam says, "than getting to answer the question 'What did your husband get you for Christmas?' with 'Tickets to an Elvis concert'?"

The ticket stubs are from a venue near the couple's Chapel Hill, North Carolina, home and remain a symbol of Adam's creative commitment to special adventures. Elvis may be the King of Rock and Roll, but Adam is the king of gift giving.

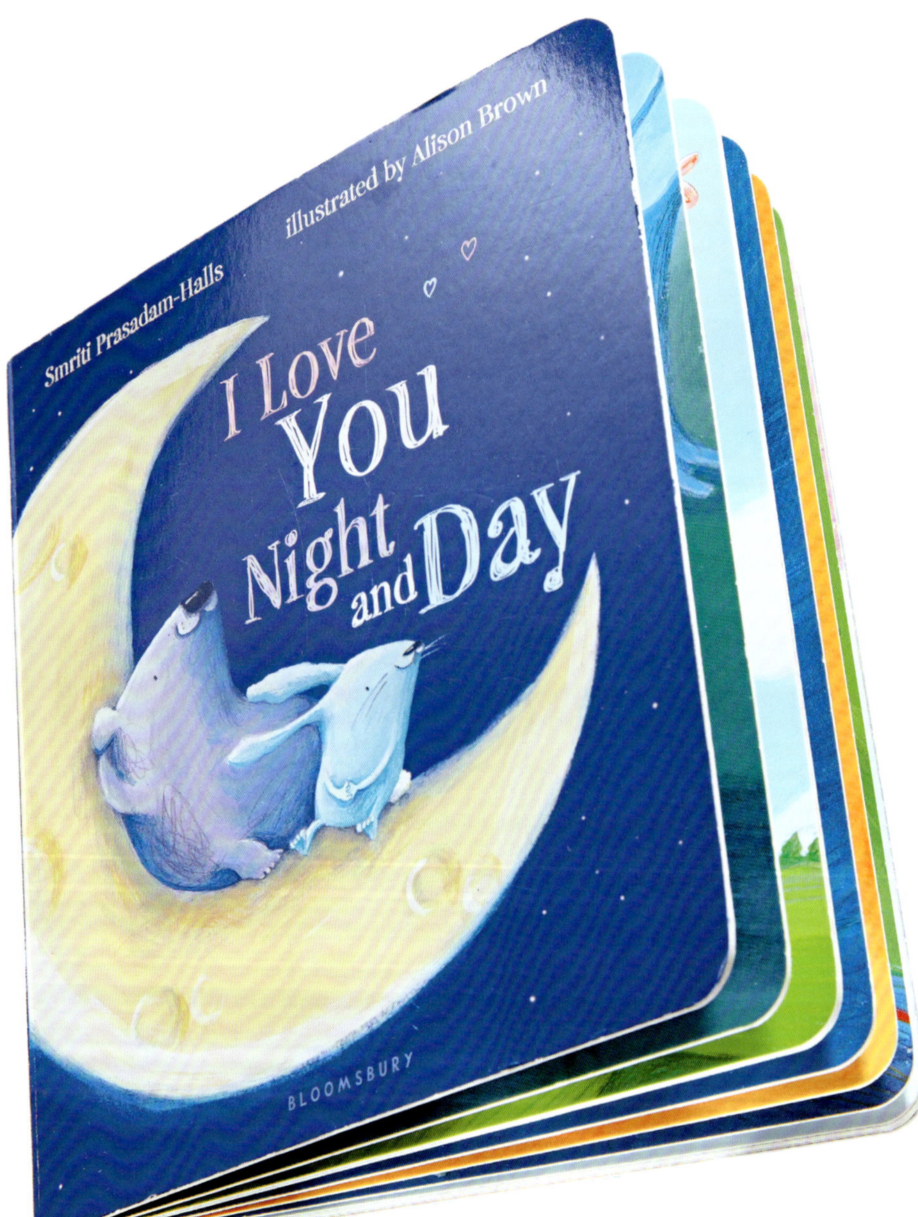
Smriti Prasadam-Halls
illustrated by Alison Brown
I Love You Night and Day
BLOOMSBURY

Nikki Cohn and her husband, Joe Knepell, went through a lot to start a family of their own. Multiple failed IVF attempts and a miscarriage of twins finally led them to a new prospect—surrogacy.

"It took me a while to wrap my head around having someone else carrying my child," Nikki says. "But I wanted to be a mom. So, after trying so hard to do it on my own, I realized that if I wanted to be one, we would have to accept a different route."

And it worked. In 2018, Nikki and Joe welcomed their daughter, Marlow. She was a miracle not only by her mere existence but also by the fact that by the age of only two, she was speaking in full sentences, commanding the table at dinner parties, and could recite the Pledge of Allegiance with only a little help. She was a tiny but enormous treasure, and they wanted more.

By August of 2020, the gestational carrier who carried Marlow was pregnant again, and Nikki and Joe were preparing the nursery for their next addition, their son, Mason Isadore Knepell. But when the surrogate hadn't felt him move for a bit, she went to the emergency room and discovered there was no longer a heartbeat. Mason was stillborn at thirty-five weeks—there was, and still has not been, any reasons or explanation.

The days after Mason's death were surreal and a blur, Nikki says. Burying a child was not something they ever expected to do.

Mason was buried with things to connect him to his family—a stuffed animal that belonged to his great-grandma, blankets his grandma and aunt had been knitting for him, notes from Nikki and Joe, and a crayon tracing of Marlow's handprint. He was also buried with one of his big sister Marlow's favorite books, *I Love You Night and Day*, written by Smriti Prasadam-Halls, illustrated by Alison Brown, and published by Bloomsbury Publishing Plc.

In time, Nikki bought Marlow another copy of her own, pictured, as a way of keeping her kids connected. "It's something for them to share," Nikki says. "She's too young to understand now. But his memory is all we have and she will know of her brother's existence."

Nikki will bravely tell you that her grief doesn't go away. "It gets to be manageable, but it will always be there," she says. She has advice for anyone experiencing the same. "Keep their memory alive, say their name, do something in honor of them every year. Mourn, grieve, and do whatever you need to do. There are no wrong emotions."

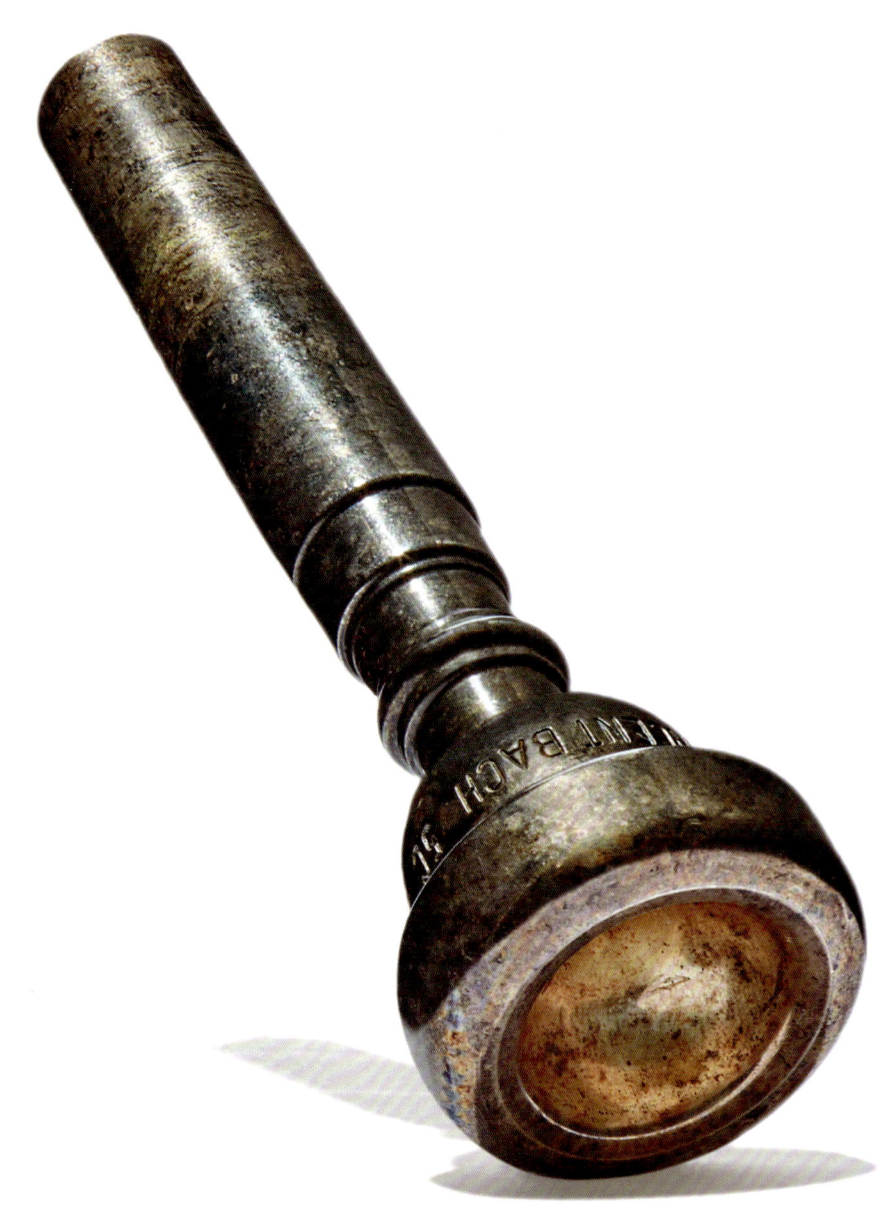
BACH

92. Ron Lieber | BROOKLYN, NEW YORK

One of Ron Lieber's earliest musical memories as a kid is the delivery of a Baldwin piano to his home, an early birthday gift from his parents. The gift of music would keep giving for generations.

Ron's father, Fred, picked up a trumpet in the 1950s during a junior high school loan program. He played in several dance bands in college, and one of them landed a single on the Indianapolis pop charts in the early 1960s. But among Fred's favorite performances were the duets he played with his son—Fred on trumpet and Ron on the Baldwin piano. The bond of music was so powerful, it didn't stop in the family living room.

Fred and all of his kids—Ron, David, and Stephanie—made a tradition of getting out into the world to see live music together for years.

"My best memories of him are those musical experiences we shared together," Ron says. "My dad was an accountant and thought about money a lot. He had concluded that experiences mattered more to him than stuff," Ron says. They attended the Newport Folk Festival and the New Orleans Jazz and Heritage Festival, and they saw the Grateful Dead, among other musical groups. They saw and did as much as possible as the years went on, even seeing the musical *Hamilton* just as the COVID-19 pandemic was beginning.

"He was an equal-opportunity music lover, and so am I," Ron says. "Seeing him light up at Jazz Fest with my daughter was the biggest possible treat."

When Ron's father was diagnosed with ALS, things changed in many ways for the family. Sometimes, just getting his wheelchair-bound father into the show venue would be the adventure.

"My favorite memory from a Bruce Springsteen show in Miami was getting him inside," Ron says. "He had been a bit skeptical of the wheelchair-accessible seats." But the experience turned out to be deeply satisfying. The seats were fantastic. Fred was grateful. The show was epic. It was one of the last shows Ron would see with his father.

"I felt like it was our responsibility to bring him to as many events as possible where ecstatic joy was likely," Ron says of the years his father fought the illness.

This trumpet mouthpiece is the last physical connection the Lieber kids have to their father's love of music. "He wasn't able to play the last couple of years, but in the first year or so after his diagnosis, he would bleat out a few notes for his delighted grandchildren and then give them a chance to try playing. He was in his element in those moments, still trying to transmit enthusiasm to the littles. Now, it's our job to keep the music playing," Ron says.

Fred passed away in 2021, and on the second anniversary of his death, Ron spent the evening in tribute—at a Bruce Springsteen show, with his father's ashes in his pocket.

I felt like
it was our
responsibility
to bring
him to as
many events
as possible
where ecstatic
joy was likely.

—Ron Lieber

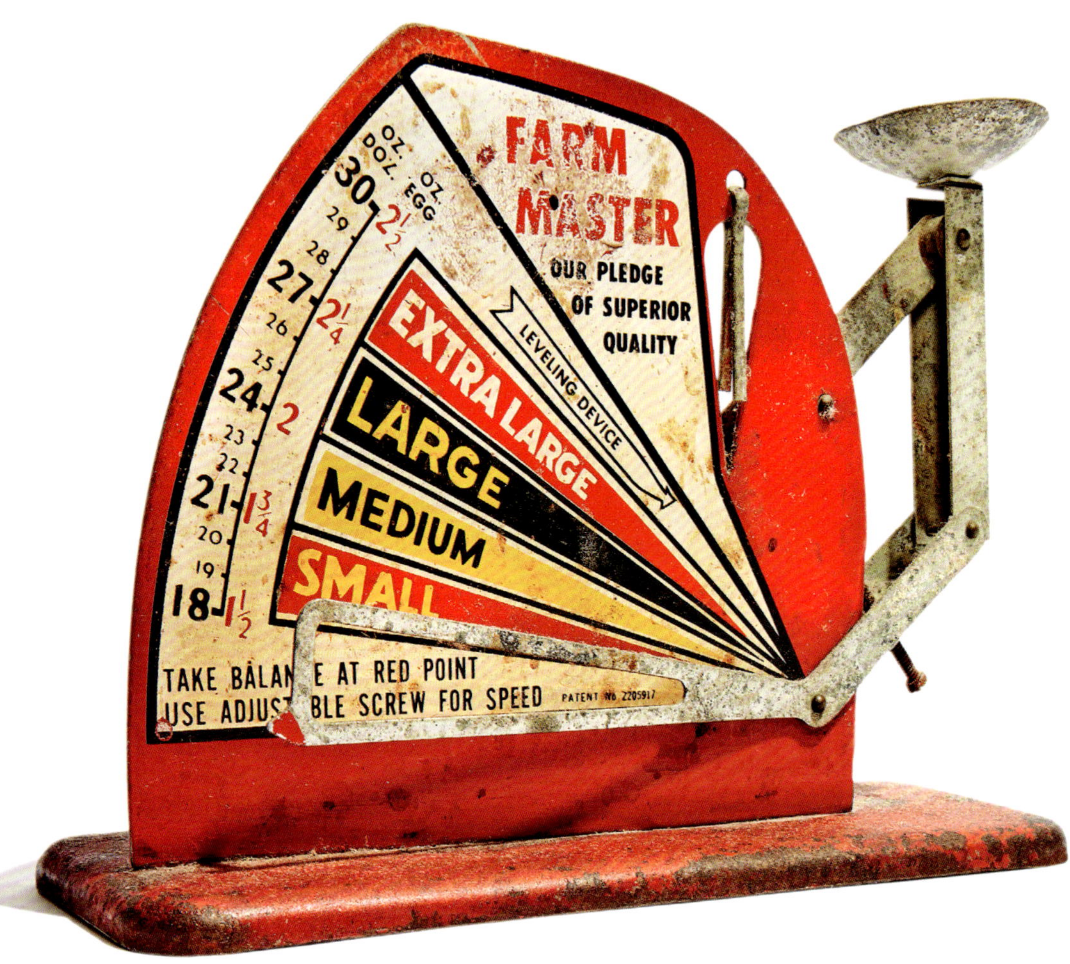

OZ. DOZ.
OZ. EGG
30
29
28
27
26
25
24
23
22
21
20
19
18
2½
2¼
2
1¾
1½
FARM MASTER
OUR PLEDGE OF SUPERIOR QUALITY
LEVELING DEVICE
EXTRA LARGE
LARGE
MEDIUM
SMALL
TAKE BALAN E AT RED POINT
USE ADJUS BLE SCREW FOR SPEED

93. Dan Kluger | NEW YORK, NEW YORK

Chef Dan Kluger is a James Beard Award–winning chef who sharpened his knives in the kitchens of some of the food industry's most beloved stars. He is now the executive chef and owner of his own restaurant, Loring Place, in New York City's Greenwich Village, and recently opened another, Greywind. But one day in 2008, he was just a guy out with some friends, huddled around a pizza.

At the restaurant that day, beyond the table full of pizza, Dan spotted a vintage metal egg scale. It was a relic from another time but felt relevant and symbolic to him. He had to have it.

"It was a reminder that certain things always stay the same," Dan says. "The scale may be old, but the egg never changes." He was a young chef at the time, pulled between the grueling pace of restaurant life and a true passion for being there. The scale, he says, reminded him of balance.

Dan found an identical scale on eBay a few days later and bid on it. Over and over, he bid, and was outbid, until he finally lost the auction. The reason he lost the auction is because his friends were on the other end, outbidding him, in order to give it to their loving foodie friend.

The scale took on a heavier meaning that day—of true friendship and hospitality, symbolic of those special days spent gathered around a pizza with good people. Those kinds of days, Dan says, are what food is all about for him—the joy of breaking bread and sharing a meal together.

While the egg scale lives in Dan's home kitchen, its meaning follows him to work. In the kitchen at Loring Place, Dan's many years of passion and hard work come together. On any given night, you'll find the dining room full of guests, all huddled around plates of conventional dishes like hummus and pizza, which turn chic with his touch, or main courses that first appear uncomplicated but then taste exquisite. This is just Dan's style. He is a fine-tuned, wildly inventive, totally balanced chef who prepares one thing over and over that, no matter the season, never seems to change—the joy of a delicious, shared meal.

"That's why I cook," he says.

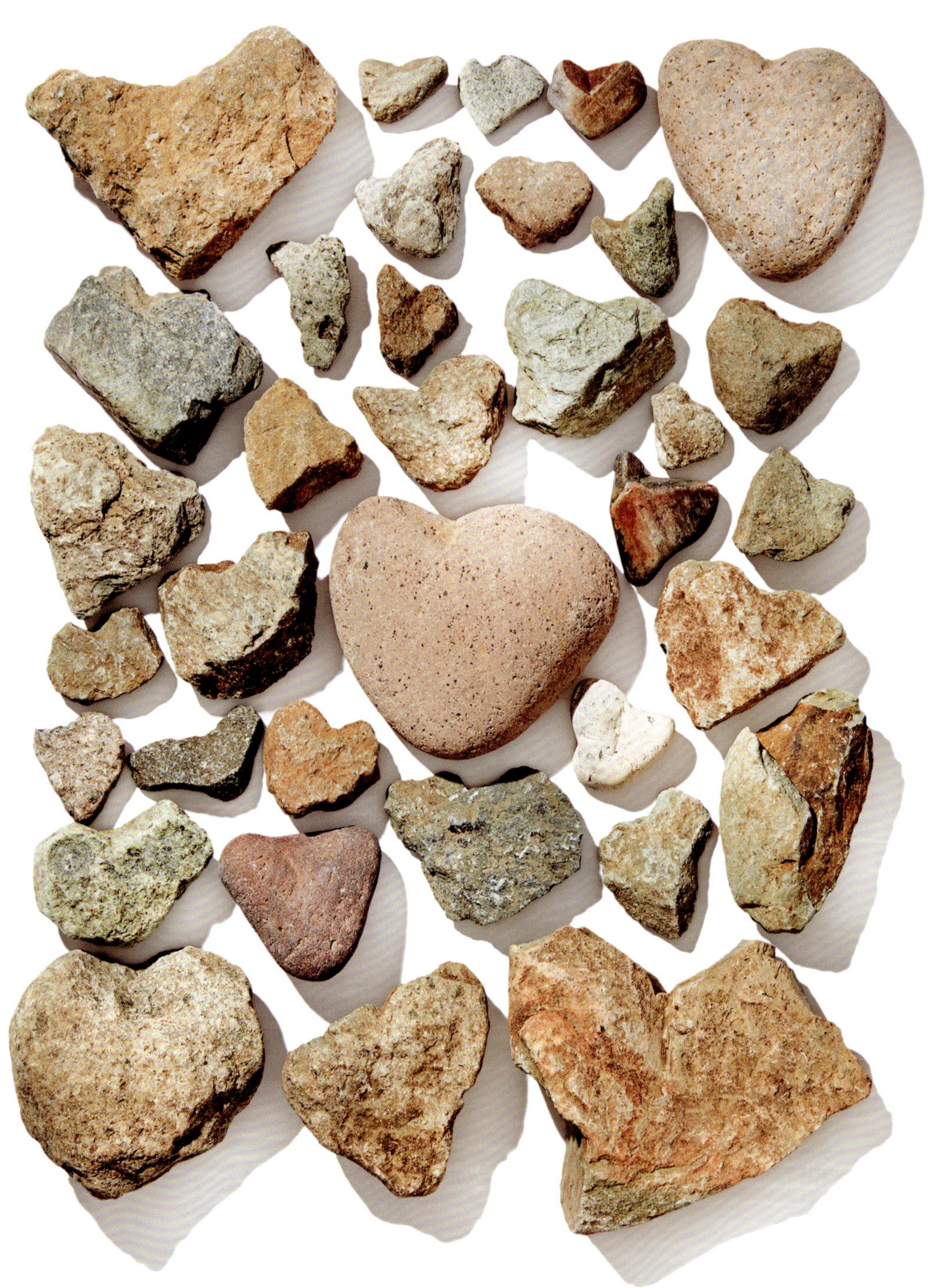

94. Jennifer Miller | ATHERTON, CALIFORNIA

The rustic Northern California family retreat called Feather River has tiny cabins, no phones, and no TVs. But there's plenty to do—enough to fill fifty years of memories for Jennifer Miller's family.

Classics such as bingo night in the lodge, Marco Polo in the pool, and bike rides to town for ice cream are some of the simple pleasures guests enjoy at Feather River. But if you were visiting with Jenn's family, you were found on the hiking trail headed for a lake—or three.

Jenn's mother, Sue, had a favorite route, on which she bestowed the name "the Bears" because it wound around three pristine alpine lakes—Cub, Little Bear, and Big Bear. Hiking this trail with family was Sue's happy place.

Jenn describes her mother as the picture of health. "She did yoga daily, walked five miles per day, and always made time for a one-hour nap from 4 to 5 p.m.," Jenn recalls. But in November of 2013, Sue was diagnosed with stage IV small cell lung carcinoma. Less than two years later, she was gone.

As the family scattered Sue's ashes in her happy place, next to one of the Bear lakes, they began to notice heart-shaped rocks around them. Jenn and her daughters began collecting them, calling them "heart rocks for Nana," pictured here.

Jenn, her dad, and her siblings have made the Bears hike an annual family tradition so the collection keeps growing—a symbol of the place their mom loved, the many memories she created for the family, and the many memories still yet to be discovered.

You got this!

I Love you!

And dont forget to move car.

95. Kate McCann | LAKEVILLE, CONNECTICUT

In a modern world where you can ask your smartphone to do just about anything for you, sometimes a good, old-fashioned handwritten note just hits different. Putting pen to paper is personal and multipurpose—love notes, reminders, or words of encouragement.

This note happens to cover all the bases. It's the triple crown of note writing. One part got-your-back, one part "I love you," finished with a dash of keeping it real.

The note is from Kate McCann's husband, Kevin. He wrote it one morning before leaving early for work. Kate was still asleep. Kate, an interior designer, still-life stylist, and Grey Dove Design founder, had a big project that day that was pulling her out of her comfort zone, hence Kevin's gentle reminder and words of encouragement. *I love you. Now move the car.*

Plus, she jokes, "If there was someone in our relationship that would forget to move the car, it would be me."

Together, Kate and Kevin have full lives—two jobs, two houses, two dogs. And though Kate says she and her husband typically have a divide-and-conquer approach to their lives, she is also quick to note that Kevin is the kind of guy who is always quick with extra support.

"It's in his core. If he can be of help or support, he steps up. He wants the best for me. We truly want to make each other's lives easier," Kate says.

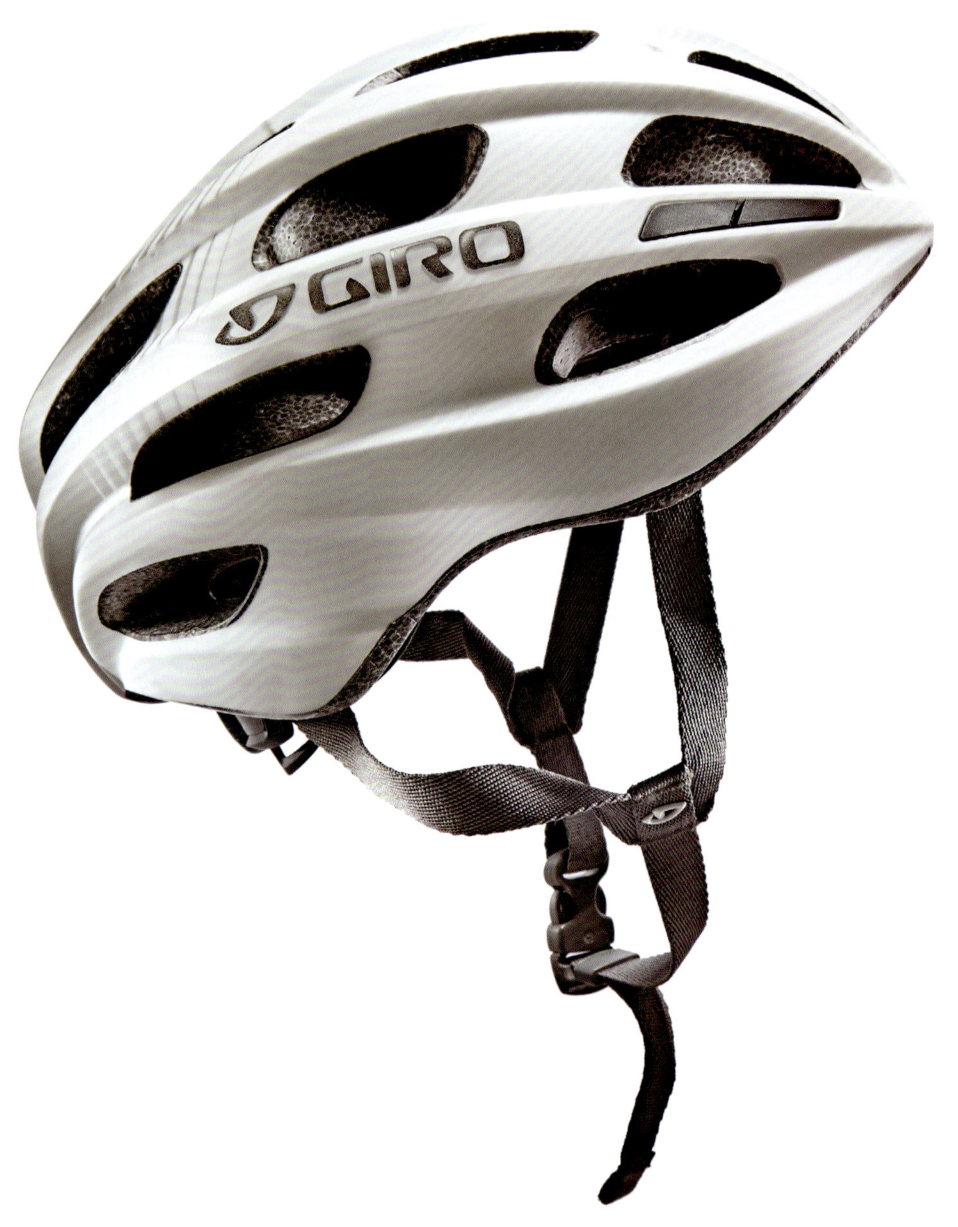
GIRO

Former congresswoman Gabby Giffords is no stranger to helmets. In 2011, doctors removed a portion of her skull after she was shot at a Tucson, Arizona, constituent-outreach event. For four months, she had to wear a helmet to protect her brain while it healed. She hated it.

"It was a reminder of everyone and everything taken from me and from our community that day," she says. Years of recovery and healing would ensue.

Thirteen years later, Gabby wears a different helmet. This one. She cycles on her three-wheel recumbent bike almost every day around her hometown of Tucson, in defiance of the partial paralysis she suffered.

She rides to reclaim her freedom and mobility. She rides to raise awareness for aphasia, a lasting language and communication impairment from her head injury. But mostly, Gabby rides out of sheer will—her personal motto is "move ahead, no matter what."

"I love cycling around the city I love so much, blasting eighties music and picking up trash. I see a lot of familiar faces and I love stopping to chat," Gabby says. "I always feel better after cycling."

One of her proudest cycling moments was a recent El Tour de Tucson, where she rode thirty-two miles. Her husband, Senator Mark Kelly, was beside her the entire way. Gabby's speech therapist, Fabi, also joined. Surrounding them was her Friends of Aphasia team. Fabi and Gabby cofounded Friends of Aphasia to raise community awareness, provide support, and conduct research for those living with compromised communication abilities due to a stroke or head injury.

The ride was a triumph for the woman who had once been in a medically induced coma. And every pedal forward changed her perspective on helmets.

"Helmets can be clunky and uncomfortable. They can remind you of your vulnerabilities and your mortality," Gabby says. "When I was in the hospital, that's what I was focused on. Now, thirteen years later and with my skull intact, I see my biking helmet as something empowering, not constraining. That's what I try to do with other aspects of my life too—to focus on what I can do and what I do have, not what's hard or missing," she says.

Gabby has another symbol of her progress. "I keep a piece of my skull in the freezer next to the empanadas. Both are reminders of how far I've come!"

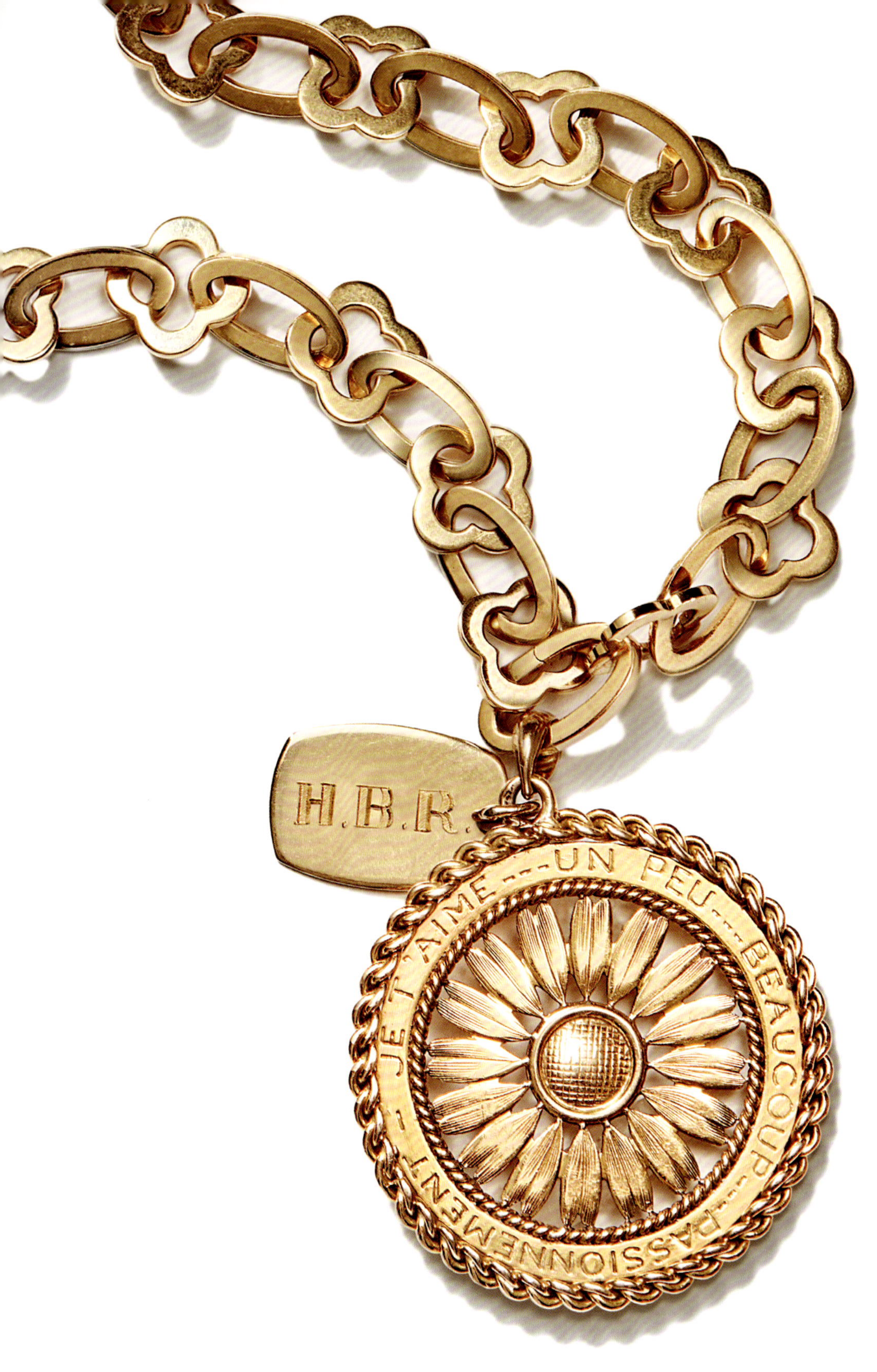
H.B.R.
JE T'AIME---UN PEU---BEAUCOUP---PASSIONNEMENT

Before her designs filled closets around the globe, before her foundation empowered thousands of women entrepreneurs, and before *Forbes* named her one of the most powerful women in the world, Tory Burch was a hardworking mom chasing a dream.

She still is. This necklace is her most treasured keepsake.

The necklace was a gift from Tory's father to her mother. Their love and worldly great taste, and their support for Tory, would inspire her to bring their brand of style and support to future generations. She credits her father for instilling in her the confidence to embrace ambition. She credits her mother for eternal optimism, effortless style, and priceless advice.

"Wear the dress, don't let the dress wear you," is one of Tory's favorite pieces of advice from her mom. Tory's namesake fashion label is an ode to this sentiment and to both of her parents.

First launched in 2004, the collection immediately hit a note many women shoppers and industry insiders liked the sound of: attainable, approachable luxury. The company continues to evolve—now on a global scale. But behind the trademark tunics, handbags, and ballet flats, Tory always had a deeper agenda. In 2009, she founded the Tory Burch Foundation to empower women and women entrepreneurs through funding, education, networking, and digital resources.

"Starting the foundation was in my business plan from day one," Tory says. "As a working mother who was raised by an incredible mom, I understood the obstacles women face, from access to capital to stereotypes, bias, and limited child-care and family support," she says.

To date, the foundation, with partners such as Goldman Sachs, Bank of America, Fearless Fund, and others, has provided support to thousands of women-owned businesses and has connected women entrepreneurs with millions in funding and low-interest loans. The foundation has long been regarded as one of the first to focus on serving women in business. But this shouldn't surprise you—Tory has always been ahead of the trends.

The necklace, which Tory's mother passed down to her, inspired the foundation's iconic logo. It remains a reminder that dreams can come true if you have the support and ambition to follow them.

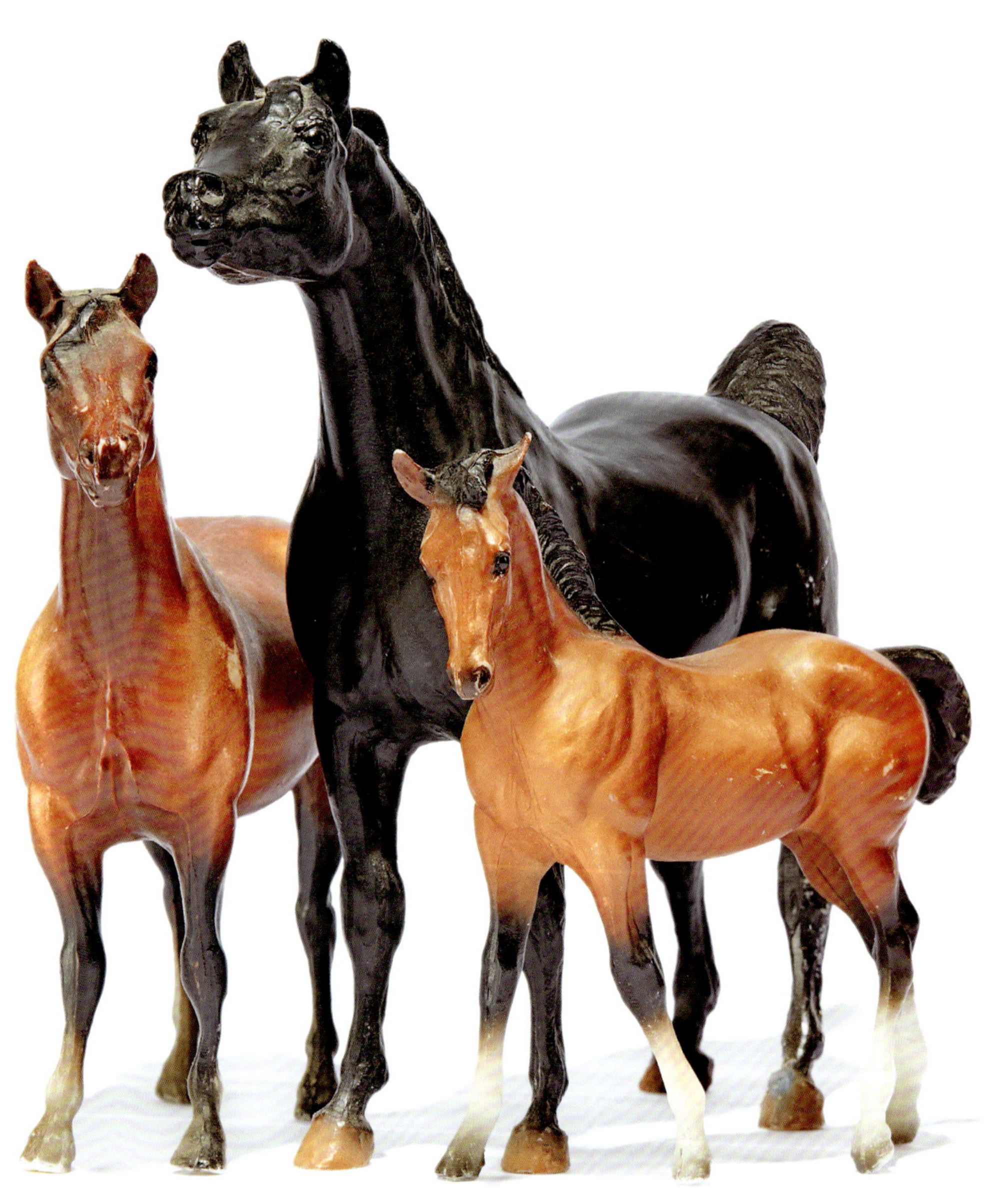

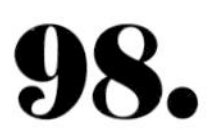 Elise Loehnen | LOS ANGELES, CALIFORNIA

Writer, editor, and podcast host Elise Loehnen has mixed feelings about having an attachment to "things," but she refuses to part with these Breyer model horses. Casually collected from eBay to use as part of the tablescapes for her wedding years ago, they now have a spot on her office shelf—a constant reminder of the animals that taught her so much about being human.

Elise thinks she was as young as ten or eleven when she and her brother would saddle up the family horses and ride into the woods near their Missoula, Montana, home. But she was old enough to understand that the horses had teachings to offer. Feeding and grooming them, even in blinding snow, was a lesson in responsibility. Simply hanging around them out in the summer pastures taught her to understand their subtle energies. Riding honed her ability to connect with other people in her life and be present in the moment.

"To work with such a large animal and to understand the dynamics of control and surrender is a pretty interesting experience, not in a dominance way but in a leaning-on-each-other-for-guidance kind of way—there's a mutual dependency," she says. "I think that early schooling in energy was instrumental in working with people."

As an adult, Elise went to work in media and made a successful career for herself in New York City and then in Los Angeles. Riding fell away from her life for a time, but it was too much a part of her for her to stay away for long. When she first rode again, she recalls, her husband had to ask if she was OK. She was crying. In a good way.

Elise freely admits she is the kind of high achiever that must make everything hard for herself in order for it to feel worthwhile. So, in the summer of 2022, back in Montana for a ride, she naturally chose the fastest and most challenging horse on the ranch. The aptly named Serrano indeed had a challenge for her. He threw her, knocking her unconscious. She suffered a concussion. (To this day she doesn't blame him for the accident.) Elise also broke her neck that day. She just didn't know it yet.

Elise will also freely admit she is the kind of person who doesn't even have the words "I'm not OK" in her vocabulary. To be back home, injured, was causing some serious anxiety. Her instinct has always been to march on and not be a burden. But she had a family to care for and a house to keep in order. Yet she was in so much pain that all she could do was give the kids an iPad and stare at the laundry from the couch.

A week later, a doctor discovered she had a broken neck. She was also a walking miracle—she should have allowed the "I'm not OK" and sought treatment immediately. But her neck could be healed with a brace, and for that she felt grateful, lucky, and humbled. Her neurosurgeon told her she needed to ride again. He literally told her to *get back in the saddle.*

Once medically cleared, Elise headed back to Montana with her son and got back on a horse. With trepidation, yes. But she was no stranger to trusting a horse's energy. This time, she got exactly who she needed in that moment—a gentle, easy soul.

"A mare named Tequila, who, as her name suggests, goes well with everything, in every situation. A horse who very much took care of me," Elise says.

And guess what? The easy ride was one of her most memorable. For the woman who admits she needs everything to be an extraordinary challenge, this was a learning moment from the incredible creatures who have been her lifelong teachers.

"It's OK to not ride the wildest horses," Elise says. "And it's OK to not be OK." She also offers some wisdom we can all identify with whether we ride or not. "It's a very different experience to go flying off a horse when you're seven than when you're forty-two!"

It's OK
to not
ride the
wildest
horses.

—Elise Loehnen

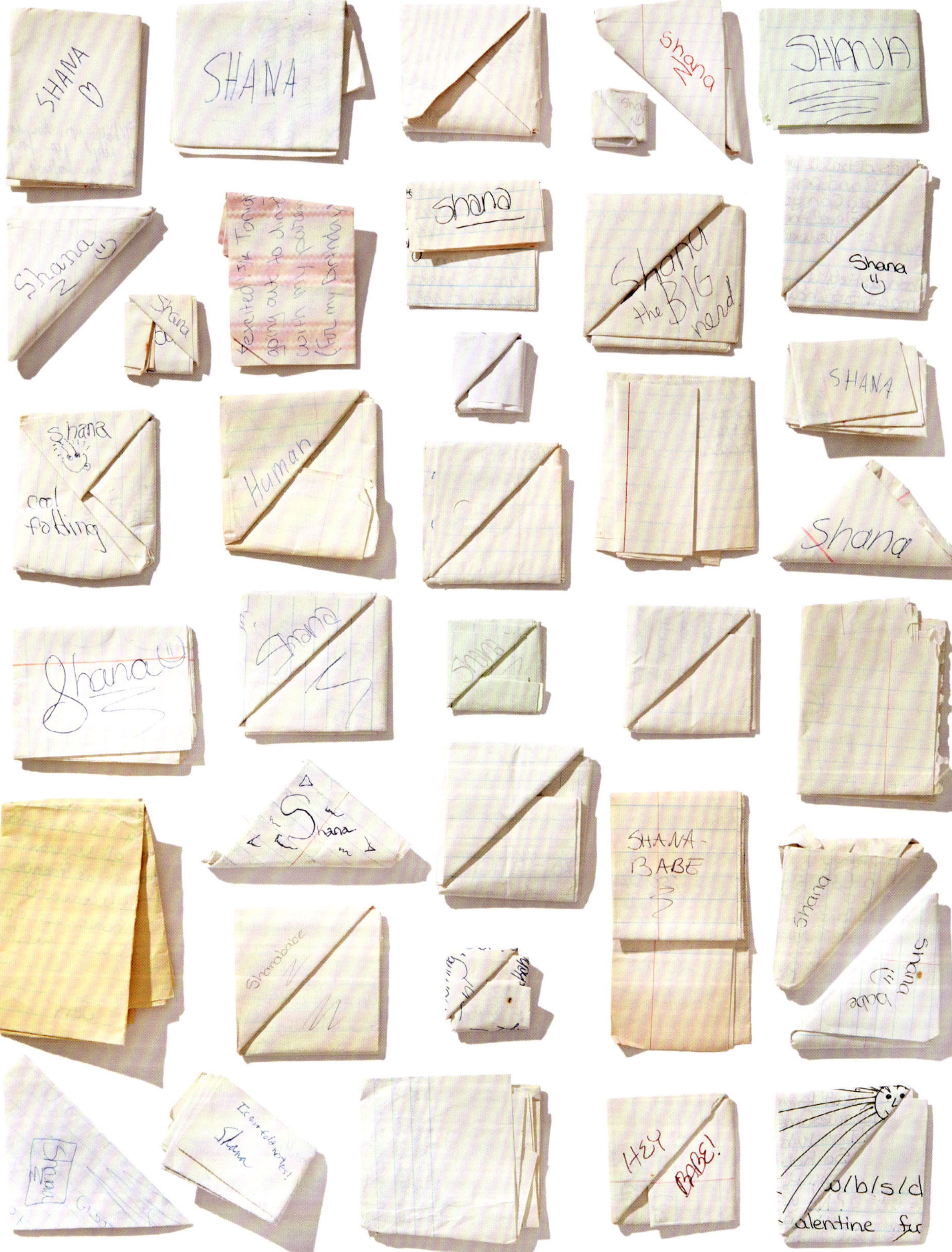
SHANA
SHANA
Shana
SHANA
Shana
Shana
the BIG
nerd!
Shana
SHANA
Shana
cool
folding
Human
Shana
Shana
Shana
Shana
SHANA-
BABE
Shanababe
Shana
babe
Shana
HEY
BABE!
alentine

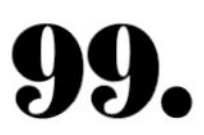

99. Shana Novak, the Author | NEW YORK, NEW YORK

One day when I was about thirteen or fourteen, a girl at my junior high school decided I was just about the right size to stuff into one of the metal lockers in the hallway. (She wasn't wrong.) Threats were made and words were exchanged but, in the end, she spared me. I would not get to see the world from the inside of a closed locker.

The locker bully was actually the least of my problems back then. There were a few other girls lined up and waiting for their turn to bully me, and theirs was a very special brand of psychological terror. Teenagers can be awful.

Pictured is a collection of handwritten notes from that era of my life. (For the kids out there, this is basically how we used to text each other.) I don't know why I kept the notes all these years, but one day, I thought it would be fun to read some. It was not.

Some of these notes are *mean*. One of them is addressed to "Shana the Big Nerd." Another is addressed to "Human" but once unfolded, it reads "Just kidding, YOU'RE A PIG!" That's rich. But I digress.

The point of telling you this is that some of the other notes are from girls who turned out to be my most cherished lifelong friends. And that is what these notes symbolize to me—that there was goodness among the bullies and that it prevailed. If not for the people who chose to be kind over mean, things could have turned out differently for me.

These notes could symbolize something for all of us—that we should lift each other up, have each other's backs, and be each other's cheerleaders. Bullying is a waste of precious time. Kindness lasts longer than you think.

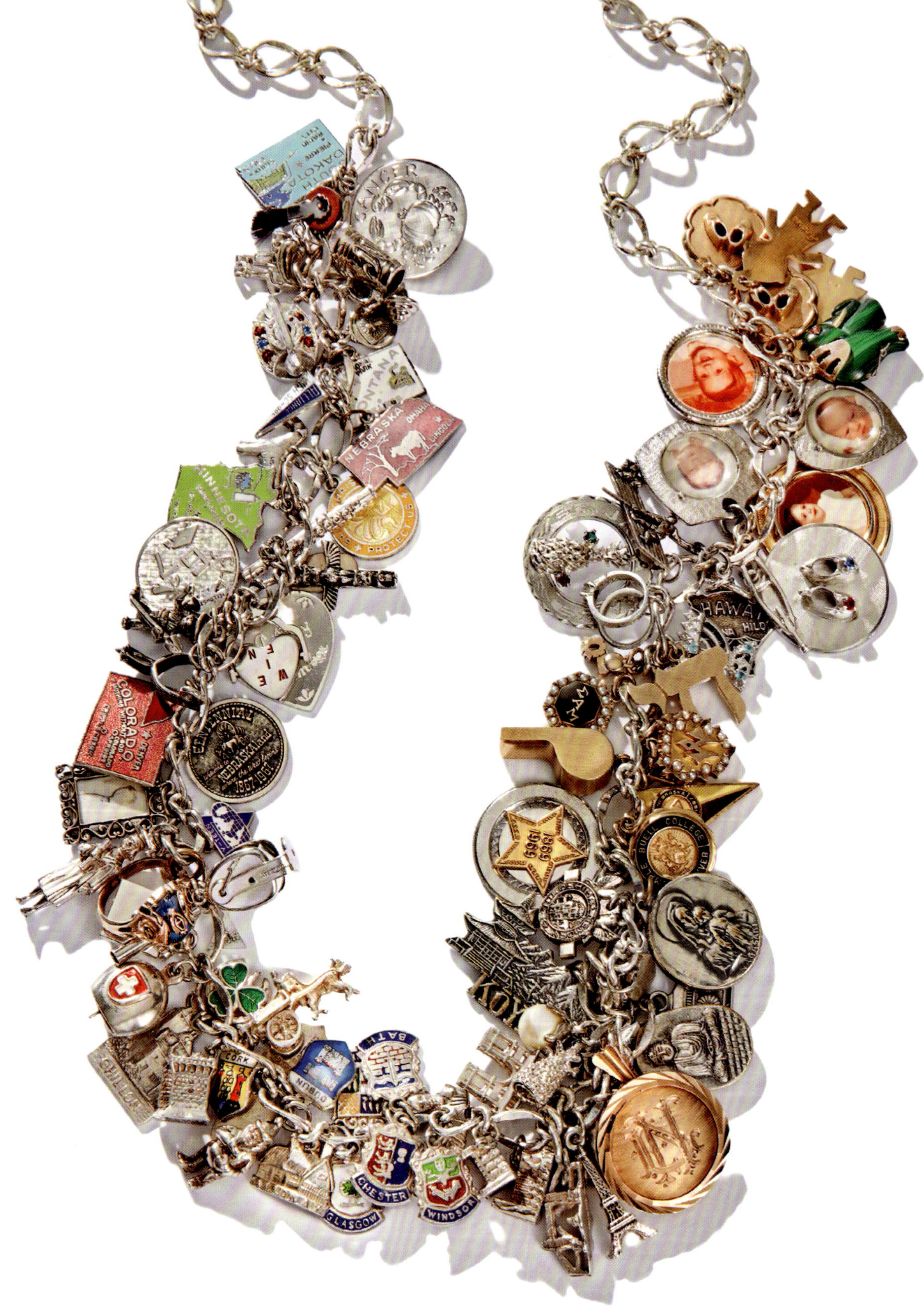

NEBRASKA
OMAHA
LINCOLN
MINNESOTA
COLORADO
PROTECT US
BATH
CORK
CHESTER
GLASGOW
WINDSOR

100. Linda Novak | OMAHA, NEBRASKA

When I asked my mother, Linda, to be a part of this book, she did not disappoint. She promptly produced a charm bracelet so heavy with the symbolism of her life's adventures, it had, at some point, been expanded to a necklace. (My mom started a charm bracelet for me when I was a kid and hers had been started by her own mom, Phyllis.) So for generations, it seems, putting charms on bracelets was the way to commemorate, document, and be grateful.

While photographing my mom's necklace for this book, I asked her if any of the charms stood out as particularly special. Charms symbolizing her faith and work educating kids and adults with disabilities were first on her list. There's a picture of an old high school boyfriend whom she will proudly remind you she's still friends with, sixty years later. It was humbling to hold an abundant life in my hands that was so familiar, yet existed long before I did.

In describing the charms, she also mentioned they were fastened in chronological order from left to right. The timeline begins at birth with a charm for her astrological sign and birth state, Nebraska. School graduations came next, some years of travel, early career trinkets, and finally, along comes my dad. His fraternity pin, and a charm from their honeymoon, lead to the inevitable—two sets of baby shoes and tiny pictures of my brother, Andrew, and me as newborns.

And that's where the charms stopped.

I can't think of a better way to end this book because the charms had stopped but my mother's story most certainly had not. She had just given her adventures and abundance over to the ones whose turn it was to write the next chapters.

My mother's charm necklace, and its symbolic end, will always be my most tangible reminder that I only have a story to tell because of hers. It reminds me that a life well lived—in kindness, love, and the spirit of adventure—is a gift that can be passed on to others. That's why our stuff is so important. Heirlooms will tell our stories long after we are gone. Future generations need our heirlooms to know that we were here, that we celebrated, loved, endured, grieved, and did things that mattered—together, and for each other.

Cristina Garces, a true master of Zoom call dogs-as-décor, your email reached me at exactly the moment I was meant to receive it. Thank you for believing in my work, even on my bad hair days. Thank you, Rachel Hiles and every single person at Chronicle Books, for trusting me to make a book and then using your talents to make it better. How wild to think that my childhood dream would come true because of all of you.

To my parents, you raised me on the wide-open plains of life choices and beliefs and always allowed me the free will to form my own opinions. You supported me wholeheartedly and didn't even flinch when I packed my car and my cat and moved to New York City a month after graduating college. Loving me for who the universe planned is the greatest gift you have given me.

To my grandparents, Max and Rose and Phyllis and Gene, all descendants of generations of family business owners and self-starters. You put the motivation and ingenuity in my DNA.

Denise, my President of Quality Control both in work and in life, thank you for supporting me without question, while also asking a lot of questions. Thank you for always seeing me for who I really am, which is Ross from *Friends*.

To the women I have the privilege of calling my friends, some since we were in diapers or needed our moms to drive us places, thank you for supporting and loving me even though you are not allowed to chew gum in my presence. It is an honor to do earth as a member of your entourage.

To the agents, representatives, and assistants who picked up the phone or answered my emails, this book would not be possible had you not entertained my demands and believed in my message. Willie Norkin at The Brooks Group, Tom Lillig at Stone Ward, and Kelly Engstrom, Director of Operations, Nate Berkus. Thank you to Julia Johns, Head of Transportation for Elephante and Lamby (a.k.a. assistant to Tig Notaro and Stephanie Allynne).

Danny Kahn of Crossroad Management, you believed in my ask and connected me with magic. Sarah Rose at Aunt Management, you are now a professional copy editor. And also, the most patient human on earth. Mary Yatrousis and Kelsey Rivera, your efforts getting Gabby to the pages of this book (and her helmet to my studio!) mean so much. Frances Pennington of Tory Burch, your support was clear from the beginning—thank you for going the distance for me. Clara Maurer of the Newport Festivals Foundation; Mel Saldaña, assistant to Christy Turlington Burns; Elizabeth Tamkin of Kule; and Corey Ruzicano, producer to Gloria Steinem; your patience deserves a trophy. Thank you for the endless coordination and bazillion emails sent.

To my clients who have trusted me with their stories and heirlooms over the years, you consistently humble me. The Heirloomist would be nothing without you.

Carrie Socol, you raised this book's bar with one email. I am in awe of your superpowers and lucky to know you.

Lee Woodruff, you trusted me with Bob's boots so long ago. Your family's story has always been The Heirloomist's North Star.

To Wendy and Jodi Kantor, for showing me the way to the heart of the story.

"Professor" Ron Lieber, for teaching me how it's done.

Pilar Queen, for your generous and early guidance.

Andee Scioli, my lifelong fashion advisor and attorney.

Paul, Jack, Dennis, and the entire team at NOHO Productions, you have given me and my camera, and so many other industry professionals, a space to learn and grow all these years. I am deeply thankful. Neil, Doug, Tony, and Baboo, you bring my images to life one print at a time, and I am endlessly grateful I get to work with your wisdom, experience, and good music.